AF386368

The Real Al Pacino

The Real Al Pacino

His Defining Roles
on Stage and Screen

Tom Brogan

WHITE OWL

AN IMPRINT OF PEN & SWORD BOOKS LTD.
YORKSHIRE – PHILADELPHIA

First published in Great Britain in 2026 by
White Owl
An imprint of Pen & Sword Books Limited
Yorkshire – Philadelphia

ISBN 978 1 03612 546 2

Typeset by Mac Style
Printed in the UK by CPI Group (UK) Ltd, Croydon, CR0 4YY.

The Publisher's authorised representative in the EU for product
safety is Authorised Rep Compliance Ltd., Ground Floor,
71 Lower Baggot Street, Dublin D02 P593, Ireland.
www.arccompliance.com

For a complete list of Pen & Sword titles please contact:

PEN & SWORD BOOKS LIMITED
47 Church Street, Barnsley, South Yorkshire, S70 2AS, England
E-mail: enquiries@pen-and-sword.co.uk
Website: www.pen-and-sword.co.uk
or
PEN AND SWORD BOOKS
1950 Lawrence Road, Havertown, PA 19083, USA
E-mail: uspen-and-sword@casematepublishers.com
Website: www.penandswordbooks.com

Contents

Introduction

This isn't a book about Al Pacino's greatest roles, or even my personal favourites, although I think all my favourite Pacino performances are in there, it's designed as a look through his career in performances that have shaped it for good or bad.

Pacino's career as a stage actor was blown apart by his leading role in what became the biggest film of its time in The Godfather. He followed that up with era-defining performances in Serpico and Dog Day Afternoon, but his career nosedived too, with some roles that were ill-fated from the start or suffered from poor decision making by Pacino and others along the way. Whether on his way up or down Pacino always returned to the stage throughout his career and this book attempts to highlight some of the important parts he played in theatre in addition to his defining roles in film.

The book also aims to shine a light on some of Pacino's collaborators through the years; the mentors, playwrights, directors and fellow actors that inspired him and his work over the decades. This is also a book about Pacino as an actor, so I have very little to say about his colourful love life that has occasionally made headlines.

Like many people when I began to get seriously into movies Pacino was an actor I naturally gravitated towards. It was many things – his swagger, his looks, the fact he always seemed to be on his own against the odds – it always felt like a ride going along with Pacino in a movie. I hope this book explains why so many people find Al Pacino such an electric presence on screen.

Note: Plays are dated in their year of performance, while films are dated to their year of release. Spellings are in UK English except where they are proper names.

Acknowledgements

Thanks to Jon, Charlotte, Olivia and everyone else at White Owl for giving me the opportunity to write this book. Thanks also to Marc Burrows.

Chapter 1

Early Days
(1940–1959)

Born in East Harlem on 25th April 1940, Alfredo James Pacino was the only child of Salvatore and Rose Pacino. His father, an insurance agent, was only 18 when Al was born, and left by the time he was two years old. 'Economics broke the marriage,' Pacino said to the *Chicago Tribune* in 1989. 'I never had much of a hangup over my dad's leaving,' Pacino told the *Daily News* in 1969. 'I saw him a couple of times a year. My mother was anxiety ridden and they didn't make it together. I always used to feel shy on visits to him and anxious to get home.'

As a child in the South Bronx, near the Bronx Zoo, Pacino described himself as 'isolated and odd.' He was kept inside the house for his own safety until he was seven. He did, however, form a close bond with his mother and his grandparents, Rose's father, James Gerard (an anglicised spelling of his Italian name Gerardi) and her mother, Kate. James, a plasterer, had immigrated from Corleone, Sicily, where he was named Vincenzo Giovanni Gerardi, to the Bronx.

Rose worked for a time as a cinema usherette, and she would take Al to see the pictures at the Dover Theatre on Boston Road in the Bronx when he was around three or four years old. When he came home, Al would act out all the parts in front of the mirror all through the week. It wasn't until he went to high school that he really began to have contact with others. The young Pacino's only exposure to the outside world throughout those years came from the movies his mother would take him to.

At six years old, Al, then known to his family as Sonny, could perform an entire scene from *The Lost Weekend (1945)*, where Ray Milland's alcoholic writer Don Birnam tries to remember where he had hidden a bottle of rye while drunk and pulls apart the whole house looking for it. It was Pacino's favourite moment from the movies, and he would re-enact the scene in various ways.

When his father took Al to visit his family, he would enjoy doing the scene for them. However, something happened. They began laughing. Al couldn't understand why. He knew it was a dramatic scene. 'This guy can't find the bottle!' His aunt was deaf, and to entertain her, Pacino naturally developed a talent for mimicry. There was no TV, so Al would lose track of time as he got so involved in his performance and his enjoyment of entertaining his older relatives.

The first time Pacino saw a TV was in a store window. 'In it was Milton Berle in black and white and it was fun to look at.' Pacino told Arlene Alda for her book Just Kids from the Bronx. 'You couldn't hear anything, because the set was in the store. I have a very vivid memory of that.'

At a press luncheon to promote *The Godfather (1972)* in 1972, Pacino said, 'When I came home from the movies, I acted out all the parts in front of a mirror, and I used the broom for a girl in the love scenes. Until I went to school, all I knew was what I had seen at the movies, and once in school, I started acting every chance I got.'

Al enjoyed listening to his grandfather's stories about what life was like in East Harlem, New York, in the 1900s. Al could get more out of him than anyone else. The young Al was more interested in the old man's stories than anybody else in the family. They sat up on their roof in the South Bronx for hours, where they could see the Empire State Building and hear the atmosphere of the neighbourhood. Pacino would recall hearing all the different accents in the neighbourhood. Italians, Jews, Irish, Polish, and German. 'It was like a Eugene O'Neill play.'

Pacino sat enthralled by these tales – running away from home, living off of farms, stealing milk, being beaten by the cops for being an Italian immigrant. They would put newspapers under their chairs to prevent the chairs from sinking into the soft tar that made the roof. Pacino's grandfather got as much out of telling these stories as Pacino did from listening to them.

In the street, Pacino would perform for his neighbours and the local kids, acting out parts from joke books and comic books. Pacino earned the nickname The Actor because of it. 'He was always full of drama,' his neighbour Kenneth Lipper told author John Lahr. Lipper would later become the deputy mayor of New York. 'He loved to take on different personae. He used to go to 174th Street and pretend he was a blind child.'

'Other things I liked to do in New York when I was a kid were jumping between the roofs of tenement buildings,' Pacino said in an interview for the book *My New York*. 'I wasn't allowed out, and it was rough, but it was a lot of fun. There is a whole life up on the roofs in New York.' Another of Pacino's favourite places was called the Dutchies, which was a swampy labyrinth on the Bronx River, where kids would hide in the marsh grasses.

Throughout elementary school, Pacino was a member of a Children's Theatre group. The young Al would read the Bible aloud in the auditorium and recite *The Rime of the Ancient Mariner*, a poem written in the late 1790s by Samuel Taylor Coleridge. When he got to school, all he knew how to do was act. He had no street smarts and would get beaten up constantly, and not just by the boys, but girls would beat on him too. But then he began to participate in school plays.

His high school drama teacher, Blanche Rothstein, noted that his Bible readings were done with passion and gusto. He would say he didn't know what he was talking about but he felt it. His teacher could see his obvious talents and so she put him in the school plays.

Someone watching him in one of the plays compared him to Marlon Brando. It was the first time Pacino had heard the name.

When he was 13, Al saved the life of his friend Brucie Cohen, who had slipped on some rocks and was hanging onto a pipe over a cliff at a Bronx construction site. As a result, Al appeared on the television programme *Wheel of Fortune*, which in its 1950s incarnation was a show intended to reward everyday people's good deeds. He won $2,500 in cash and $1,000 worth of prizes. With the money, he and his mother went to see *Cat on a Hot Tin Roof* on Broadway.

By then, Pacino was also drinking hard liquor and roaming the streets with the Red Wings, the Police Athletic League baseball team for whom Al played third base. They were seen as a quasi-street gang. It was a great time in Pacino's life. The young Pacino would have loved to have made it as a baseball player, but he knew, despite his enthusiasm, he wasn't good enough.

Around that time, Pacino also had a life-changing experience when he saw a travelling production of Anton Chekhov's play *The Seagull* in a nearly empty Elsmere Theatre in the South Bronx. It was an old vaudeville theatre that had been turned into a movie house. A travelling theatre troupe came to play it. Although Pacino had been on stage himself, he had never seen grown-ups act on stage before. There were only around fifteen to twenty people in the audience of an auditorium that held thousands. 'The play started and then it was over,' Pacino told *Esquire* in 2002. 'That's about how fast it went for me. It was magical.'

Pacino was fascinated by who wrote the play. He went out and got a book of Chekhov's stories. Sometime later, Pacino, on his lunch break from Herman Ridder Junior High School, went into a Howard Johnson's. 'And the star of that show is pushing coffee behind the counter. My jaw dropped. I was in awe of this guy. I had to tell him. I remember that exchange. He was so grateful in a way, kind and understanding. He had to be all of twenty-five.'

By now, Al had friends, but studying roles helped him with his loneliness. Pacino's teachers kept urging his mother to let him act. They would write letters and come over to the house. Pacino recalled that Blanche Rothstein came by to talk to his grandmother about his proficiency in acting. He was around twelve and remembers it as the first time he ever had encouragement.

Ms Rothstein sat and had coffee with Al's grandmother and told her that Al should pursue acting. Later, Pacino would say that Blanche recognised that there was hope in the young Al, when he himself thought he was hopeless. The gesture gave Pacino a lifelong affection for the work of teachers.

'I never wanted to be an actor, really,' he said in 1973. 'It wasn't the practical thing to do, I mean, coming from my background, a lower-middle family.' He enrolled in the High School of the Performing Arts in Manhattan, the only school that would take him; he would later say. There, he first encountered Stanislavski's Method. It didn't chime with Pacino. The notion of having to feel it, Pacino, now around thirteen or fourteen, just didn't get. He was looking to have fun, and he found it boring. He wanted to imitate and enjoy himself, but the introspective method he was being shown nullified him.

When his mother's health deteriorated, when he was 16 Al had to find work. She had particular problems with her blood and went to the hospital. Rose's enthusiasm for Al's acting pursuits dissipated as the need to find a regular income became more prevalent. It would be a long time before Pacino had a financial breakthrough, and the lack of money became a bone of contention between him and his mother. However, he was also failing every subject except English. He was astonished that the Spanish class was conducted entirely in Spanish.

Pacino moved out of the family home and to Greenwich Village when he was 17. 'Living the Bohemian life with actors, poets and artists.' He continued to send money back to his mother and grandparents, but he was now having the time of his life. 'We had the theater,' he said to the *Associated Press* in 1996. 'There was this energy. It was a very fruitful time, a very rich time and I've never quite felt that again. Even with all the success that came.'

Pacino said to *New York Magazine* in 2018, 'I've lived all over the city, but the Village at that period of my life is the memory that seems to keep – it repeats itself. It makes me feel good to think about that time.'

It was the time of cafe theatre, and Pacino would go to coffeehouses in the Village, and wherever he went, he could see actors performing all for the price of a coffee. Afterwards, the actors would pass a hat around to collect money so they could eat. It was where Off-Broadway was born. Pacino was seventeen, wide-eyed and awed by what he saw happening. It wasn't long before Pacino was just like them, making his living the same way, performing in coffeehouses for up to 16 performances a week.

He worked hard to support his mother, holding various jobs, including shoeshine boy, furniture mover, movie usher, theatre usher at Carnegie Hall, messenger, and building superintendent.

For a time, he delivered a trade paper called Show Business to newsstands. His pay was twelve dollars. Paid as a ten and two singles. Pacino would cash the ten, so he had twelve singles. 'Then I could peel off the singles at a bar and it looked like a bankroll.'

For two years, he was the mail boy at *Commentary* magazine. The essayist Susan Sontag and Norman Podhoretz, the editor-in-chief, were there at the time. Pacino would attend their parties and take advantage of the free scotch on offer. He was tolerated as they saw him as an energetic young kid. It was one of the few places Pacino wasn't fired from, and he loved the atmosphere there.

Working as a movie usher at Cinema 1 on Manhattan's 3rd Avenue, one of his co-workers was another young actor called Martin Sheen. The pair would spend their shifts talking about acting. In October 1963, the movie

Tom Jones, starring Albert Finney, played at the theatre. It was an unexpected smash hit and Cinema 1, an arthouse cinema, was the only place in New York that took it. People queued around the block. 'It turned out later a big scandal developed because some of the people working there were taking money on the side,' Sheen said in 1995. 'And it turned out that Al and I were the only ones that weren't involved in it. It just never occurred to us to ever do anything like that.'

Pacino and Sheen lived together in the South Bronx around that time and formed a bond as they attended acting classes together. Pacino recalls the 18-year-old Sheen telling him about meeting the woman he would marry.

At around 19 years old, Pacino worked as a bicycle messenger for Standard Oil at Rockefeller Plaza, cycling around for 12 hours a day. It was how he became familiar with New York. There, he got to know a fellow messenger named John Cazale. He recalled in 1978, 'I think he suspected I was an actor, just as I suspected he was, but I didn't know until much later.' Pacino said, 'For the next seven years, I waved to him in Central Park.'

Chapter 2

Beginnings
(1959–1967)

In 1959, Pacino worked with the Living Theatre on 530 Sixth Avenue as an unpaid stagehand. 'It was like walking into somebody's heart,' he said to *The New York Times* in 2000, 'the thing was that alive.' 'The Living Theatre was most influential to me in my life as a young actor,' Pacino wrote in the dedication to Judith Malina's book *Full Moon Stages*. 'As I laid the rugs on their stage for the nightly productions, cleaned the hallways of their Magic Box Theatre or stacked programs, I knew it was all worth it just to have the experience of seeing whatever they put on each night.'

'I was sixteen years old when I went to the Village,' Pacino said on the Maltin on Movies podcast in 2018. 'I was so affected by that renaissance that was going on at that time in the 60s with the Living Theatre, and Judith Malina and Julian Beck.'

Malina and Beck were a married couple; radical Jewish intellectual artists and pacifists deeply committed to peace and social justice through non-violent political activism, they were the Living Theatre's co-founders. It had begun in 1951 in their living room, hence the name.

The big play there that year was *The Connection* by Jack Gelber, about junkies waiting on their dealer so they could get a fix. Pacino spoke to NPR in 2013. 'I was there,' he said. 'I used to clean toilets there with Marty Sheen. And we both were backstage, putting the sets on for The Connection and all this great theatre.'

The Connection, which starred Garry Goodrow and Warren Finnerty, opened in the summer of 1959 and was initially dismissed by the newspaper critics as junk. The production, though, caught on with audiences and gained favourable magazine reviews, leading to word-of-mouth success. As the show entered its second year, many dismissive critics returned to see the production and changed their minds. Gelber began to be bracketed with Edward Albee, who was enjoying success with *The Zoo Story* and Jack Richardson, writer of *The Prodigal*, as playwrights revitalising American drama. It would win Obie awards for Finnerty as Best Actor, Beck and Malina for Best All Around Production, and Jack Gelber for Best New Play.

Pacino and Sheen weren't paid much. Pacino recalled years later that maybe they got some food to eat. However, what they did get to do was watch the show. Pacino and Sheen crouched down at the back of the theatre and watched *The Connection*, to Pacino's reckoning at least one hundred times. One night, Sheen leaned into Pacino and asked him 'How would you like to do that?' pointing to Goodrow on stage. Pacino felt at the time he wasn't anywhere near the standard of what he was watching. Sheen initially surprised him by saying, 'I'm gonna do it.' Pacino would say that he could see in Sheen's eyes that he was. Sheen took over the part of Ernie from Garry Goodrow when the play's cast went to work on the 1961 film version of the play. Sheen then toured Europe in the role.

Another play at the Living Theatre that had an influence on Pacino was 1968's *Paradise Now*, where both the 34-strong cast and the audience were encouraged to lose their clothes. 'The audience became the theatre,' Pacino said in his 1996 documentary *Looking For Richard*. 'They were the event. They were the play.' On either side of the theatre were Judith Malina and Julian Beck, orchestrating and controlling it. 'And it was literally the most exciting, vibrant, alive thing that I…I can only describe it as changing my life.' In the *Rutland Daily Herald* Tom Slayton described the show. 'In essence Paradise Now is a beautifully controlled four hour exercise in anarchy.'

It may seem unusual to audiences who know his later work, but Pacino spent a lot of his early years working in comedy. He was in a double act with his friend Brucie Cohen. He told ABC News in 1983, 'That's what I did, the first part of my life. I did only comedy. I wrote my own revues and I directed them and I cast them and I put them on. I got a storefront and invited people. I guess from 23 to 26 I did that. It sort of saved my life at the time, because I was I guess so depressed. So unhappy that anything funny was…it's good therapy.'

Pacino, though, realised that he couldn't be funny on cue. He then discovered what he called solace and joy in playing great material, whether he was reading it or acting it. That discovery, he said, was the luckiest thing that ever happened to him.

Pacino recalled the day he decided acting had to be his number one focus. He was in downtown New York handing out circulars. He suddenly had a moment of realisation and went back to tell his boss he was finished. He called a friend when he went home and he said, 'Either I act, or I die.' From that point on Pacino worked steadily as an actor.

The Actors Studio was founded in 1947 in New York City by Elia Kazan, Cheryl Crawford, and Robert Lewis. The Studio began as a place where theatre artists could gather, privately, to explore new and deeper connections to the work. Kazan wanted to create a not-for-profit organisation providing a private workshop in which the professional actor could work on his or her craft, far away from the commercial pressures of casting, rehearsal and performance. The following year Lee Strasberg was invited to join the studio as a teacher and in 1951 he became its Artistic Director.

Membership of The Actors Studio was achieved through an audition process of preliminary and then final auditions where the only requirements were talent and the possibility of improvement.

Pacino auditioned for the Actors Studio. He got through the preliminaries but was rejected. He shrugged off the rejection thinking 'What do they know?' At the age of 18, Pacino enrolled at the Herbert Berghof Studio.

Berghof was a leading actor on the European continent in the 1920s and 1930s. Born in Vienna, he escaped to England in 1938 when the Nazis moved into Austria. The rest of his family were wiped out. He soon moved on to New York, where he grew a reputation as an actor and director on Broadway. He appeared in the original Broadway production of *Oklahoma!* and performed as Gustav Eberson in Arthur Miller's 1944 Broadway flop *The Man Who Had All the Luck*.

As a director, Berghof took on the first Broadway production of *Waiting for Godot* in 1956, having been approved after a 90-minute interview by Bert Lahr, who played Estragon. In 1957, Berghof also staged a production of the play in Boston with an all-black cast.

In 1945 he founded the Herbert Berghof Studio in the Chelsea area of Manhattan. Although an alternative to The Actors Studio, the two were never rivals and respected each other. Berghof became a charter member of

The Actors Studio in 1947, but he was never as entrenched in Stanislavski's Method, as those teaching at the Actors Studio. Berghof preferred an emphasis on actions rather than thoughts and reactions.

In addition to Pacino, Berghof's students over the years included Steve McQueen, Robert De Niro, Anne Bancroft, Liza Minnelli, Bette Midler and Prunella Scales.

Ed De Leo, who also took classes at HB Studio, recalled watching Al performing a scene in the class from the Broadway hit *Mr Roberts*. Berghof reprimanded Al and his scene partner for attempting a difficult scene they didn't have the technique for. 'He told them they weren't mature enough for such dramatic material,' De Leo remembered in his co-authored memoir *When I Knew Al.* 'How could they be at 18? They didn't understand that this was part of Berghof's modus operandi to shake up the students so the next time they'd select material more close to type, something with which they could identify.' De Leo recalled that Pacino was nervous and inhibited.

At HB Studio, Pacino met Charlie Laughton, who became his mentor and close friend. Laughton was around a decade older than Pacino and taught an acting class there. Pacino would call him a great actor, although Laughton never pursued a career as an actor. Pacino connected with him because, in acting class, he talked to the young actor as if he were a person, not a student.

Laughton introduced Pacino to books, of which he didn't have much access to growing up. It was an education for him, and Pacino absorbed everything Laughton put in his path – books, plays and music.

Pacino also lived with Laughton, his wife, actress Penny Allen, and their baby girl. It was good for Pacino to see a settled happy home and he felt their warmth as he knew Laughton and Allen believed in his talent.

Laughton nicknamed Pacino 'the wild square'. Bohemian on the outside, traditional on the inside. 'In life, Al's speech wasn't that good,' Laughton told the *New York Times* in 1977, 'but when he acted Strindberg, it was like Frank Sinatra when he sang – like an angel!'

Speaking with John Lahr in 2014, Pacino recalled a time in Laughton's class when he performed a scene from Reginald Rose's *Crime in the Streets* in front of Berghof and the rest of the class. After Pacino finished, he said, 'Berghof got up there and started to put me down. He started screaming at me, "How dare you!" He was absolutely flipping out.' Pacino later asked Laughton what had happened. 'A new era,' Laughton said. 'He saw a new era.'

Pacino's mother, Rose, died in 1962 when he was 22. She was only 43. Not long before she passed, Pacino had an audition for Elia Kazan's *America America*. Pacino fantasised that the audition would go well and he could go back home to his mother, tell her he got the role and they were going to be okay. Pacino arrived late and missed the audition.

Pacino was doing children's theatre at the time including *The Adventures of High Jump* directed by Tullio Garzone.

Within a year, his grandfather had also died. His death made Pacino feel a little more fragile. His death was the loss of a positive force in Pacino's life. His grandfather's devotion to him was a great driving force in Al's life. While his grandfather was alive he never felt alone. Pacino would reflect on his relationship with his grandfather a lot throughout his life. When he made the low budget movie *Two Bits (1995)* Pacino aged up to play a character he based on his grandfather.

Pacino felt that the grief he felt from his grandfather's death affected him mentally and it resulted in the Army rejecting him classifying him 4-F.

In a 2002 interview with Esquire, Pacino recalled a key memory he had of his mother. As a ten-year-old the neighbourhood kids called round asking him to go out carousing with them. His mother wouldn't let him go. Pacino was incensed and screamed at her. 'She saved my life. Because those guys down the alley – none of them are around right now. I don't think about it that much. But it touches me now as I'm talking about it. She didn't want me out in the streets late at night. I had to do my homework. And I'm sitting here right now because of it. It's so simple isn't it? But we forget, we just forget.'

In 1963 Laughton directed Pacino in his first public performance in William Saroyan's *Hello, Out There*. Saroyan was a noted short story writer, first coming to prominence in 1934 with his short story *The Daring Young Man on the Flying Trapeze*, published in the magazine *Story*. He wrote his first play in 1935. Saroyan later said that while passing through New York, he had read in *The New York Times* that he was working on a play. In order to save the newspaper from error, he said, he spent five days writing *Subway Circus*. Saroyan won the Pulitzer Prize for *The Time of Your Life*, which opened in October 1939. However, he rejected the prize and the $1,000 that went with it on the grounds that businessmen were not qualified to judge art.

Hello, Out There was a short one-act written in 1941 and first seen on Broadway in September 1942 as a curtain raiser to Gilbert Keith Chesterton's 1913 comedy *Magic*.

The show grew out of Laughton's classes. Laughton asked Joe Cino at the Caffe Cino to come over to see the readings they were doing. Cino agreed to stage the play at his cafe for three performances a night.

The show would have a profound effect on Pacino. At his first line the audience laughed. It was supposed to elicit a laugh, but this was Pacino's first time in front of an audience with the play. He had no idea it was funny. At the moment he realised he didn't know the part properly. After the show, shattered, Pacino sat on a stoop in the street outside the theatre. Laughton approached him. He reminded Pacino that with sixteen performances a week he was back on stage later that night. After the run finished Pacino would say he stayed at home for months.

Next for Pacino was a production of August Strindberg's 1889 play *Creditors*, again directed by Laughton, out of necessity this time as the original director quit. Once more, Pacino had jitters. The cast was made up of classical actors and in rehearsals Pacino became overwhelmed and wanted to quit the show. Laughton sat down with him and went over the script. With time and patience, Al began to understand what was going on. Laughton encouraged him to read it naturally, not act, and say the words out loud in his own speech. The pair discussed the meaning of the words as they went through them. Laughton would say that by the time of the production Pacino was better than any of the classically trained actors but he had a better handle on the play's story. The play became a turning point for Pacino, 'When I knew that nothing mattered except that I became at one with the play.'

The play was put on in what Pacino described for Esquire as 'an obscure theatre in the bowels of SoHo, which at the time wasn't SoHo but just a bunch of warehouses.' It was staged by The Actors Gallery, 414 West Broadway, which, in 1962, had been found guilty of performing theatrical performances without a licence.

The play was set in Sweden at the turn of the twentieth century. It was an introduction for Pacino to becoming part of a world he didn't know. Acting for him now was transformative. It was like falling in love. For Pacino, acting wasn't about getting paid or becoming successful or famous. 'It was as they say, no longer the destination but the journey.'

He expanded on this realisation in an interview with Leonard Probst for his book *Off Camera*, 'I'm from the South Bronx, I didn't know anything about the Strindberg world. I felt this great sense of saying, I can talk, I can speak, I've got something to say. I knew that I would do nothing else but that.'

Pacino was homeless at the time, and in addition to staying nights with Laughton and his family, he would occasionally sleep in the theatre. His situation would help Pacino feel a connection with what he was doing.

In 1966, Pacino appeared in *Why is a Crooked Letter* by Fred Vassi at Caffe Cino. Pacino played the part of John. Also in the six-strong cast was John Medici, who would later play opposite Pacino in *Serpico*. The production by the Theatre of Encounter was directed by Alec Rubin, the company's founder and a long-time member of the Actors Studio.

Around this time, Pacino was working as a building superintendent. A friend told him about a job with a rent-free apartment and fourteen dollars a week. Pacino got a boiler's permit and got the job. He had no money and little to eat but now had a roof over his head. For the year he worked the job Pacino would say it was both 'a very fruitful time' and 'the lowest time in his life'. He pinned an eight by ten glossy of himself on the door.

'The guy came out and started talking about me a few years back,' Pacino said to Conan O'Brien in 2024 of the building's owner. 'Saying, "He was a terrible super," or something like that. I thought, "Why? Why would he say that?" I was a terrible super! I'm sure there's a lot around.'

Playwright Israel Horovitz saw Al in a production of *Why is a Crooked Letter*[1] in an apartment on 87th Street. The audience was in single figures. 'It had a symbolic orgy scene,' Horovitz recalled for the *Boston Globe* in 1982,

---

1. Andrew Yule's biography of Pacino suggests that he was Obie nominated for this performance. However, no contemporaneous news reports could confirm this. In an email received in December 2022 Pie Soto Producer and Project Manager for the Obie Awards wrote: 'Sadly there are no records going back that far back and no way to know who were the nominees for that year.'

'in which Al and these young actresses were rolling around on the floor. It was hideous, but he had moments that were absolutely amazing.'

Horovitz spoke to a disconsolate Pacino after the performance. 'Don't give up now,' he told him. Horovitz was impressed enough by Pacino's performance to hand him a script he had just written called *The Indian Wants the Bronx*. 'There was no question that Pacino was the right actor for my play.' Pacino read the script that night, and the pair met the following day to discuss Al doing the role[2].

On the 6th of December 1966, *The Peace Creeps* opened at the Off-Broadway Theater Four under the sponsorship of the non-profit New Theater Workshop. The play was written by John Wolfson, a 27-year-old Harvard graduate who studied playwriting with John Gassner at Yale. Wolfson was the son of Erwin S Wolfson, one of New York's most prominent skyscraper builders. At the time of Erwin's death in 1962, he was overseeing his project to build the 59-storey Pan Am building in Manhattan.

The production was directed by John Stix and produced by Ivor David Balding.

The Peace Creeps concerned a group of Freedom Riders, who were civil rights activists, stranded on a South Carolina beach and an attack on them by a band of Southern draftees. Also in the cast were James Earl Jones, who would win a Tony in 1969 for *The Great White Hope*, Don Scardino and Matthew Cowles, who would star alongside Pacino in *The Indian Wants the Bronx*. Scardino would feature alongside Pacino in 1980's *Cruising* and go on to become a noted television director, helming shows such as *The West Wing* and *30 Rock*.

Martin Sheen had begun to make his name on and off Broadway, playing Timmy Cleary, the son in *The Subject Was Roses* by Frank D. Gilroy for which he received a Tony nomination and appeared in *The Wicked Cooks* by Gunter Grass at the Orpheum in early 1967. Sheen would offer Pacino the job of understudying him in *The Wicked Cooks*. Pacino accepted and then discovered he had to be in the play as an extra. When Sheen contracted laryngitis and Pacino had to go on in his place, Pacino refused, saying he didn't know the lines. Director Vasek Simek fired him.

---

2. In his autobiography *Sonny Boy* Pacino writes that Penny Allen recommended Pacino for the role to Indian's director Tullio Garzone.

In 1966, Pacino was accepted into the Actors Studio. He performed two different characters. The first was from the movie *Counsellor at Law (1933)* written by Elmer Rice and the second was *Look, We've Come Through, a 1961* play by Hugh Wheeler. 'It was a glorious feeling. I'd hardly ever felt anything like that,' Pacino told *Playbill* in 2022. Pacino borrowed $50 to pay his rent from the Studio's James Dean Memorial Fund. Pacino's work there had a formative effect on him. 'I could try things out that I knew I would never have a chance to do in the professional world,' he said to *Playbill*. 'I got to play roles I didn't dream I would ever play without the pressure of having to succeed or having to do something in such a way that it's applauded. It was all about developing, finding out, and searching.'

One of those roles was King Oedipus in the Greek tragedy by Sophocles, which Pacino did at the Studio with a young Dianne Wiest and Estelle Parsons. Oedipus wasn't a role he ever thought he would do, but at the Actors Studio he could step into those shoes.

There he met Lee Strasberg. Strasberg was an icon, and Pacino felt afraid to let Strasberg see him in anything. He would even stand at the back hoping not to be noticed. It was six months before he would perform a scene. When he stepped on the stage it was revelatory. Pacino did two monologues. He only did them because he was too shy to ask another actor to share a scene with him. The first monologue was as Hickey from Eugene O'Neill's *The Iceman Cometh*, the second as Hamlet. Pacino had been amazed by Jason Robards' portrayal of Hickey when he saw the 1960 television movie as a teenager. It stayed with him over the years. *Hamlet* was Pacino's favourite play. Lee Strasberg looked down at Pacino's card and said, 'Al Pacino? Hickey and Hamlet? Where are you from?'

The date was 17th January 1967, and although against a long-held Studio tradition, the audience of actors applauded Pacino's performance. Strasberg asked Pacino, dressed in cut-off jeans, to now play Hickey as Hamlet and Hamlet as Hickey. The object of the exercise was to be as real as Hamlet as he was playing Hickey and to give Hickey the same kind of intensity he gave his Hamlet.

Pacino's throat was dry, so he had a cup of coffee and then performed the parts again as Strasberg suggested. Pacino heard a few people ask, 'Who is that?' Strasberg coyly teased, 'See, we take anyone.'

Strasberg began his assessment of Pacino's performance by telling him that he had chosen a tough problem and had shown real acting courage. He told Pacino that the actors' applause corroborated the judgement of the directors [in accepting Pacino to the Actors' Studio]. It was evident that Strasberg enjoyed Pacino's performance, an emotion he rarely showed to his students. However, as detailed in Foster Hirsch's 1984 book on the Actors Studio, he did provide some criticisms. 'When you did Hamlet, there were many casual, unnecessary movements – yours not the character's. Naturalness pours out of you without regard for its significance. What seems lacking is a sense of situation. You're aware of an audience, of people around you.' He told Pacino that he didn't need as much movement and to focus his concentration and that his behaviour was too general. Strasberg finished by wishing Pacino good luck and saying, 'We hope to see your work again soon.'

Strasberg spoke to Pacino afterwards, 'The courage you have shown today is rarer than talent.' Pacino didn't look back. He had his identity. He knew now he was an actor.

The Actors Studio meant a lot to Pacino over the years. He said it was the only place he ever had that he could just go to. It was a place where the greats mingled with the unknowns. In Pacino's time as a young actor stars like Rod Steiger and Paul Newman were around the building.

Pacino credited the Actors Studio, along with Laughton, for launching him into the acting world. 'It was directly responsible for getting me to quit all those jobs and just stay acting.'

Laughton would say that Pacino didn't attend the Studio all that often. Despite how much he was influenced by Strasberg their relationship wasn't one of student and mentor, it was more personal. Pacino would hang around in the lobby to go and get lunch with Strasberg or go to Strasberg's apartment where they would listen to classical music together.

Pacino realised years later that his relationship with older men like Laughton and Strasberg was his unconscious search for a father figure.

Strasberg would give Pacino a motto to live by. 'Don't do what you can do. Do what you can't do. That's how you learn.'

Pacino did just that by performing in a variety of scenes at the Actors Studio. On 26th May 1967 for example he performed a scene from J. D. Salinger's novel *Catcher in the Rye* with Sally Alex and Allen Garfield. Earlier in the month he had done Rodgers and Hammerstein's *Carousel* with Clifford David, Sylvia Miles and Mimi Turque. He also performed *Armstrong's Last Goodnight*, a 1964 play by John Arden set on the border of Scotland and England in the year 1530, with Penny Allen on 20th June. Pacino and Allen also performed *Doctor Zhivago* in April 1968.

Sometimes after a scene had ended the discussions would become intense and emotional. Once at an Actors Studio party they gave out some just for laughs awards. Pacino won best after-the-scene-was-over actor.

Pacino came to Boston in 1967 to work at the Charles Playhouse. He borrowed money to get there and slept on floors once he arrived. At his audition Pacino was handed a script of Bertolt Brecht's *The Caucasian Chalk Circle* and offered him a small part paying $50 a week. Despite having everything he owned in a paper bag Pacino turned it down. Having already been working in the theatre he felt he shouldn't be doing small parts. He wouldn't learn from watching others in the cast, Pacino believed that the only way he could learn and improve was by acting himself.

Pacino pretended to producer David Wheeler that he had something else waiting for him in New York. Wheeler seemed puzzled and assured Al that there would be other plays after this. Despite having the conviction that small parts weren't for him Pacino couldn't bring himself to say that to Wheeler insisting that there was something better waiting for him in New York. After that audition, he returned to New York, but despite turning the small part in Brecht's play down, he impressed Wheeler enough to be asked to return.

Pacino reflected on his approach to selecting roles to the *New York Daily News* in 1999 emphasising the importance of passion in his choices. However, he discovered an interesting paradox early in his career while working in repertory theatre. During this formative period, he often found himself excelling in roles he hadn't initially sought out, while struggling with parts he had specifically chosen and felt passionate about.

This pattern became particularly clear during his time in Boston, which he later described as very important to his development as an actor. Working in repertory theatre exposed him to multiple productions simultaneously, where actors would rehearse one play during the day while performing another at night. Pacino experienced this dynamic first-hand when he auditioned for the role of Ralph Berger in Clifford Odets' 1935 drama *Awake and Sing!* – a character name he would sometimes use as an alias later in life. While he was excited about this particular role and focused his energy on securing it, he was also assigned smaller parts in *America Hurrah*, which held little initial appeal for him.

The outcome surprised him completely. Despite his preparation and enthusiasm for *Awake and Sing!* Pacino found himself lost and struggling in that role, unable to connect with the character or find his footing in the performance. In contrast, he felt liberated and performed exceptionally well in the two different roles he played in *America Hurrah* – the very parts he had considered unimportant. This experience taught him a valuable lesson about the unpredictable nature of acting and the importance of remaining open to unexpected opportunities, as he realised he never would have discovered this about himself without trying roles outside his comfort zone.

America Hurrah was a trio of satirical one-acts written by Jean-Claude van Itallie, a Brussels-born Harvard graduate. The first one act was *Interview* where interviewers, the bottom half of their faces in smiling masks, ask job seekers a series of questions. The questions begin innocently but steadily become dehumanising. The second was *TV* in which the characters monitor television shows for ratings but slowly get more involved in the mundanity of their own lives. The third one-act was *Motel*, with doll-like people who rip up motel furniture and write on the walls. The show opened at the Charles Playhouse in Boston on Thursday, 28th September 1967. Pacino played 2nd Interviewer in *Interview* and Hal in *TV*. Jill Clayburgh, who had parts in all three one-acts, played opposite Pacino in *TV* as Susan. They would be a couple for the best part of five years. 'I never had a boyfriend before Al,' Clayburgh said in 1972. 'We got along splendidly right from the start.'

Also in the cast was Eda Reiss Merin, a member of New York's legendary Group Theatre throughout the 1930s who had appeared in the US premiere production of Bertolt Brecht's *Galileo* in 1947.

The production was directed by Thomas Bissinger. It was produced by Frank Sugrue and Michael Murray, the co-founders of the Charles Playhouse. As with November 1966's Off-Broadway production, the producer was Stephanie Sills, formerly a writer of Department of Agriculture pamphlets, including one entitled 'Help Stamp Out Hog Cholera'.

Kevin Kelly's review in the *Boston Globe* called the Playhouse production 'much slicker than the original Off-Broadway version.'

This was the first time in Pacino's life that he felt like he had money. 'Before that the closest I'd come was bus transfer slips,' he said in 2002. As a kid he had found a place where there were rejected slips. He filled his pockets with them and imagined what it was like to walk around with pockets stuffed with dollars.

Early in his career, journalists and moviegoers commented on Pacino's resemblance to Dustin Hoffman, who was a little older than Pacino and was also a few steps ahead in his career. Hoffman's first hit film, *The Graduate*, appeared in 1967. 'A couple of times people have asked me if I was Dustin,' Pacino said at a press luncheon in 1972. 'And when I finally met him I said to myself, "God, do I look like that?"' Pacino noticed the journalists present quickly scribbling in their notebooks. 'No, I am only kidding, I really didn't think that,' he hurriedly assured them.

'They asked me to understudy Dustin in Jimmy Shine, but I was busy,' Pacino said to the *New York Times* in 1969 talking about the play Hoffman starred in which opened in December 1968. Around the same time Pacino was in the audience at the Royale Theatre for Robert Shaw's play *The Man in the Glass Booth*. A lady came up to him asking, 'Aren't you Dustin Hoffman?' She wouldn't take no for an answer, repeatedly pulling on Pacino's shirt and demanding he admit he was Hoffman. 'I'll bet nobody's pulling on his shirt and saying, "You're Al Pacino." I love his work, and I think he's brilliant. But when we act, I think a whole different thing comes across. And he is older – and shorter.'

Chapter 3

The Indian Wants the Bronx
(Stage, 1968)

Written by: Israel Horovitz
Directed by: James Hammerstein
Cast: John Cazale, Matthew Cowles, Al Pacino

The *Indian Wants the Bronx* was set at a bus stop, a study of urban savagery, its themes still echo in the present landscape. A pair of young hoods torment an Indian who is also waiting for a bus on a chilly September night.

Horovitz based the play on an incident he had witnessed in London. While studying at the Royal Academy of Dramatic Art, Horovitz would eat in the cafeteria at the Commonwealth Institute on Kensington High Street. He was outside one morning waiting for the staff to open for breakfast. As the meals were cheap, there was already a queue, mainly unremarkable students and older locals. A young Indian student, a Hindu, who wore a turban, stood in line peacefully waiting as the group stood in silence. The silence was shattered by a group of Teddy Boys who had pulled up in a car. They hurled insults at the young Indian while the rest of the queue stood frozen. Their insults rose in volume and expletives. Surprisingly, however, the young man laughed and nodded at them. Not receiving the expected response, the Teddy Boys lost interest and drove off. Horovitz said he was left with one question: 'What the hell just happened?' Horovitz asked the young man, only to find that he didn't speak a word of English. When Horovitz returned to America, *The Indian Wants the Bronx* was the first new play he completed while writing at nights as he juggled two day jobs.

In 1978, Pacino recalled his first thoughts on being cast, asking, 'Who's going to do the Indian? Who knows Hindu?' Someone in the room replied that there was an actor sitting practising his Hindu with a tape recorder right at that moment. Pacino was impressed by the dedication. When the actor walked into the room, Pacino pointed at him and declared 'You! You!' It was John Cazale, the messenger Pacino knew from Standard Oil at Rockefeller Plaza.

Cazale had first worked with Horovitz in the 1950s at the Charles Playhouse. Pacino found that Cazale had an unusual way of working. He wouldn't simply run lines in rehearsal, Cazale would discuss the scene, the intentions of the characters, the choices they made. Soon they had slipped into the scene. Pacino embraced this method throughout his career.

Pacino developed a close friendship with Cazale that began during this production and continued throughout their careers. In a 2018 interview with *New York Magazine*, Pacino described their unique working dynamic. When Pacino would begin a scene, Cazale would challenge him directly, questioning what he was actually trying to communicate rather than simply reciting dialogue. Cazale's approach was serious and uncompromising – he refused to accept mere line delivery without genuine understanding of the material's meaning.

This would often lead to heated exchanges between the actors, with Cazale pushing Pacino to dig deeper into the text's intentions. Their confrontational discussions would evolve into improvisational exercises, during which Cazale would gradually guide them in circles back to the original scene material. Pacino recalled this process as producing remarkable results, transforming their understanding and performance of the work through Cazale's methodical and insightful approach to acting.

Tullio Garzone, who directed *The Adventures of High Jump*, would be the play's original director. They rehearsed at a loft on Bleecker Street. Charlie Laughton and Penny Allen came to see rehearsals and liked what they saw. Laughton told Al that now he had arrived.

The Indian Wants the Bronx didn't initially go into a legitimate theatre. There were staged readings to begin with in Waterford, Connecticut with the run of the show beginning in Provincetown at the Gifford House. Pacino and the cast spent more than a year performing the play in lofts, living rooms, basements and small theatres, 'Wherever and whenever somebody would let us do the play,' Horovitz recalled, garnering little to no attention.

Horovitz said later, 'The New York producers thought it was too violent.' The writer and the cast's most disheartening experience took place at the Canoe Place Inn on the Shinnecock Canal on Long Island, where the ballroom was set up as a theatre. It was a massive space and the audience was made up entirely of three little old ladies in big hats. In the middle of the play they got up and left. Pacino carried on for a few minutes before addressing the fact that 100% of his audience had departed. Horovitz said, 'Let's go home.'

The playwright and his star drove home together in silence. As he dropped Pacino off Horovitz promised he would find a producer to give the play a full-scale production if Pacino would stay on board. Pacino committed, and Horovitz found his producer in the shape of Ruth Newton Productions in association with Diana Mathews.

While Newton had multiple Obie awards and had performed every role from stage manager to actress to director to producer in a long theatre career it was Mathews's first venture into production. Born as Ofelia Cornejo, she had previously been an actress.

However, the producer initially wasn't keen on Pacino's participation and told Horovitz so when Pacino auditioned for her. At that time, she hadn't actually seen Pacino play the part; she had only met him. 'She thought he was too short and not handsome,' Horovitz recalled in 2005.

Mathews had an alternative in mind, an actor who was tall and blonde, quite unlike Al Pacino. Horovitz was adamant he wouldn't play the role. Mathews said that she wouldn't produce the play in that case. Horovitz suggested that both actors audition and then they could make a calm rational decision on which one was better. The playwright went to his actor and explained what was happening. Horovitz would say that Pacino was furious with him for putting him in that position.

As Pacino was not yet a member of Actors Equity, he was made to audition at an open call. By now, it wasn't just Al and the one alternate; the play had made the rounds of the talent agents in New York City, and several non-union actors showed up. Actors who had auditioned previously were also there to be seen.

Horovitz had insisted that the producer's choice and his be the first two actors up. Horovitz described Mathews's choice as 'boring.' Pacino though was determined to show that the part was already his. He stepped onto the stage singing. He moved downstage into the centre and addressed Mathews, delivering his opening line of the play with panache. 'Hey, Pussyface, can you hear us? Can you hear your babies singin' to ya?' Horovitz would say that Mathews was terrified, but it was all he needed to indicate that his choice was justified. 'You see it right?' he asked, almost rhetorically. Horovitz received the affirmative answer he was looking for, and he bounded onto the stage to hug Pacino and announce to Al and all the other actors waiting to be seen, 'You got the part Al! She said yes!'

The Indian Wants the Bronx cost $13,000 to produce. It would run under the banner Ruth Newton Productions in association with Diana Mathews.

Pacino portrayed Murph, a part he connected with as it reminded him of his childhood friend Cliffy. Matthew Cowles was Joey, and Cazale played Gupta.

Director James Hammerstein was the son of Oscar Hammerstein, the multiple Tony Award winner best known for his collaborations with Richard Rodgers, which included *Oklahoma!*, *South Pacific* and *The Sound of Music*. James only decided he wanted to go into directing shortly after his father's death in 1960. He told journalist Sandra Knipe in 1989, 'The only advice he ever gave me was, "There are no rules in theatre." He said, "If you're going to direct, I can't give you any advice." That's the best advice he gave me.'

The Indian Wants the Bronx opened off-Broadway at the Astor Place Theatre on Wednesday, 17th January 1968. The top price ticket was $5.95. It played with another one-act play by Horovitz, *It's Called the Sugar Plum*. That play featured Marsha Mason and John Pleshette. Jill Clayburgh later replaced Mason.

The casting of Cazale, wearing a turban, drew criticism for the use of 'brownface'. Horovitz defended the casting in print, writing, 'True, John's Italian not Hindu…from Winchester, Massachusetts, not Delhi. But it's also true that John Cazale is a fine, sensitive actor.'

Some newspapers had incorrectly reported that Bombay-born actor Shelly Desai was to open in the role. Horovitz recalled for the *Village Voice* in 2019, 'I thought it was going to be insulting to East Indians to have a Caucasian play the role. I insisted on finding a real Hindu and did: an accountant who lived in Queens and had a penchant for the stage.' But that actor only lasted one performance, and Cazale would make the role his own.

The Associated Press Drama Critic William Glover was in attendance on the opening night. He contended there was a 'high contrast' between the two plays. Hammerstein's direction he wrote was full of 'crispness and vigour'.

George Oppenheimer, a playwright and Academy Award-nominated screenwriter, was *Newsday's* regular drama critic. He was also among the audience on opening night and wrote about the double bill in his *On Stage with Oppenheimer* column. His criticism was both cutting and eloquent. 'Credit to Mr Horovitz,' he wrote, 'despite my hearty dislike of his second and longer one-acter, of having an ear for the speech of the gutter and an eye for the malignity of the current scene.'

Oppenheimer felt that both plays fell into a group of plays which looked to assert their quality by arousing revulsion. He cited *The Toilet* by LeRoi Jones and George Tabori's *Niggerlovers* as two recent works of that nature. Oppenheimer praised Hammerstein for his 'relentless photographic fidelity to the violence in our streets by directing this short but much too long item.' Oppenheimer felt that the sadism on show by the two hoods lost its point and came to exist for its own sake. The work, though, was 'extremely well directed and played' by the director and cast.

In 2014, John Lahr wrote, 'Of all the débuts I attended in more than fifty years as a theatre critic, Pacino's was the most sensational: immediate, arresting, and inexplicable.'

James Davis in New York's *Daily News*, felt both plays carried little if any plot. Pacino and Cowles he felt were 'credible' while Cazale played a 'thankless' role. 'Off-Broadway remains in good supply of competent players – and woefully short of playwrights who know how to fashion a plot.'

Variety called the opener 'an implausible, thin black comedy' and 'the work of a beginner.' Indian, however, it felt was 'compelling theatre.' *Variety's* 24th January 1968 review is notable given that the stereotype of Pacino's later film acting is a shouty overblown style. *Variety's* reviewer wrote, 'Pacino is particularly effective in the use of an uncommonly naturalistic, unstagey style which works well in the small Astor Place Theatre, where there is little need of vocal projection.'

In *The Village Voice*, Ross Wetzsteon wrote, 'Al Pacino gives a fascinating performance, all cool, fluid, swaggering mannerisms, as graceful and gratuitous as smoke. But what I liked best was the subtlety of his broadness, the naturalness of his fakery – years ago, actors adopted the mannerisms of hoods, and now the mannerisms have returned to the hoods by way of the movies.'

During the run of the play, Pacino would take long walks with Horovitz as part of his character development process. Horovitz explained in a 2014 *New Yorker* interview with John Lahr that Pacino was searching for his character through real-life observation. When Pacino spotted someone interesting on the street, he would insist on following them for hours to study their walk and posture. The costume was equally crucial to his method – he needed to discover the right costume, rehearse while wearing it, and essentially live in it to fully inhabit the character.

Horovitz was 28 at the time and was working a $50,000-a-year job in advertising. He would quit, becoming a full-time playwright. The production allowed Pacino to leave his janitorial job and obtain his first Equity card.

Laughton would say that with *The Indian Wants the Bronx* Pacino 'seized the power.' In conversation afterwards Pacino was positively glowing. They both knew that this was where the life he wanted to live was beginning.

In February, an invitation came in for the production to perform for two weeks in June and July at the Festival of Two Worlds in Spoleto, Italy. It was the only New York production invited, and the box office at the Astor Place Theatre remained open while the show was abroad. Pacino called performing for an Italian audience 'a marvellous experience.' 'We were reviewed by a great number of European critics,' Horovitz said. 'In a word, our careers happened.'

In all *Indian* ran at the Astor for 177 performances. Ruth Newton said in an interview with the *Miami Herald* in 1970 that the production had 'went far over budget'. She took a position as Theatrical Production Supervisor with Theatre Now Inc after it finished to help clear her debts.

For Pacino, the show became the catalyst for his whole career as someone who would become pivotal to his success over the years came into his life because of it. Faye Dunaway, then a major star following her success in *Bonnie and Clyde (1967)*, attended one of the shows, although she and Pacino didn't know each other. Though she didn't meet him backstage, Dunaway recommended the young actor to industry professionals, telling them to 'go down and see this kid.'

This recommendation reached Martin Bregman and David Begelman, head of Creative Management Associates, who subsequently attended Pacino's performance. During that particular show, Pacino was performing with a limp due to a leg injury sustained the previous night. Coincidentally, Bregman himself walked with a limp as a result of childhood polio. This physical similarity Pacino felt created an immediate connection between the two men.

Following the performance, Bregman invited Pacino to his office. The 42-year-old Bronx native ran Artists Entertainment Company from offices on Fifty-Fourth Street between Lexington and Third Avenue. For Pacino, a downtown theatre actor, venturing uptown to meet with industry executives was unfamiliar territory. He wondered if the building's doorman would even let him in.

Despite Pacino's initial uncertainty about what Bregman could offer, the meeting established a crucial professional relationship. Bregman recognised Pacino's artistic talent and saw potential for developing his film career. The manager explained how he could serve as an intermediary between Pacino and the entertainment industry, helping to launch the actor's transition from stage to screen. Both men acknowledged the importance of trust in their partnership. Bregman emphasised that while he couldn't give Pacino acting ability – that talent already existed – he could provide the industry connections and guidance necessary to establish a film career. Although not quite sure what the businessman could do for him Pacino signed with Bregman as a client, beginning a relationship that would prove transformative for his professional trajectory.

This meeting represented a pivotal moment when Pacino's focus shifted from simply finding individual acting jobs to building a sustained career in entertainment, marking his entry into the film industry that would define his legacy.

On the afternoon of Saturday, 25th May 1968, the 13th annual Village Voice Off-Broadway Awards ceremony was held at the Village Gate in Greenwich Village. More commonly known as the Obies, it honoured *Indian* with multiple awards. Pacino won Best Actor, while Cazale won for distinguished performances in both *Indian* and another Horovitz play, *Line*. Horovitz was one of three playwrights honoured for distinguished playwriting, the others being John Guare and Sam Shepard. Among the other acting winners was Roy R. Scheider for *Stephen D.*

In June of 1968, the Peter Witt Agency put together a package for presentation to distributors and producers. Horovitz was touted to adapt his play and direct the movie with the leads being Pacino, Kevin O'Connor and Dustin Hoffman. The film, however, didn't happen.

In October of 1968, *Variety* announced that Pacino would play Feisel, the lead in *Huui, Huui*, a play by 31-year-old Iowa housewife Anne Burr. It was due to open as the seasonal opener at the New York Shakespeare Festival's Public Theater on 2nd November. It was directed by Joseph Papp, the executive producer of the festival. Papp had bought an old library building near the Bowery and remodelled it to house five theatres, which he called the New York Shakespeare Festival Public Theater. He would later sell the building for a profit but keep a lease on it.

Playwright Julie Bovasso recalled for *New York Magazine* in 1974, 'Every actor in the business knows Joe and it has become something of a running gag by now that Joe once fired Al Pacino from a play called Huui, Huui. "He can't act," Joe said. So Joe fired him. But Al Pacino adores Joe, and it is safe to say the feeling is mutual.'

Papp assured Pacino he would be a big star one day. Pacino felt that he could have done the role if only Papp had the necessary patience.

Barry Primus took over the role. Primus would later star alongside Pacino in films *Righteous Kill (2008)* and *The Irishman (2019)*. Pacino said in his autobiography that it was a sobering experience, coming off the back of his success.

Pacino had been offered a co-starring role in the musical *Zorba*. 'After Indian I was offered exact opposite roles,' Pacino said to the *New York Times* in 1969. 'I turned down a part in the movie Catch-22 and in Zorba on Broadway.'

Pacino would make his movie debut soon after with a small role in a film directed by Fred Coe. 'I played a gigolo in a movie with Patty Duke called Me, Natalie. I think I'm the first guy who ever said, "Do you put out?" on the screen.' Matthew Cowles also made his film debut in the movie. The film, released in the summer of 1969, featured a number of actors familiar to Broadway, including Martin Balsam, Nancy Marchand and Bob Balaban.

That was no coincidence as the movie was cast by Marion Dougherty, who began her career working in television in New York. When she moved to work in Hollywood she took with her, her index-card file filled with the names of promising actors she had spotted Off-Broadway, in regional theatres and in summer stock.

Pacino wouldn't work on stage with Horovitz again. However, in 1982, he played playwright Ivan Travalian in the film *Author! Author! (1982)* which was written by Horovitz.

In August 1993, Bill Marx of the Boston Phoenix wrote two articles outlining complaints of sexual harassment by Israel Horovitz at the Gloucester Stage Company. The allegations covering the period 1989 to 1992 ranged from offensive language to inappropriate kissing and repeated acts of sexual fondling. Horovitz protested innocence, and the allegations were dismissed by the board of the Gloucester Stage Company, which Horovitz founded in 1979.

In November 2017, Jessica Bennett of the *New York Times* ran an article where she spoke with nine women who accused Horovitz of sexual misconduct. This time the accusations were treated more seriously. Horovitz issued a statement apologising, 'with all my heart to any woman who has ever felt compromised by my actions.' His son Adam, best known as Ad-Rock, of the group The Beastie Boys, issued a statement of his own, 'I believe the allegations against my father are true, and I stand behind the women that made them.' At this point, the Gloucester Stage Company cut ties with Horovitz, who had been their artistic director for 28 years.

When Horovitz died of cancer aged 81 in 2020, the accusations featured in the first paragraph of his obituaries.

Chapter 4

Does a Tiger Wear a Necktie?
(Stage, 1969)

Written by: Don Petersen
Directed by: Michael A. Schultz
Cast: Hal Holbrook, David Opatoshu, Al Pacino, Roger Robinson, Lauren Jones, Jose Perez, M. Emmet Walsh, Jon Richards, Kenneth Rosaly, Hector Toy, Bob Christian, Laura Figueroa, Caitia Lord, Michael Brandon, Bruce Scott, Lazaro Perez and Sam Watson

The success of *The Indian Wants the Bronx*, and its 204 performances had already left Pacino grappling with newfound recognition. 'I won an off-Broadway Obie for Murph,' he told the *Daily News* in 1969. 'I got so uptight I had to go to a shrink. I didn't know what was expected of me as a success.' In a separate interview with the *New York Times*, he revealed that he had injured his knee and hip during this period. 'I knew it was because I couldn't cope with the success, so I went to a psychiatrist. I saw him about four times and quit.'

Pacino made his Broadway debut in February 1969 in *Does a Tiger Wear a Necktie?* as Bickham, a hot-headed student harbouring deep-seated resentment toward his absent father. The play was set in the jail school for young prisoners on New York's Rikers Island. Although the program describes the setting as 'An island on a river bordering a large industrial city.'

Associate Producer Jay Weston and director, Michael Schultz, were struggling to find a young actor for the pivotal role of Bickham for the production at the Belasco Theatre, Manhattan. Hal Holbrook and David Opatoshu were already cast and they struggled to find a talent to match theirs. They then received a tip about a brilliant young actor performing in an Off-Broadway show. Weston and Schultz wasted no time and went along to see Indian that evening. Weston would say both were 'deeply moved by the intensity of his work.' When the show ended they went backstage and approached Pacino telling him, 'If you're interested in auditioning for this role, here are the sides. We'll be at the Broadway theater all afternoon tomorrow.'

Nearly 300 actors auditioned for the role, including Jon Voight. At 5 PM, Pacino arrived, shuffling into the theatre wearing a long Army overcoat and a wool hat. Having studied the sides Pacino launched into the tirade where Bickham explains to the psychiatrist his bitterness toward his errant barber father. One minute into watching him Weston turned to Schultz and whispered, 'That's our Bickham.'

Does a Tiger Wear a Necktie? centred on an idealistic English teacher attempting to connect with troubled students in a correctional facility. The play emerged from the rich experiences of its creator, Don Petersen, who was born in Davenport, Iowa, and graduated from the Rodney Theater program at the University of New Mexico.

Music ran in his family – his father was a cellist with the Tri-City Symphony Orchestra, and Petersen himself played violin with the orchestra in his twenties before joining the Navy during World War II. His passion for theatre developed while playing in orchestra pits for touring productions such as *Oklahoma*! and *Kiss Me, Kate*.

Following a brief stint at a television acting school, Petersen found work in Chicago's summer stock theatre circuit. When the Korean War erupted, he discovered his World War II service had left him just three days short of an exemption. Enlisting in the Army, he was appointed entertainment director at Sandia Air Force Base in New Mexico.

In 1952, Petersen left New Mexico for Hollywood. 'I tried to get into the movies,' he told the *Quad City Times* in 1967, 'but I didn't have the push, the toughness, or the resilience to be an actor.'

Returning to New Mexico, he enrolled in the University of New Mexico's Department of Theater Arts, where he discovered his true calling as a playwright. During this period, he had two one-act plays produced and began teaching. 'I want to be known as a playwright,' he explained. 'I teach to eat.' He graduated in 1956.

Petersen relocated to New York in 1959, where he worked as a copywriter and art layout designer at an advertising agency. He expanded his writing portfolio by working on several films for Allied Artists, co-authoring *The Courtship of Harmony Treadwell* with his wife, Valerie, and ghost-writing for the television series *The Doctors*.

While teaching during the day and writing at night, Petersen worked at Riverside Hospital on North Brother Island in New York City. The experimental facility treated young drug addicts through a combination of rehabilitation, psychotherapy, and education. In 1963, the facility closed amid allegations of staff corruption and mounting operational costs, leading to the island's abandonment. Petersen's two-year experience there would later inspire *Does a Tiger Wear a Necktie?*

Like *The Indian Wants the Bronx* before it, *Does a Tiger Wear a Necktie?* underwent extensive development before reaching Broadway. Beginning around 1964, the play went through multiple iterations. 'I rewrote it four times,' Petersen revealed in 1967. The work caught the attention of prestigious literary agent Audrey Wood, who most notably represented Tennessee Williams.

Through Wood's influence, Petersen gained membership in the New Dramatists Committee, an elite group of about thirty playwrights established in 1950. The organisation's members had collectively authored over 100 Broadway productions and nearly 70 Off-Broadway plays. Notable alumni included acclaimed writers Paddy Chayefsky and Muriel Resnik.

Following a reading at the New Dramatists Committee, Petersen substantially revised Tiger, 'tearing out whole scenes.' Yale University offered him a $5,000 fellowship based on the work – an offer he declined, saying, 'I didn't want to live in New Haven.' He did, however, accept a $500 loan from the Dramatists Guild, noting wryly, 'It's the kind you pay back later when you're rich.' His talent earned further recognition through the 1965 John Golden Playwrights Award, and the New Dramatists selected him as their representative at the prestigious Eugene O'Neill Writers Conference.

The play attracted significant early interest, with options for both Broadway and Off-Broadway productions, but these opportunities failed to materialise. Among the notable figures interested in *Tiger* was Jerome Robbins, the creative force behind *West Side Story*. 'It got kind of upsetting,' Petersen admitted. 'You know. It affects your other writing.'

But things turned around for Petersen and his play when the newly established National Foundation for Arts and Humanities began offering $25,000 grants to university theatres to encourage new playwrights and productions. At Brandeis University in Waltham, Massachusetts, Howard Bey – head of the Department of Theater Arts and an established New York scene designer – began searching for a suitable script for the grant program. His criteria were specific: he needed a large-cast production that could combine professional actors with graduate and undergraduate students. When Bey contacted the New Dramatists' office in New York, they immediately recommended *Tiger*, with its seventeen-person cast.

Bey submitted the script along with his production plan to the National Foundation, securing a $25,000 grant. Petersen received $7,500 of the award, enabling him to pursue writing full-time. The play's potential was further validated when it won the American National Theater and Academy's inaugural Bishop Award.

Does a Tiger Wear a Necktie? premiered at Brandeis University in February 1967 under Charles Werner Moore's direction. Peter MacLean, who later became a familiar face on television series like *The A-Team*, *Wonder Woman*, and *Fantasy Island*, portrayed Bickham. *The New York Times* offered a mixed assessment. 'His play limps; it also swings,' wrote Dan Sullivan, who criticised Petersen's comprehensive but unfocused approach: 'One of his problems is that he wants to tell us everything he saw, which makes his play a shapeless and unfocused work.' Sullivan felt that there were too many stories being told, and it wasn't until the third act when the focus lands on Linda and Conrad, who wants to marry her when they've kicked the habit, that Petersen hits on the story that matters most. 'From then on we've got a play.'

Tiger ran for two weeks at the Berkshire Playhouse in Stockbridge, Massachusetts, beginning 22nd August 1967. The production featured William Devane, later known for *Knots Landing*, as Bickham and Cleavon Little, who would achieve fame in *Blazing Saddles*, under Jim Ambandos's direction. *The Berkshire Eagle* review of the opening night notes that Pacino had a supporting role in this production, something that Petersen's *New York Times* obituary confirms.

Despite its harsh subject matter, the play maintained an underlying thread of hope. When Pacino later took on the role of Bickham in the Broadway production, he portrayed him as a complex character – a snarling yet sensitive young addict, an Irish youth without hope who harboured a killer's instinct.

Petersen emphasised that addiction merely served as a backdrop – the play's true focus was survival. Despite its dark themes, the December setting and Christmas-adjacent finale symbolise hope and renewal.

The play's provocative title originated from an early scene where a teacher assures his students they can overcome their addictions. One student's cynical response – 'Does a tiger wear a necktie?' – captured the essence of their struggle.

The production brought together accomplished theatre professionals. Director Michael Schultz came with impressive credentials, having won an Obie Award for *The Song of the Lusitanian Bogey* with the Negro Ensemble Company, where he served as resident director. Producer Philip Rose, a former concert baritone turned music publisher, had already established his theatrical reputation by producing the 1959 Broadway hit *A Raisin in the Sun*.

Does a Tiger Wear a Necktie? opened on 25th February, 1969. Weekday tickets topped at $7.50, with premium Friday and Saturday night seats priced at $8.25. Pacino's agent presented him with six bottles of Piper Heidsieck champagne to mark the occasion.

CBS Cinema Center secured the film rights for $125,000, with an escalator clause potentially raising the price to $350,000 based on the play's success. Producer Jay Weston, who reportedly signed Pacino to reprise his role, had backing from Cinema Center, which had already invested $75,000 in the $150,000 stage production.

During rehearsals, Pacino's unpredictability and tardy arrivals concerned the production team, as his artistic process remained unrefined. Weston later reflected, 'But slowly the performance began to build into something special.' He vividly recalled opening night: 'I will never forget when this young actor made his first appearance onstage. He has an appointment with the psychiatrist and slowly shuffles into his office. After a moment, he viciously kicks the door shut with his foot. The audience, startled, inhaled with a gasp, and the actor had them in the palm of his hand from that moment on.'

The critical response was overwhelmingly positive. *The New York Times* critic Clive Barnes wrote, 'Al Pacino as Bickham is magnificent—a lumbering, drug-sodden psychotic with the mind of a bully and the soul of a poet.'

The Daily News predicted, 'The stars Hal Holbrook and David Opatoshu may get them to the box office, but they'll come out talking about Al Pacino.' In *The Sunday News*, John Chapman noted, 'The most lively character, both in the writing and playing, is a young Irish junkie…Al Pacino, an interesting young actor, portrays him with almost too many nervous mannerisms, but his performance is vivid.' Chapman characterised Bickham as 'a fidgety cocky monster if you ever saw one.'

Variety praised Pacino as 'eloquently menacing' and lauded Hal Holbrook for delivering one of his career's most moving performances. 'There are several upsetting scenes, and also one or two lovely ones. It is a worthwhile evening,' noted the reviewer. Holbrook, who had made his Broadway debut in 1961's *Do You Know the Milky Way?*, was fresh from his role as Don Quixote in *The Man of La Mancha*.

For his portrayal of Bickham, Pacino gained 25 pounds, reasoning that a young addict in withdrawal would overcompensate through excessive eating. When he started to build the character, he remembered the junkies he saw in his neighbourhood when he was a kid.

Pacino emphasised that his understanding of addiction came from observation rather than experience. He explained to the press that he never touched dope, reasoning that he didn't want to disgrace his Italian family. But he acknowledged that it was all around him in every neighbourhood he lived in. He could look back and feel lucky that he found acting so was never tempted to fall into the drug world.

When journalist Robert Wahls inquired about his method-acting approach, Pacino responded, 'I have my own formula.' He read a few books, and that was it for his research. He didn't feel the need to visit any narcotics centres. He was from New York and when you're from New York you've seen everything. He had friends who were addicts, so he'd done the research, even if he didn't realise he was doing it. The part though did make Pacino more aware of his own anxieties, acknowledging in interviews that he drank to calm down.

The play reaches its emotional peak during a confrontation between Pacino's Bickham and the institution's psychiatrist, played by David Opatoshu. Though Bickham attempts to intimidate the composed doctor with threats and vitriol, the psychiatrist maintains his resolve to reach the troubled youth.

Director Michael A. Schultz also received a nomination for dramatic direction. Although admitting to being disappointed at losing, Schultz took pleasure that *Tiger* and Howard Sackler's *The Great White Hope*, which won best play, stood as powerful, hard-hitting dramas in the days when Broadway was mainly a place for musicals.

The July *Variety* critics poll for the 1968–69 season further cemented Pacino's success. He dominated the Actor in a Supporting Role category with eight votes, outpacing runner-up Ron Liebman (*We Bombed in New Haven*) by six votes. Pacino also claimed the Most Promising New Broadway Actor award, ahead of notable contenders: Rene Auberjonois for *Fire*, Richard Dreyfuss for *But Seriously*, and Dustin Hoffman for *Jimmy Shine*.

This made Pacino the first double winner in a *Variety* critics poll since 1963–64 when Barbara Loden was named both best supporting actress and most promising actress for her performance in *After the Fall*. Previous winners of the Most Promising Actor award included Michael Crawford in 1966–67, Martin Sheen in 1963–64 and Peter Fonda in 1961–62. Pacino's co-star Lauren Jones, Schultz's wife, won the Most Promising New Broadway Actress award.

The growing success Pacino had experienced was now leading to job offers, but while other actors might be counting the dollar bills and leaving the stage behind for the big screen Pacino wasn't rushing into anything.

Pacino confirmed to *Variety* in March 1969 that he turned down the role of Arthur in Otto Preminger's film of Marjorie Kellogg's 1968 novel *Tell Me That You Love Me, Junie Moon*. He disputed the money offered saying that the figure quoted of $150,000, saying 'let's say it was several thousand dollars.' Ken Howard, who had been in the hit Broadway show *1776*, took the role opposite Liza Minnelli. Pacino felt the part, an epileptic who lives in an institution, wasn't suitable for him.

It wasn't the first big role he had turned down, telling *Variety* that he had refused a role in Mike Nichols's film of Joseph Heller's novel *Catch-22*. The difference there was that it was a role that he wanted. Paramount would not give him a contract for one picture without options. Pacino didn't want to be tied down by a long contract. It didn't worry him that he was allowing motion pictures to pass him by. He felt he was making decisions that were right for him, and his instinct was what he could trust.

Pacino went back to the theatre in a play that would become a long held personal project. On 30th October 1969, *The Local Stigmatic* opened at the Actor's Playhouse in New York. Pacino played the leading role of Graham, with Michael Hadge as Ray, Joseph Maher as David and Paul Benedict as Man. Arthur Storch directed. It was a co-venture between Len Gochman and James Stevenson of Lenja Productions and Jon Peterson. It played as a double bill with seven Harold Pinter sketches, some of which had appeared on television as animated features in NBC's *Experiment in Television* programme. Maher and Benedict also featured in the sketches with Susie Bond. The top weeknight price for a seat was $6.50 with the price going up by a dollar at the weekend.

The Local Stigmatic was a one-act drama by Heathcote Williams. It was first produced by Jim Haynes on 1st March 1966 at the Traverse Theatre in Edinburgh. Again playing as a double bill with Pinter, on this occasion with his play *The Dwarfs*. The part of Graham was played by Oliver Cotton. It moved later that month to London's Royal Court.

Director Storch joined Erwin Piscator's Dramatic Workshop fresh out of the Army after World War II. There he counted among his fellow students Harry Belafonte, Elaine Stritch, Rod Steiger and Walter Matthau. In 1951 Storch joined The Actors Studio. There he put on a workshop production of Calder Willingham's novel *End As a Man*. The production went on to Broadway in 1953 but without the actor who played a court clerk in the workshop – James Dean. Storch also appeared in the world premiere of Tennessee Williams's *Night of the Iguana* in Spoleto, Italy in 1957.

The central premise of *The Local Stigmatic* wasn't far from that of *The Indian Wants the Bronx*. Pacino was once more cast as one of a pair of rudderless, frustrated young street toughs intent on projecting their frustrations on someone else. Pacino again played the more vicious of the duo. This time though, the action was set in England, and Pacino used a working-class London accent.

The duo, on their way back from losing money on a greyhound race, stop in at a London pub. There they meet a movie star, a man whose lifestyle they envy. They beat him up and carve him with a blade. Months later, they call him by telephone, mocking him.

Variety led their opening night review with a gloomy paragraph. 'A series of early skits by Harold Pinter, and a Pinter-esque drama about violence equal unlikely box-office and The Local Stigmatic looks doomed.'

In the *New York Times*, Clive Barnes wrote that Pacino's accent, 'off-beat and with his gutter underlines, is impeccable.' He was less impressed by the play, calling it 'half-interesting…remarkable far more for what it promises than for anything it delivers.' Barnes also felt that the role of Graham was now something audiences had seen Pacino do in both of his recent hit plays. 'I would like to see what else Pacino can do in this world besides scaring babies, old women and me. I wouldn't even dare say he can't do something else – but I just want to see it.'

In *New York Magazine*, John Simon had similar criticism. '…there is Pacino doing his exactly identical bit from The Indian Wants the Bronx and Does a Tiger Wear a Necktie?, and though his characterisation is again quite terrifying, it is even scarier that an actor whom you are seeing only for the third time is already as unsurprising as Sam Levene or Helen Hayes.' Levene had made his Broadway debut in 1927, originated the role of Nathan Detroit in 1950, and had just opened in *Three Men on a Horse*, his 34th Broadway production. Helen Hayes made her Broadway debut in 1909, appearing in her 46th Broadway role with *The Front Page* in May 1969.

Simon also picked out the pauses in the play, a feature certainly of Harold Pinter's work. Simon speculated on who authored the pauses and arrived at the thought it was the actor. 'Pacino pauses hammily, hysterically, noiselessly clattering around the stage. If Pacino is an actor, not merely a highly efficient robot programmed for psychosis, evidence is urgently required.'

The Associated Press Drama Critic William Glover was also less than impressed. He wrote, '…Heathcote Williams, a Pinter protege, whose use of "stigmatic" instead of the prosaic "twisted" or "deformed" is a tip-off on his self-indulgent put-on about backstreet hoodlums.' Glover was also aware of Pacino going over old ground, writing, 'Pacino…seems in danger of becoming over-adept at projecting effete but brutal insanity.'

The reception was so poor, in fact, that the show faced closure after only one night. However, the play had a benefactor. Jon Voight, an actor Pacino beat out for the part of Bickham, was fresh from the success of the movie *Midnight Cowboy* and, out of his own pocket, paid for a run of one week.

The show closed on 9th November after eight performances.

From the heights of a Tony win only a few months earlier, Pacino was now at a professional low. He put his finger on the failure of *Local Stigmatic* as a lack of rehearsal time.

Pacino pondered what to do next. He read plays including a new one by Murray Schisgal, the author of *Jimmy Shine*, and Israel Horovitz's *Rats*.

What Pacino chose to do, though, was not work. For a few months, he sat around. It was a period where he became depressed and drank heavily. He would tell the *New York Times* in 1972 that he was feeling uncomfortable about his success. He had gone from being a struggling anonymous actor to becoming well known, and it was difficult for him to adjust.

Al wanted to be anonymous, but he also realised that acting work didn't have value if nobody knew about it. He needed recognition and work, but that also came with an increased visibility he wasn't always comfortable with.

Around about this time Pacino got fired from a play again, and once again it was Joseph Papp who dismissed him. He laughed about it in a 2022 *New York Times* interview with Dave Itzkoff, who he would work with on his autobiography *Sonny Boy*. Pacino also talked about being fired with *Playbill* in 2022. 'I don't think Hamlet was my role; I have to be honest. Hamlet speaks to the ghost, and I remember saying to [director] Joseph Papp, "I'm not interested in speaking to my father right now as the ghost. I want to save that. I'm interested in speaking to my father before he became a ghost." Shortly after that, I was fired.'

In January 1970 Pacino appeared in a revival of Tennessee Williams's 1953 play *Camino Real*. Williams's agent Audrey Wood personally selected Pacino for the role. However, Pacino initially refused to audition. He was receiving so many scripts that he had no need to do an audition to land a part. Not giving up on the man she wanted, Wood had artistic director Jules Irving ask Pacino to come to Lincoln Center and meet with her. At the meeting, Pacino read the play and said, 'Okay, I'll read for you.' Pacino loved the script and signed off on the part there and then.

Rehearsal time was limited. Pacino would say that going on stage on opening night was like 'going out in the cold without a coat.'

Pacino and director Milton Katselas clashed over the way the part should be played, Katselas thinking it should be done for laughs, while Pacino played the role straight.

Pacino's entrance involved him riding a hook and line down into the audience from overhead. Reviews were mixed with Pacino being praised for his deftness and the play receiving decent notices, but again critics suggested that Pacino's nervous tics, berserk gesturing and mannerisms were similar to his last two roles. In *Newsweek*, Jack Kroll felt that Pacino was turning the ensemble piece into his own star turn and suggested that he 'ought to be read the riot act' for relying on the same acting tricks audiences had already seen him display. Camino Real closed on 21st February 1970 after 52 performances.

In March, Pacino was back at the Charles Playhouse in Boston. This time he wasn't on stage but directing a production of Israel Horovitz's *Rats*. Pacino had directed a production of *Rats* previously, in April 1969, at the Loft Theater Workshop in New York and at the Brecht West Cultural Center in New Jersey. In Boston, *Rats* played in a double bill with *The Indian Wants the Bronx*, although Pacino didn't feature in either play. *Rats* was an unsettling play concerning an old grieving rat who has witnessed his wife and their 60 children exterminated. Fleeing from their house in Upper Montclair, he holes up in a baby's room in a Harlem tenement. There he is visited by a young rat who wants to take over the house. The older rat has now mellowed and has become domesticated, while the young rat wants to taste the baby's blood.

In November of 1970, it was announced that producer Dominick Dunne had signed Pacino to play the lead in his film *The Panic in Needle Park*. Adapted from James Mills' novel by Joan Didion and John Gregory Dunne, it told the story of two drug addicts in the midst of a drug shortage that sweeps New York.

In a 1995 *Playboy* interview, Dominick Dunne recalled Pacino's casting. The New York production had such a low budget that the production office was actually Dunne's apartment. They got down to two actors for the lead, and did screen tests. 'One of them knelt down on the floor and put his hands around my knees and said to me, "Dominick, don't give it to Al! Don't give it to Al!" That was Robert De Niro.'

Don Petersen only had one more play produced, *The Enemy is Dead*, which went to Broadway in 1973. Of the many screenplays he wrote, only three were filmed: An Almost *Perfect Affair*, *Deadly Hero* and *Target*, which was directed by Arthur Penn and starred Gene Hackman. A project that never got off the ground Petersen collaborated on with Penn was an adaptation of Tom Wicker's book *A Time to Die* about the inmates' uprising at Attica prison. Petersen passed away from lung and liver disease in 1988, aged 70.

Among the people who went to see *Tiger* was the 29-year-old director of *Finian's Rainbow (1968)*, Francis Ford Coppola. Impressed by Pacino's performance he contacted him and said he had a script he wanted Pacino to look at. Pacino went out to San Francisco and spent five days working with Coppola on the script, the story of a college professor who falls in love with a student, a desire that ultimately ruins his life. It didn't get made but Pacino and the director got on well and got to know each other. The following year Coppola called Pacino with another film. It was *The Godfather*.

Chapter 5

The Godfather
(Film, 1972)

Directed by: Francis Ford Coppola
Screenplay by: Mario Puzo and Francis Ford Coppola
Based on the novel *The Godfather* by Mario Puzo
Produced by: Albert S. Ruddy
Cast: Marlon Brando, Al Pacino, James Caan, Richard Castellano, Robert Duvall, Sterling Hayden, John Marley, Richard Conte, Al Lettieri, Diane Keaton, Abe Vigoda, Talia Shire, Gianni Russo, John Cazale, Rudy Bond, Al Martino, Morgana King, Lenny Montana, John Martino, Salvatore Corsitto, Richard Bright

Mario Puzo's novel *The Godfather* became a publishing phenomenon upon its 1969 release, remaining on *The New York Times* Best Seller list for 67 weeks and selling over nine million copies in two years. In his essay *The Making of The Godfather* Puzo contends it wasn't as good as either of his first two novels *The Dark Arena (1955)* or *The Fortunate Pilgrim (1965)*. Paramount Pictures' interest in the property began in 1967 when they offered Puzo a $12,500 option for his unfinished manuscript, then titled *Mafia*, with an additional $80,000 if it became a film. Despite his agent's advice to decline, Puzo, facing gambling debts, accepted the deal.

In 1969, Paramount confirmed their intention to adapt the novel, aiming for a Christmas 1971 release. Albert S. Ruddy was appointed producer in March 1970, chosen for his ability to work within budget constraints. Paramount, wanting to avoid the failures of previous mafia-themed films like *The Brotherhood*, sought an Italian-American director to ensure cultural authenticity.

Several prominent directors declined the project, including Sergio Leone, Peter Bogdanovich, Arthur Penn, and Otto Preminger. Peter Bart, a Paramount executive, suggested Francis Ford Coppola, an Italian-American director who would work for a modest fee. Despite initially rejecting the project, considering the novel 'pretty cheap stuff,' Coppola's financial struggles with his American Zoetrope studio led him to accept the position in September 1970 for $125,000 plus six percent of gross rentals.

Paramount hired Puzo for $100,000 plus profit participation to adapt his novel. Puzo and Coppola worked separately on the screenplay – Puzo in Los Angeles and Coppola in San Francisco. Coppola rewrote one half and Puzo rewrote the second half. Then the pair traded and rewrote each other. Puzo suggested they work together. Coppola immediately said no.

Coppola approached the material as a family chronicle and metaphor for American capitalism rather than a mere crime story. He created a detailed notebook analysing the novel's fifty scenes, focusing on themes and cultural authenticity.

The final screenplay, completed on 29 March 1971, ran 163 pages, with uncredited contributions from Robert Towne, particularly in the scene where Michael speaks with his father as he recovers from the assassination attempt in the garden.

Numerous debates between director Francis Ford Coppola and Paramount executives marked the casting process for *The Godfather*. For the pivotal role of Don Vito Corleone, Mario Puzo championed Marlon Brando from the start, considering him the only actor capable of portraying the character. Despite Paramount's initial resistance due to Brando's difficult reputation and recent box office failures, he secured the role after an impressive screen test where he transformed himself using cotton balls in his cheeks and darkened hair. Brando ultimately accepted a lower salary and posted a bond to guarantee he wouldn't delay production, earning $1.6 million through net participation.

The search for Michael Corleone proved equally challenging, remaining unresolved until just before filming began. Several prominent actors were considered, including Jack Nicholson, who declined believing an Italian-American should play the role. While Paramount pushed for established stars like Warren Beatty or Robert Redford, and producer Robert Evans favoured Ryan O'Neal, Coppola insisted on Al Pacino despite executives' concerns about his height.

When Coppola read the novel, he kept picturing the young actor he had seen onstage in the 1969 Broadway run of *Does a Tiger Wear a Necktie?* as Michael Corleone. He hadn't considered who else might be suitable. For Coppola, it was always Al Pacino. But the actor had no track record in the movies, and from what little experience he had up until this point he wasn't all that comfortable in them. It wasn't like theatre. He had to do it again and again. It wasn't as visceral as the stage, and it was taking some getting accustomed to.

When Coppola called Pacino to tell him he was directing *The Godfather*, Pacino thought the director was going through a breakdown. Pacino didn't consider that Paramount would trust the adaptation of a massive book like *The Godfather* to a director with Coppola's track record. He had made a Roger Corman-produced movie *Dementia 13 (1963)*, *You're a Big Boy Now (1966)*, the musical *Finian's Rainbow (1968)* and *The Rain People (1969)* with Robert Duvall and James Caan. When Coppola told him he would play Michael, Pacino really thought he had lost it. As a young actor, Pacino didn't even see himself in the conversation for a role as coveted as he felt this one would be. Soon, though, he realised that Coppola was serious. He was the actor he wanted, and he would put his neck on the line to make sure Pacino got the part.

Pacino didn't want to fly out to the West Coast to test for the role. Martin Bregman, though, told him to get on the plane. He bought him a bottle of whiskey to settle his nerves for the plane ride.

'Paramount wanted to test every guy in Hollywood for every part,' John Cazale told the *Pittsburgh Press* in 1973. 'Most of the screen tests were terrible and the studio began to wonder if it was his [Coppola's] fault.'

The screen tests consisted of Michael sitting with his wife-to-be Kay, played by Diane Keaton. The scene chosen was exposition heavy and gave Pacino no chance to display any of his ideas of how the character would transform throughout the movie.

Despite the fact Paramount auditioned a number of big-name actors for the role, Pacino knew that the director wanted him, and that gave him the resolve to go through the numerous rounds of tests, which were, according to producer Robert Evans, 'each worse than the last.'

Puzo backs that assertion up in his essay. 'He didn't know his lines. He threw in his own words. He didn't understand the character at all. He was terrible.'

Through it all Pacino knew that Coppola wanted him. It was a great feeling for an actor to know that the movie's director had faith in him. However, at this point in time Coppola was very much on his own.

Evans was dead set against Pacino's casting, writing in his autobiography that 'Puzo's depiction of Michael in the book was diametric in every way to Pacino.' Evans, though, said that Coppola could have Pacino on one condition – that James Caan play Sonny. Coppola was shocked. Carmine Caridi was signed to the role. Coppola didn't think Caan was right at all. He wanted an Italian and Caan was Jewish. As Evans tells it in his book there was a stand-off; Coppola left his office, only to return ten minutes later and agree to the parts.

Evans now had to get Pacino out of the contract he had signed in February 1971 with MGM and Chartoff-Winkler Productions to do *The Gang That Couldn't Shoot Straight*. While MGM were looking for $2M an out-of-court settlement would clear the way for Pacino to begin on *The Godfather*. *The Gang That Couldn't Shoot Straight* found a replacement in Robert De Niro.

Other key roles fell into place more smoothly. Robert Duvall, Coppola's first choice for Tom Hagen, won the part, while Diane Keaton was selected as Kay Adams for her eccentric reputation.

The role of Johnny Fontane went to Al Martino – who had the UK's first ever number one single in 1952 – following some controversy. Ruddy had given Martino the role, despite not having a track record as an actor. When Coppola came on board he dropped Martino and cast Vic Damone. Martino had mob connections himself and got them involved to get back into the picture. 'I went to my godfather, Russ Bufalino,' Martino told Vanity Fair in 2009. Bufalino was the head of the Pennsylvania-based Bufalino crime family. Damone dropped out and Martino stepped back in.

John Cazale joined as Fredo Corleone after casting director Fred Roos saw him in Israel Horovitz's play *Line*, Off-Broadway. Roos had been in attendance to see Cazale's co-star Richard Dreyfuss. Cazale called his casting,

'Plain, dumb luck.' Gianni Russo secured the role of Carlo Rizzi through a screen test featuring the character's fight scene with Connie.

Pacino did not like to use extensive script analysis or affective memory exercises – which drew on real past experiences. His own process was far more intuitive; he worked 'from the unconscious …what you hope happens is your unconscious is freed, you trust that part of you.'

The scene that Pacino's involvement in the film hinged on has gone on to be acknowledged as one of the most iconic in cinema history. At the time, though, Pacino and Coppola's cards were marked. Paramount executives were looking at what Coppola had shot and, not for the first time, were pondering if Pacino was suitable for the role.

In his 2024 autobiography, Pacino noted that discomfort had grown amongst people on the set, and he could feel a loss of momentum. It didn't take long for him to hear the rumours that he would be fired. Coppola was going to feel the studio's wrath for insisting that Pacino was his man, and he was also feeling the pressure.

Coppola called Pacino to a meeting at the Ginger Man, at 51 West 64th Street, near the Lincoln Center for the Performing Arts, although for Coppola, it was a family dinner that he had asked Pacino to stand aside from. The director unequivocally told his actor that he wasn't working out in the role and to go away and look at the rushes Coppola had put together from his performance.

When Pacino watched the footage, he saw no standout moment. Pacino's plan for Michael, which he hatched as he walked around Manhattan for hours pondering, was for him to emerge from the shadows, for the unremarkable kid to develop the resolve to show the Family what he was capable of; how they had underestimated him. The power of the role for Pacino was in the character's transition. He could see, however, that none of that arc was on the screen yet. Michael had no charisma; there was no presence. It was coming, but it would have to come much quicker if Pacino was to stay in the picture.

Coppola, though, wasn't sitting around waiting for his actor to save him. As he said on the 2001 DVD commentary for *The Godfather*, he knew that directors weren't fired midweek. So he moved up the filming of the Italian restaurant scene, the twenty-sixth scene in Coppola's schedule which he had marked 'Key Scene.' It was a scene that Coppola remembered from his first reading of the novel. He was instantly excited that he would film it. The scene was where Michael had his sit down with Sollozzo, the rival who took a hit out on his father, and McCluskey, the crooked police captain in Sollozzo's pocket, who had recently broken Michael's jaw. Michael, now stepping up from all-American Kid to doing real work for the family, volunteered to kill both of them. The scene was to be shot on Wednesday 31st March and Thursday 1st April 1971, in the first week of the film's production.

The inspiration was the meeting in April 1931 between Lucky Luciano and Joe Masseria at Nuova Villa Tammaro in Coney Island. Luciano excused himself to go to the bathroom, while a firing squad entered and gunned down Masseria. On his working copy of the novel Coppola wrote: 'Where did Luciano have Masseria killed?'

Coppola had taken Pacino to Patsy's in Harlem in order to show him the old-fashioned toilet where the gun would be hidden. However, the restaurant's owner wouldn't allow for the scene to be shot there out of respect for the real mobsters who frequented the establishment, including Frank Costello, Tommy Lucchese, Carlo Gambino and Joe Colombo. Shooting a cop just wasn't done in that world. Mario Migliucci, who ran Mario's, mentioned in the novel, also turned down the opportunity, saying he'd rather his restaurant was known for its menu than a murder. But then Production Designer Dean Tavoularis came upon Louis' Restaurant in the Bronx. When he went inside he realised it was perfect for what the movie needed.

Pacino's co-stars in the scene were Al Lettieri and Sterling Hayden. Lettieri's brother-in-law was Pasquale "Patsy Ryan" Eboli, who, according to an article in the *New York Times*, was 'a reputed capo in the Genovese crime family.' A fluent Italian speaker Lettieri helped Pacino with the Italian he would have to speak in the scene, and also taught him how to handle a gun.

Hayden interrupted his movie career to serve in the Marine Corps during World War II. He became a notable leading man throughout the 1950s before retiring in the 60s, only to reappear in Stanley Kubrick's *Dr. Strangelove (1964)*. By the time of *The Godfather*, Hayden, who had become a sailor and adventurer, lived on a diet of rice and nuts on the Seine on a barge called WW Griessandi. Lettieri and Hayden were acutely aware that Pacino was under pressure and offered him support. Pacino would call Hayden one of the greatest people he'd ever met, a bona fide movie star who was happy to make the young actor comfortable.

Coppola needed the scene to be tense and terrifying. The word TENSION is written all over Coppola's notes on the scene and the lead up to it.

The scene took around fifteen hours to film. Pacino stumbled over his Italian during the close talking moments with Sollozzo, and had to do the scene again and again. Eventually he thought on his feet and quickly switched into English midway through. Coppola felt that Al Lettieri's performance perfectly complemented what Pacino was doing in the scene.

Michael gets up to go to the toilet in order to locate the gun he'll use which has been hidden earlier. The tension increases when momentarily it appears that the gun isn't there as Michael frantically fumbles behind the cistern, not feeling anything. But then he stops, and the gun is in his possession.

The camera follows Michael out of the bathroom stalls, with the feeling as if it's just creeping over the top of the stalls to snatch a look. Michael runs his hands through his hair. The camera is still behind Pacino's Michael when he returns to the restaurant. McCluskey swivels his head around suddenly to stare at him. Sollozzo half turns his body around to look at him. Then the camera faces Michael.

Returning to the table the acting is all in Pacino's eyes, as they dart around, as Sollozzo resumes speaking in Italian. The camera focuses only on Michael, who doesn't speak. The cinema audience knows now he has the gun and the anticipation is building. Pacino shows intensity as Michael – not debating if he should do it – but waiting for just the precise moment to stand and fire. The sound of the L train rises, until Michael stands, his right arm raised. In his notes for preparing the movie Coppola wrote of the moment Michael fires 'Time stops short.'

He fires a bullet into Sollozzo's head and Michael's rival falls back as a red mist sprays over the white jacketed waiter. Sterling Hayden's McCluskey has a look of bemusement on his face as he frantically begins to work out what's happening. At close range Michael fires the gun into McCluskey's throat and the police captain makes a choking sound. A further shot enters his forehead and he falls head first onto the table dead. In the background can be seen Coppola's parents Carmine and Italia Coppola as a pair of the restaurant patrons.

In his book *The Method: How The Twentieth Century Learned to Act*, Isaac Butler wrote, 'The scene is a wonder of Strasbergian internalisation. You see Michael's entire decision-making process, his fears over his safety and his future, and his eventual rage and resolution, travel through Pacino in a few wordless seconds.'

Michael seems to forget to drop the gun as he begins to leave. Coppola wanted the audience to be willing him to 'Drop it! Drop it!' After a moment he does.

While making his getaway, Michael leaps into a moving car. No one had told Pacino what to do when he came out of the restaurant. The driver of the getaway car had not been told to stop. As the car slowed down, Pacino decided to leap onto the running board. But the car picked up pace and Pacino's jump fell short. He collapsed into the street having twisted his ankle so badly he couldn't move. He suddenly felt relief as he lay there with the cast and crew looking down on him. It was over. He could leave the film thanks to this injury. He could escape this environment where he wasn't wanted or rated. The studio would get what they desired all along – another actor to play Michael. But that wasn't the case. Paramount executives watched the footage, and they saw something. They saw that Pacino was right for Michael Corleone after all.

Despite Puzo describing Pacino as terrible at the screen test he would later say that Pacino was everything he imagined Michael would be on screen. He happily went around telling people he was wrong until Al Ruddy had a word with him and told him that if he wanted to be a movie producer he couldn't go around admitting he had got anything wrong.

When Ruddy passed away in May 2024, Pacino said in tribute that Ruddy, 'was absolutely beautiful to me the whole time on *The Godfather*, even when they didn't want me, he wanted me. He gave me the gift of encouragement when I needed it most, and I'll never forget it.'

Chapter 6

The Basic Training of Pavlo Hummel
(Stage, 1972)

Written by: David Rabe
Directed by: David Wheeler
Produced by: The Theater Company of Boston
Cast: Al Pacino, Irma Sandrey, Carolyn Pickman, Gustave Johnson, Walter Lott, Jack Kehoe, Barry Snider, Jan Egleson, Lance Henriksen, Tom Bower, Matthew Chait, Joseph Wilkins, Marc Frasier, Brent Jennings, Marc Sachs, Ron Hunter, Andrea Petersen, Josephine Lane, Richard Lynch, James Spruill, Steve Evets, Jon Terry, Gary Halcott

The Godfather was released in cinemas in America in March 1972. It turned Pacino from a noted theatre actor to a bona fide movie star. Lines to see the picture stretched for blocks as box office records were being broken all over the country.

In its first week alone, The Godfather brought in $465,148 from just five Manhattan theatres. By the end of its second week, now playing in 322 theatres in the US and Canada, the total was $7,397,164. Before long, The Godfather was making $1M a day. Some theatres were showing it around the clock, beginning with a 9am screening and closing for the day only when the audience came out of the 3.30am screening at 6.30am.

In short, this was about the biggest movie America had ever seen, yet its breakout star wasn't lapping up the acclaim. Pacino was in rehearsals for Theater Company of Boston's production of *The Basic Training of Pavlo Hummel* which was taking place at the Charles Playhouse Open Circle Theatre on Warrenton Street. Pacino showed up to Sack Savoy One's opening night screening of The Godfather on 21st March in aid of the Kidney Foundation. He was joined by co-star, singer Al Martino who was in Boston for a show at the Empire Room.

Pacino wasn't at home with the increase in interest in him, feeling that casual conversation wasn't one of his skills. He worried he'd be a disappointment to people.

While *The Godfather* allowed Pacino more visibility, it didn't leave him much richer, despite being paid $35,000. 'I wound up losing money,' he said. The deal struck to get Pacino out of The Gang That Couldn't Shoot Straight saw him having to pay MGM's lawyers' costs, as well as being committed to making a movie for them.

Pavlo Hummel wouldn't help his finances out much. His salary was $200 a week. '…I never worry about money,' Pacino said to the *New York Times* in May of 1972. 'I've done a lot of things in my life for money; the one thing I haven't done for money is act.'

When Gregg Kilday of the *Los Angeles Times* went to visit Pacino in the rented flat above Boston Common where he was living for the duration of the production, he found him eating his lunch straight out of the saucepan while on the phone with Marty Bregman. In her autobiography *Then Again* Diane Keaton observed that Pacino didn't eat sitting down with others. Eating while standing up at home alone was where he was more comfortable. Kilday asked him why he wasn't in New York lapping up the plaudits for his role as Michael Corleone. Pacino's answer was he didn't intend to build a career, so he wasn't following any prescribed path. He really wanted to avoid the film's massive impact. He wanted something to concentrate on, and what he really wanted to do was act, not appear on talk shows or speak to interviewers. He liked the play's director David Wheeler and he felt comfortable in Boston, so it was a good fit to dodge *The Godfather*'s overwhelming success.

The stage revitalised Pacino and after working in an unfamiliar setting such as a big motion picture he jumped at the chance to go back on stage when Wheeler suggested Pavlo Hummel.

William B. Collins of the *Philadelphia Inquirer* suggested that Pacino must now have his pick of projects. But Pacino countered that wasn't the case. People were making assumptions over what he would do or how big his fee would be, so he wasn't being inundated with projects. Pacino told Collins the thing he wanted to do most was repertory, playing different roles in succession. He said in particular he would like to do Richard III.

Chris Chase of the *New York Times* also visited Boston to see the play and talk with Pacino. Chase discovered that despite the play starring one of the leads from what was shaping up to be perhaps the biggest movie of all time, it was a task to find out how to see it. The telephone number listed for the theatre, Chase discovered, gave a recording saying the line had been disconnected at the customer's request. When he found the Charles Playhouse off an alley behind the larger Shubert Theatre, Chase discovered that the box office employee wasn't sure if there was a Sunday night show. When Chase told Pacino of his travails before he eventually saw the show, he laughed. 'If you want to see this play, you can't. That's the Theater Company of Boston.' Chase asked Pacino why he was playing to 'maybe 85 seats filled out front' when he could be reaching millions doing another movie. Pacino's reply was simple: he was being an actor. The stage was, Pacino believed, where the core of the actor's craft lay.

Playwright David Rabe was 31, a native of Dubuque, Iowa. He graduated from Loras College there. He enrolled in graduate studies in theatre at Villanova University in Pennsylvania and began writing plays. He spent two years feeling suffocated. 'I felt I didn't know enough about anything to write,' he told John Lahr of the *New Yorker* in 2008. Rabe dropped out and supported himself with various odd jobs, including as a parking valet and bellhop. Then, in 1965, at the age of twenty-five, he was drafted.

He served two years in the army, including a year in Vietnam at a hospital field unit. His military service involved clerical work, guard duty, and hospital construction in what became the US Army base Long Binh Post. Since his unit faced no threat, Rabe's Vietnam experience wasn't combat but rather witnessing uninhibited behaviour where normal social restrictions had broken down. He described the atmosphere as having barriers and restrictions removed, creating a chaotic environment where one could encounter both horrific and thrilling scenes around different corners; to Rabe it felt a little like the Wild West.

After returning to Villanova in January 1967, Rabe spent eighteen months in Philadelphia, during which he remained psychologically immersed in his Vietnam experience. He would tell Ellen Kaye of the Philadelphia Inquirer magazine, that after his return he felt he was still living in Vietnam one hundred percent of the time. It was three years, he said, before he felt it was anything like 50/50.

He worked as a feature writer for the New Haven Register, earning an Associated Press award. During this period, his anger about US involvement in Vietnam intensified as he perceived that Americans at home had nothing at stake in the conflict, living in abundance while others suffered. This realisation provided him with his subject matter.

Rabe channelled his experiences into writing *The Basic Training of Pavlo Hummel* and *Sticks and Bones*. His writing process involved completing a draft of one play before moving to the other, then returning to refine the first. A third Vietnam-related play, *Streamers*, was completed in 1975. Rabe viewed writing as essential for processing his emotional trauma, describing the material in his plays as too difficult to discuss casually with others.

Rather than creating protest theatre, Rabe aimed to authentically portray what Vietnam was actually like. His journalistic background influenced his approach, and he had attempted to keep a journal during his service. He observed that most young soldiers lacked understanding of their situation in Vietnam, which became central to developing the character of Pavlo Hummel.

A Rockefeller grant enabled Rabe to focus on playwriting, despite his initial doubts about producing commercially viable work in a theatre world he perceived as overly focused on form and technique. He returned to Villanova as an assistant professor, teaching drama and film courses, though he found that student work sometimes interfered with his own creative process when students explored similar themes to his own ideas.

Pavlo Hummel premiered at Joseph Papp's New York Public Theater in 1971 with William Atherton in the title role, though it had first been performed at Villanova Theater. Pacino had been offered the role, but was committed to *The Godfather*.

Rabe had sent his script to a number of producers, both on and off Broadway. No one was interested. Rabe would say it was rejected by almost all of America's regional and experimental theatres – including Long Wharf, the American Place, Chelsea, Yale, the O'Neill, Lincoln Center, and the Arena Stage.

Papp enjoyed discovering new writers through the mail. It was estimated that at that time, around 1500 scripts were posted to his desk. They would be handed over to readers for their initial assessments, and from there, Papp would personally read around 200.

'You create a certain ambience, and you begin to attract certain writers,' Papp told the *Philadelphia Inquirer*. 'Suddenly, you don't have to seek writers, they are seeking you.' For some reason he couldn't put his finger on, Papp picked *The Basic Training of Pavlo Hummel* out of the pile himself. What piqued his interest on that first reading was that he didn't understand it. He couldn't place the play in any particular context. 'That meant that Rabe was doing something different.' Although it was about Vietnam, it didn't feel like propaganda, nor did it have an agenda. Rabe wrote the play to show that soldiers were neither monsters nor heroes. 'There are people who wait around for the great play,' Papp said, 'but play production is a process of life. Nobody comes in full-blown. It develops like life itself.'

Initially, Rabe's first act had a documentary feel. Papp urged him to break down the play's linear nature, which Rabe resisted initially, having already written another play – *The Orphan* – based in theatricality, so he felt that *Pavlo* had to be rooted in realism. During rehearsals though, he began to realise that Papp was right.

Papp put it on at the 299-capacity Estelle R. Newman Theatre at the Public Theatre, making it a showcase performance. It had its world premiere on 20th May, 1970, running for 363 New York performances before moving to Philadelphia's Locust Theatre for two weeks.

In *Newsday*, George Oppenheimer wrote that Rabe was, 'the most potentially powerful American playwright since Eugene O'Neill.' Oppenheimer would later ask Rabe how it felt to be compared to O'Neill, noting 'quite a few critics' including New York magazine's John Simon, had done so, though neglecting to mention he was one of them. 'Enormously flattered and terribly embarrassed,' was Rabe's response. 'I wish they wouldn't.'

David Rabe's experience serving with the Army's 68th Medical Group significantly shifted his perspective on the Vietnam War, transforming him from someone who initially supported American involvement to holding drastically different views upon his return.

Rabe resisted characterisations of *The Basic Training of Pavlo Hummel* as simply an anti-war piece, arguing that such labeling missed the deeper point. He contended that while people readily accept family dysfunction in plays like *Long Day's Journey Into Night* or *Death of a Salesman* without dismissing them as anti-family works, they struggle to view war as an inherent aspect of human experience. Rabe believed this resistance stemmed from society's reluctance to acknowledge war as a permanent fixture of human existence, unlike other social institutions and even criminal behaviour.

Regarding his protagonist, Rabe presented *Pavlo Hummel* as a fundamentally flawed individual rather than a sympathetic victim of military circumstances. He described Hummel as someone incapable of meaningful connections whether in civilian life or military service, consistently deflecting responsibility for his own shortcomings. Rabe characterised Hummel's defining trait as his tendency toward self-destructive behaviour, describing his propensity for putting himself in dangerous situations.

Director David Wheeler had completed a nine-month stint at the Guthrie Theatre in Minneapolis, but was keen to return to the Theater Company of Boston, for Rabe's play.

Pacino told Chase that he had always wanted to work with Wheeler, who was the man he had auditioned for years earlier when he turned down $50 a week because he wouldn't do small parts. This part, however, was different. 'It's the best thing that's happened to me in years,' Pacino said. The Theater Company of Boston were routinely described as embattled, continually up against it financially, and the rumour at the time was that Pacino was there to help them out.

The Basic Training of Pavlo Hummel opened on 6th April 1972, running initially for six weeks, before playing for four extra weeks. Rabe's follow-up *Sticks and Bones*, also concerning Vietnam, was running on Broadway at the same time.

The play begins with the unheroic death of Pavlo Hummel, then flashes back to his Army basic training in Georgia. Here, Hummel, a Chaplinesque social failure, weird, quirky and odd, buys into his drill instructor's army logic as he seeks acceptance and manhood from the life of a soldier. The second act, more brutally direct than the first, moves to Vietnam.

In one scene, Pavlo attempts to convince his fellow soldiers that his uncle has been put to death in San Quentin for murdering several people. Pacino related that scene to his childhood, where he'd invent tales for his friends in the Bronx, telling them he had ten dogs, or he was from Texas or he had a job.

Pavlo is naive rather than genuinely innocent. Rabe recalls being drafted and being bemused by his sergeant talking about Vietnam. Pavlo lies, steals, is incompetent, and contemptuous of others. Incapable of forming relationships, the army offers him companionship and a role he has failed to find elsewhere.

Pacino was a revelation in the role.

In the *Boston Globe*, William A Henry wrote, '…the evening belongs to Al Pacino. Pacino's manner is engaging, his timing virtually flawless. His range is vast, yet he never seems to strain.' The really important detail for Henry though was that Pacino didn't dilute the failings of his less than heroic character with his own boundless charm.

Of Pacino's performance, Kevin Kelly wrote in the *Globe*, 'Pacino creates Pavlo as a dreadful human being, but not so dreadful that our pity is withheld.' He summed up by describing Pacino's journey as Pavlo from shiftless lout to rampant soldier wide-eyed with murder as 'subtle and awesome. The performance is a non-stop tour de force.'

In the *Harvard Crimson*, Whit Stillman, later to become a noted film director with *Metropolitan (1990)* and *The Last Days of Disco (1998)*, wrote, 'Al Pacino gives a performance that can have no equal. "You're weird, Hummel," Kress, the squad bully tells him. "You don't even talk American, you talk Hummel – some god damned foreign language." And Pacino acts his own language, with a nuance and virtuosity that is wonderful.'

The role was a departure from what Pacino had been earning his name for on stage with his last few performances. In *The New York Times*, Chris Chase called back to Clive Barnes' comment about seeing what else Pacino could do besides scaring babies, old women and Barnes. Chase suggested Barnes should get up to Boston to see exactly what else Pacino could do. 'Seeing him act in Boston, you get some idea of the moves the guy has.'

Pacino had a ritual during the show's run. Every night before going on he'd go into the bathroom backstage to prepare. He'd put his fingers to his face, look in the mirror and recite a line from the play to himself. 'I'm all right. I do all right.' On the last night of the run there was a wrap party. Pacino slipped out of the party and went into that bathroom. He looked in the mirror and said for the last time. 'I'm all right. I do all right.' It was his way of saying goodbye and letting go of the character. Later after *Richard III* closed Pacino found himself, at 8 at night, walking around with a limp. 'The body doesn't know a role is over until the mind tells it,' he told Paul Rosenfield of the *LA Times* in 1986.

Pacino returned to *Pavlo Hummel* for a Broadway run in 1977 where he would win a Tony award for Best Actor.

Pacino shared his theatrical ambitions with the *Boston Globe*, expressing his desire to perform *Richard III* with the Theater Company the following year and his dream of eventually tackling Henrik Ibsen's 1867 play *Peer Gynt*. Despite his emerging success in cinema, Pacino maintained his preference for stage work, citing the greater control, freedom, and physical engagement it offered, along with adequate rehearsal time. He observed that film stardom didn't necessarily correlate with acting ability, noting how some talented stage actors struggled in movies while certain film actors appeared lost on stage. Pacino believed that working exclusively in films could cause an actor's physicality to deteriorate.

The Mark Taper Forum was the location for the mooted *Peer Gynt*, while Pacino was also being lined up for a film with Gene Hackman called *Scarecrow*. The movie would film in the fall of 1972 with Jerry Schatzberg directing.

During this period of his career, Pacino was dealing with significant alcohol dependency. In a July 1972 interview with journalist Bob Lardine, he openly discussed how the demands of theatrical performance left him physically and mentally drained, making alcohol seem necessary for unwinding. He referenced a comment by Laurence Olivier suggesting that post-show drinks were theatre's greatest pleasure and praised whisky's effectiveness, claiming it helped him more than therapy sessions with psychiatrists. Pacino credited alcohol with improving his social abilities and communication, though he acknowledged that most people lacked proper drinking skills. While he had moved beyond destructive three-day drinking sprees, which he recognised as depressing experiences, he still felt dependent on alcohol after performances. He told Chris Chase, 'I need that drink after the show, I really need it.'

In January 1973 Pacino opened in *Richard III* at the Loeb in Cambridge in a Theater Company of Boston production. It moved to the Church of the Covenant in the Back Bay area of Boston for shows from 3rd February to

4th March. Pacino had performed the first half hour of *Richard III* at The Actors Studio around three or four years earlier.

On 12th February 1973, Pacino discovered he had been nominated for an Academy Award for Best Supporting Actor in *The Godfather*. He was nominated alongside his co-stars Robert Duvall, and James Caan along with Eddie Albert for *The Heartbreak Kid (1972)* and the eventual winner Joel Grey for *Cabaret (1972)*.

Pacino felt he was a stage actor, but he knew he had to do films because of the money. He had never done Shakespeare and really felt it was time, although he told the *Boston Globe* he would have preferred to start with a smaller part, something less demanding than Richard. He went into this production with the outlook that it would be preparation for *really* doing *Richard III* one day.

The production and Pacino were well received, but soon it was time for Pacino to return to the movies.

Chapter 7

Serpico
(Film, 1973)

Director: Sidney Lumet
Screenplay: Waldo Salt and Norman Wexler,
Based on the book *Serpico: The Cop Who Defied the System* by Peter Maas
Cast: Al Pacino, John Randolph, Jack Kehoe, Biff McGuire, Barbara Edayoung, Cornelia Sharpe, Tony Roberts, John Medici, Alan Rich, Norman Ornellas, Ed Grover, Al Henderson, Hank Garre, Damien Leake, Joe Bova, Gene Gross, John Stewart, Woodie King, James Tolin, Ed Crowley, Bernard Barrow, Sal Carollo, Mildred Clinton, Nathan George, Gus Fleming, Richard Foronjy, Alan North

On 1st August 1972, the *New York Times* reported that Bantam Books, a company that usually only bought reprint rights to bestsellers, had sold a book it commissioned in 1971 to Viking Press, a leading hardback publisher. It was unusual then for paperback houses to buy original material, which was solely the domain of hardback publishers. It was a strategy Bantam had used recently with William Peter Blatty's novel *The Exorcist*.

The book was *Serpico*, written by Peter Maas, a 43-year-old journalist who had worked for *The Saturday Evening Post* and *New York Magazine*. It was a biography of Frank Serpico, a New York City cop who fought on his own against corruption in the police department. Maas disclosed that he had sold the film rights to Dino De Laurentiis Productions. His fee was reported to be in excess of $400,000. Maas split the fee with Serpico. 'After all, it's his life,' Maas said.

Frank Serpico had joined the police department in 1959. Working in the 81st Precinct in Brooklyn to his bemusement, he found that the beat cop's life was full of free meals, small bribes to look the other way, and your feet up on the dashboard. When he stepped up to work in plain clothes, he found that corruption, too, was promoted. He attempted to have his bosses do something about it, but of course, he found many of them were also on the take. 'Like an Army private attempting to court martial four star generals.' Their stonewalling – even the Mayor wasn't interested – led to Serpico taking his concerns to the *New York Times*.

In 1970 the NYT ran a series of front-page stories on corruption in the New York Police Department. It led to the formation of the Knapp Commission, where wide scale corruption was publicly exposed, with many cops losing their jobs. For his book Peter Maas had access to transcripts of closed sessions of the commission.

Peter Maas said that most people who spoke to him about Frank Serpico had one common question: 'What was wrong with him?'

The 51-year-old Italian De Laurentiis produced his first movie at 19 years old and dominated the Italian film business throughout the 1950s. In 1969, De Laurentiis bought Maas' previous book, *The Valachi Papers*, the story of mobster Joe Valachi and his decision to turn federal informant. 'It turned out the [American] studios were afraid of the Mafia, afraid to touch it,' Peter Maas recalled for Marie Brenner's book *Going Hollywood*. 'Remember, this was before The Godfather.' It was filmed with Charles Bronson in the lead role. In 1972, De Laurentiis sold Dinocitta, the sprawling studio complex he built on the outskirts of Rome to the Italian government and moved to New York, setting up the De Laurentiis Entertainment Group.

Maas had written only one chapter of *Serpico* when De Laurentiis inquired about his current project. Maas explained he was writing about a courageous Italian-American police officer whose parents likely came from the same Naples neighbourhood as De Laurentiis's family. This brief description immediately captured De Laurentiis's interest.

De Laurentiis found himself fascinated by Frank Serpico's character based solely on Maas's initial twenty pages. He believed that compelling personalities and strong characters were the essential ingredients for successful films, reasoning that an exceptional book wasn't necessary if you could build a story around such a powerful character. This philosophy convinced him that *Serpico* had the potential he was looking for.

Without hesitation, De Laurentiis decided to purchase the film rights on the spot. Maas was stunned by this immediate commitment, pointing out that the book remained unfinished and that De Laurentiis was essentially making a blind purchase. De Laurentiis dismissed these concerns, emphasising his confidence in the project's potential. True to his word, he completed the deal by noon the following day.

There was someone else on Maas's trail. Martin Bregman was looking to get into filmmaking, and was searching for good material to develop. He was focusing on the type of things he felt Pacino would be exceptional in and more importantly something he would identify with. Bregman had zeroed in on two things – a gangster film or a cop film, something set on the streets. Serendipitously Bregman met with Sam Cohn, who represented Maas. Maas had written a piece for *New York Magazine* about Serpico. Immediately Bregman related to the story. It was different from the kind of cop tales he had read before. The man at its centre was unusual – unique. He was, Bregman felt, exactly the type of character Pacino would click with.

Maas had allowed Bregman to read the first chapter while he was midway through writing the book. Bregman knew instantly that it had cinematic potential and *Serpico* would be a role perfect for Al Pacino.

At that point Maas had been thinking of Dustin Hoffman to play Serpico. Maas was told that Pacino liked the book. 'That's all I needed to know,' Maas told Bob Talbert of the *Detroit Free Press*. 'Pacino reads four chapters of the book and he thinks he's Serpico. He is, let me tell you.'

Pacino read a treatment, as a script wasn't yet written. Pacino thought it was interesting, but it didn't read well, and he couldn't commit based only on a treatment. What sold Pacino was Frank Serpico himself. When they met Pacino felt that there was something in Serpico he could play. At first glance with his long hair and earring he looked a little strange, but there was a look in his eye that made Pacino feel that he could serve Frank Serpico as a man.

Peter Maas said there was such a connection that within twenty minutes Pacino was virtually absorbing Serpico through his pores.

Pacino invested significant time with Frank Serpico, even living with him. As Maas observed, both men shared similar Italian-American backgrounds. This direct access to Serpico provided an invaluable advantage for Pacino, allowing characteristics to absorb subliminally and strengthen his portrayal.

Unlike theatre where the material serves as the primary source, Pacino observed that film often lacks that textual strength, making Serpico himself an essential reference point.

Access was also available to working cops, and Pacino did go out on a ride along for one night, but quickly realised that way of preparing wasn't for him, and he went back to spending time with Frank.

During one memorable evening at Pacino's rented Montauk beach house, he and Serpico were sitting out gazing at the water. Pacino took a breath and asked something he felt Serpico must have been asked many times before. 'Why did you do it? Why make a stand against corruption?' Serpico pondered for a moment, and thought about his answer. What he said hit Pacino as something profound. 'If I didn't, who would I be when I listened to a piece of music?' Pacino found this response perfectly characteristic of Serpico's nature.

Speaking to the *Associated Press*, Pacino explained how their relationship differed from natural friendships, being artificially constructed around the film project. 'Unfortunately our relationship was vague at the end,' Pacino said. 'It's not like how we pick and choose our friends; we were put together out of an unnatural situation.' Pacino though always enjoyed being in Serpico's company.

Waldo Salt, who had won the Best Adapted Screenplay Oscar for *Midnight Cowboy (1969)*, was brought on to adapt the book. Salt had been blacklisted in Hollywood in 1951, having refused to testify on purported Communist affiliations before the House Un-American Activities Committee. Salt was named by Richard J. Collins, a fellow screenwriter and the best man at his wedding. 'One man's subversion is another man's patriotism,' Salt said when he was questioned at the inquiry in April 1951. 'I consider the activities of this committee subversive of the Constitution.' Salt's blacklisting lasted until 1962. If there was anyone who could identify with Frank Serpico it was surely Waldo Salt.

John G. Avildsen, who had helmed *Joe (1970)*, was set to direct. He and his chosen screenwriter, Norman Wexler, went to stay with Serpico in his home in the Swiss mountains. Waldo Salt wrote the first script. Wexler, *Joe's* screenwriter, came on board to offer some humour.

Wexler, an award-winning playwright, was also known for being arrested by the FBI on a flight from New York to San Francisco, having told stewardesses and fellow passengers that he was going to shoot Richard Nixon. He was thrown into city prison for a time. Wexler denied planning an assassination and insisted he was merely discussing ways of 'saving the country', one of which was to kill the president. 'You've heard of street theatre, well this is airplane theatre.' he said. The truth was that Wexler suffered from regular psychotic mania.

In the 1970s, producer Bob Zmuda worked as Wexler's assistant. Wexler had earned the nickname 'The Doctor' for his exceptional ability to write authentic street dialogue. According to Zmuda's 2012 appearance on the *WTF with Marc Maron* podcast, Wexler's talent stemmed from his understanding that people speak differently when they're upset – their breathing patterns change along with their speech patterns.

Wexler's method for capturing this authentic dialogue was unconventional: Zmuda would follow him throughout each day with a Panasonic tape recorder, documenting the frequent confrontations that Wexler would initiate with people on the street. 'I mean big-time confrontations when people wanted to kill him, and I would record it.'

Every four days, Zmuda would send the accumulated recordings to a stenographer for transcription, and Wexler would use this real-world dialogue as source material for his screenplay writing.

This approach gave Wexler's scripts a distinctive authenticity that other writers couldn't replicate, making him the go-to screenwriter when films required realistic street-level conversations and dialogue.

Maas wasn't happy with how the adaptation of his book *The Valachi Papers* turned out. 'I had some say-so in casting and some script approval,' he told Bob Talbert of the *Detroit Free Press*. He wasn't happy with the first few versions of the screenplay, so in his words, he 'structured' the final draft.

Soon, though, Avildsen fell out with Bregman and the film's line producer over locations and departed the production. Pacino had been reading other actors with Avildsen ahead of rehearsals starting. Then one day he didn't turn up. Bregman hadn't mentioned the director's dismissal to Pacino.

De Laurentiis was furious. He wouldn't let Bregman appoint another director, insisting instead that Pacino do it. Pacino, baffled and unhappy with the request attempted to fulfill it. He spoke with Peter Yates who had made films as diverse as *Summer Holiday (1963)* and *Bullitt (1968)*, and Mark Rydell the director of *The Reivers (1969)*.

Pacino met with Sidney Lumet, who directed *12 Angry Men (1957)* and the movie adaptation of Eugene O'Neill's *Long Day's Journey into Night (1962)*. Pacino felt that Lumet was critical of his performances previously. But when Pacino watched his work he knew he was a great director.

Lumet took over as director of *Serpico* with only six weeks remaining before the scheduled shooting date. He later recalled having just five weeks for preparation, with no locations selected, despite 107 being required and nothing accomplished beforehand. The script remained in draft form, leaving Lumet feeling he lacked sufficient time to consider his approach properly. He characterised the experience as frantic, noting there was essentially no usable script since Waldo Salt's three successive drafts had grown progressively weaker. Lumet found the process both physically brutal and emotionally demanding. 'It's all up there on the screen, all the intensity,' he told the *Daily News* in December 1973.

It was Pacino's first-time meeting with Sidney Lumet. 'It was an interesting meeting,' he told *GQ*. 'I grew to love him naturally, but the first impression of him was, he said a couple of things that seemed a bit, a bit off putting about me. So I felt a little, "Who does this guy think he is?" or something. Then I started seeing some of his films, and I thought, "He's a great director, that's who he is."'

Lumet made Pacino rehearse the script like a play, which, although Pacino found it tough, he responded to. He loved Lumet's extraordinary energy and began to feel a kinship with his director.

Paramount Pictures came on board as the distributor and fronted the $3M to make the movie.

'I always had a feeling about him,' Lumet said of Frank Serpico when he spoke to David Schwartz of *Pinewood Dialogue* in 2005. 'I don't know, Al and I talked about it; I don't know whether Al agreed with me. I always felt he was a rebel, period. That he would've behaved that way if he'd been a baker. That anybody above him was his automatic enemy.'

Serpico, sat in and contributed ideas for the film. 'He's bottomless,' Lumet said of him, 'It keeps pouring out.' Lumet was happy to have him there as he said it helped him get 'at the inner truth of the man' and avoid making 'just another cop picture.'

However, Lumet had to draw the line on Frank's involvement somewhere. He warned Pacino not to get too close to Serpico. With his anti-corruption stance Serpico had upset a lot of people. Lumet cautioned Pacino that close proximity to Frank Serpico came with a lot of risk. Lumet told Serpico that he couldn't be there for rehearsals or on the set of the movie. People would be too self-conscious. 'I broke his heart,' Lumet said.

Pacino was locked into a shooting schedule as he was committed to filming *The Godfather Part II*, so delays were not welcomed. 'Al and I were both determined to do it right,' Lumet told film historian Robert Osborne in 1974. 'We felt an extraordinary obligation to Serpico himself. When you're dealing with the life of a real, living man, you don't dare take that dramatic licence you feel free to use in a falsely made piece of work.'

Cinematographer Arthur J. Ornitz was behind the camera, editor Dede Allen was hired, and Michael 'Mikis' Theodorakis provided the music.

Serpico featured 107 different locations. Serpico's apartment was built in the studio, but all the other locations were in Manhattan. The production had an average of three moves per day. Lumet felt that the character demanded mobility, and that was integrated into the style of the movie. The director told Kenneth M. Chanko of *Films in Review* in 1984, 'I had wheelchairs. I had rollerskates. Anything that was necessary to move the camera. Rather than tell Al to slow down I'd rather put the cameramen on rollerskates and have them pulled.' That became part of the style of the movie, camera movement that was naturalistic to make it look like it was filmed by a news crew fighting their way through the crowds.

Pacino said years later that he never knew where the cameras were.

The film featured 110 speaking parts, and they were all filled with actors from New York, with around 5000 being auditioned. 'We wanted the sound and look of New York,' Bregman said to the Daily News, 'and New York has more and better actors than any city in the world.'

Lumet wanted to use actors that weren't widely known by the movie-going public. He was going for realism and knew that would be shattered if an audience recognised an actor because they were in a commercial or had a stand-out part in another movie.

The film covers eleven years, from 1960 to 1971. The production discovered that there was no graffiti in the early sixties; it had only arrived in New York around 1966, so graffiti on walls had to be cleaned up for the early parts of the movie. The film was shot in reverse order. Pacino begins the shoot with a full beard and long hair, then trims it down to his Zapata moustache before finishing the shoot with scenes of Serpico as a short-haired, clean-shaven rookie.

Perhaps surprising, as the movie was about police corruption the New York Police Department were co-operative. Lumet shot in four live station houses while the NYPD carried their work around filming.

The film was shot throughout summer, but Lumet wanted to ensure that seasons changed during the story. The crew uprooted trees and replanted them later in order to give the summer locations a winter look. 'I don't even want to discuss that,' associate producer Roger Rothstein told *Filmmakers Newsletter* in 1974. 'I don't want to tell you what we spent defoliating trees, cutting down shrubs etc.'

For Pacino, one of his concerns was not sweating in July's New York heat. 'The makeup man put some special stuff on us so our faces wouldn't sweat,' he told Marty Campbell of the *Associated Press*. 'It's very refreshing and it dries you. He comes around with a rag just before they shoot. One time I was on a roof in winter clothes, gloves and hat and I sat on a chair to rest and it sunk into the tar at an angle, and it was at the edge of the roof.'

Lumet clarified that his intent with Serpico was not to create an anti-police film, but rather to expose how the acceptance of corruption had become ingrained in American society as a whole. He viewed this resigned attitude of helplessness against institutional power – you can't fight city hall – as the fundamental problem underlying many of America's issues. For Lumet, the police department served as just one illustration of a broader systemic corruption that, if it infected both law enforcement and the courts, left citizens with nowhere to turn for protection.

The director emphasised his commitment to presenting Frank Serpico's story authentically, avoiding dramatisation or exploitation in favour of simply showing what the man actually accomplished. Lumet praised Al Pacino's performance, attributing its power both to the actor's shared sense of obligation to truthful storytelling and to Pacino's inherent inability as a performer to portray anything false. According to Lumet, Pacino completely inhabits his characters and maintains that authenticity throughout, making him an ideal collaborator for the director's vision of honest filmmaking. Lumet said after filming that he could work with Pacino forever.

Maas recalled being on set with Pacino. While waiting on the sets being changed Maas and Pacino sat at a bar which happened to be one of Frank Serpico's old hangouts. A stewardess walked in. Maas would learn that she had been one of Serpico's girls. She spotted the pair and walked up to them. 'Why didn't you call me Frank? I thought you were in Switzerland!' the woman said. Maas corrected her, pointing out it wasn't Serpico but Al Pacino. The woman shyly asked for Pacino's autograph. Maas knew Pacino had done a great job if he could fool one of Serpico's former girlfriends.

'Yeah my friends say Pacino was more me than me,' Frank Serpico said in 1997.

In advance publicity for the film, Bregman insisted it would be as big as *On the Waterfront (1954)*. 'It's the same kind of fight,' he said. 'One man who couldn't accept a system that was corrupt.'

Lumet added a score even though he didn't feel the film needed one, simply because he felt Dino De Laurentiis would put one in. 'He'd take it back to Italy and Nino Rota would lay in a score like wall-to-wall carpeting,' Lumet said to *Pinewood Dialogue*. Lumet discovered by accident that the Greek composer and political activist Mikis Theodorakis, had just gotten out of jail after just over a year. Greece at the time was run by a right-wing military junta. Lumet surmised Theodorakis must need some money. He found that Theodorakis had immediately left Greece for Paris. Lumet located him there and Theodorakis provided the score. Lumet calculated that there was around fourteen minutes of music in the entire picture.

Lumet completed the film in 71 days. It had been budgeted for 75. Serpico opened in December 1973, just before Christmas.

In the *Daily News* Kathleen Carroll wrote of Pacino's performance: 'No longer does he have to stand in Hoffman's shadow. He is an important actor in his own right.'

In *The Record*, John Crittenden wrote: 'Salt and Wexler have produced dialogue that is rife with obscenities, yet it is so perfectly naturalistic, so right in its echoing of the way people actually talk, that it never grates on the ear.'

Pauline Kael wrote in her book *Reeling* that 'scene after ragged scene cried out for retakes.' Kael also wrote that Lumet directed, 'sloppily but effectively.'

In December of 1973, the National Board of Review Awards awarded Pacino the Best Performance by an Actor jointly with Robert Ryan for his performance as Larry Slade in *The Iceman Cometh (1973)*. It was a posthumous award for Ryan who had passed away in July of that year.

Serpico topped Judith Crist's 10 Best of 1973 list, with *O Lucky Man (1973)* and *Sleeper (1973)* taking the second and third spots. Rex Reed also included Serpico in his 'in no particular order' 10 Best of 1973 list. Charles Champlin of the *Los Angeles Times* also chose Serpico in his 10 Best of 1973 list.

On 26th January 1974 at the Beverly Hilton Hotel, Pacino won the Golden Globe for Best Actor in a Drama. Joyce Haber in *The Los Angeles Times* suggested that Pacino won ahead of Jack Lemmon for *Save The Tiger (1973)* because Paramount had put their money behind Pacino instead of Lemmon as he was due to open in *The Godfather Part II*. Robert Blake, Jack Nicholson and Steve McQueen were the other nominees. *The Exorcist (1973)* was the night's big winner taking home four awards.

On 19 February, the Academy Award nominations were announced. Pacino was nominated for Best Actor alongside Marlon Brando for *Last Tango in Paris (1973)*, Jack Lemmon for *Save the Tiger (1973)*, Jack Nicholson for *The Last Detail (1973)*, and Robert Redford for *The Sting (1973)*. A heavyweight group of big name actors, it was Redford's first nomination.

At the ceremony, Pacino took time away from filming *The Godfather Part II* in New York to attend. He applauded enthusiastically from the front rows when Jack Lemmon was announced that year's recipient of the Best Actor award.

Maas said the movie had a positive effect on those who saw it. 'It's made people think of behaving better,' he told the *Newspaper Enterprise Association* in 1974.

Chapter 8

The Godfather Part II
(Film, 1974)

Directed by: Francis Ford Coppola
Screenplay by: Francis Ford Coppola and Mario Puzo
Based on the novel *The Godfather* by Mario Puzo
Cast: Al Pacino, Robert Duvall, Diane Keaton, Robert De Niro, Talia Shire, Morgana King, John Cazale, Mariana Hill, Lee Strasberg, Michael V. Gazzo, Richard Bright, Bruno Kirby

'I don't like to repeat myself,' Pacino said to *Playboy* while drinking Wild Turkeys in a bar in La Guardia in 1973. For that reason when he was presented the script for The Godfather sequel he said no. Soon though, another offer was made. It was one Pacino couldn't refuse. He was reportedly earning $500,000. At thirty-two he realised that his career struggle was behind him, although he was still talking about playing Peer Gynt, or Oedipus and 'daring to fail.'

Pacino was eager to resume working with Coppola. He knew that the director almost lost his job by insisting Pacino was the right man to play Michael Corleone. Modestly Pacino told the press that without that insistence he would still be doing repertory in Boston.

In the spring of 1971 Coppola set up pre-production offices in Los Angeles. The film took Coppola two years of preparation although he still found time to direct *The Conversation (1974)* with Gene Hackman and John Cazale, Noel Coward's *Private Lives* at the Geary Theatre in San Francisco for the American Conservatory Theatre and Gottfried von Einem's *The Visit of the Old Lady* for the San Francisco Opera Company. Filming on *The Godfather Part II* began in Lake Tahoe, California and for seven months continued in Las Vegas, Paramount Studios and locations in Los Angeles, the Caribbean city of Santo Domingo, New York City, Trieste, Sicily, and brief location shooting in Rome, Miami and Washington, D.C. Filming began in October 1973.

The sequel was more epic in scope as Coppola opted to take in Vito Corleone's childhood in Italy and his rise to power in New York's Little Italy in the late 1910s and early 1920s. This wasn't simply a film about organised crime and gang warfare, it was a study of how power corrupts.

Coppola had been impressed by Robert De Niro in Martin Scorsese's *Mean Streets (1973)* and had cast him as the younger Vito. De Niro travelled to Sicily and tape recorded the locals to capture their unique Italian dialect.

For the role of the Jewish mob figure or 'investment financier' Hyman Roth, Pacino and Charlie Laughton came up with an idea – Lee Strasberg. Pacino's old acting teacher had given up acting in 1929, only once returning to the stage when in 1936 the Group Theatre struggled to find someone to play a part in a Clifford Odets one act and Kazan stepped in. Coppola had wanted Elia Kazan for the role. Pacino turned up at Strasberg's apartment where he was holding a party, with the script, only to find Kazan was also in attendance. Pacino found a quiet moment to push the script in an unmarked manilla envelope onto him. Strasberg wasn't looking for a movie career, and was reluctant to accept the package telling Pacino he'd been handed things like this before. Pacino insisted that the part was right for him.

While Strasberg wasn't keen on acting in movies he was interested in how his methods might be used on film. Students had told him that The Method didn't translate well to filming schedules and with all the machinery they had to perform in front of. It would be interesting he thought to find out for himself.

Pacino though knew Coppola was intent on casting Kazan and would have to work on his director if his idea would be approved. Pacino engineered a meeting between Coppola and Strasberg, being careful to ensure that both men didn't realise they were being set up. He enlisted Strasberg's wife Anna to take him to the wrap party for John Schlesinger's movie *The Day of The Locust (1975)* which was shooting on the adjacent lot to *Godfather Part II*. When they left the party Anna suggested looking in on the adjacent set. A conversation between Coppola and Strasberg began naturally, and Coppola offered Strasberg the role, only for Strasberg to turn it down due to the salary being only $10,000. It was soon upped to $60,000 and Strasberg accepted.

Strasberg would tell the Associated Press in 1979, 'I figured it was a small part and if I were bad in it nobody would care too much. If I was good the results might be interesting.' Strasberg would end up with an Academy Award nomination for Best Supporting Actor.

Pacino would later say he didn't need any thanks from Strasberg. He wasn't doing anyone any favours, Strasberg was right for the part and proved it in his performance.

Pacino's Michael was now undisputedly the head of the family, and a different character from the one which began the first picture. He wasn't a gangster, he was working his way towards respectability. Pacino listened to a lot of Mozart and Stravinsky while preparing to play Michael Corleone again. It put him in the character's mindset. He would try different pieces to see where they'd put him.

The Godfather Part II is chock full of great scenes and dialogue so quotable that along with some lines from the first film they have become part of the language.

Perhaps the finest scene in the picture comes late on, and features only Pacino and John Cazale. The scene is an acting masterclass featuring two of the best actors of the era performing at their best. Michael confronts his brother Fredo about his loyalty to the family. Fredo's jealousy of his younger brother has made Michael and the Corleone family vulnerable. Michael stands and barely opens his mouth. Fredo slouches in his sun lounger and finally has the fortitude to tell his brother what's been rattling around his head for years. Cazale flopped in the chair, making the character seem limp, which was perfect. Michael stands and gazes out of the window, the power dynamic obvious yet subtle.

Fredo explains that he felt his business dealings – which Michael knows were to the detriment of the Corleones – were good for the family. It soon becomes apparent that Fredo was seduced by the idea that Hyman Roth had dangled an enticement in front of him which made him feel wanted, and independent from the family which had carried him. So much so that Fredo was part of a conspiracy to have Michael murdered.

Michael is unmoved and counters that he has always taken care of him. This is the moment that the put-upon hard done by Fredo explodes. 'You're my kid brother, and you take care of me? Did you ever think about that, huh? Did you ever once think about that? Send Fredo off to do this; send Fredo off to do that. Let Fredo take care of some Mickey Mouse nightclub somewhere. Send Fredo to pick somebody up at the airport. I'm your older brother, Mike, and I was stepped over!'

Pulling himself up from his chair he shakes and even though he's finally asserting himself he still comes off as mostly pathetic; his broken heart is almost visible. Michael changes the subject without a care, asking what Fredo can tell him about his forthcoming senate investigation. Fredo slumps back exasperated. He swallows and gives Michael the little piece of information he has.

Michael coldly dismisses him by telling him he is nothing to him now. Not a brother or a friend. It's devastating to watch.

'It's weird for me that he's an actor that tends to play weak people,' Richard Shepard, director of a 2009 documentary on John Cazale said to the *LA Times* about the actor, 'but there is something about him that is just so incredibly compelling. You can't take your eyes off of him.'

'John felt very strongly that finding the character, you had to find the pain first,' theatre producer Robyn Goodman said in Shepard's documentary *I Knew It Was You (2009)*.

The scene was filmed at the Fleur du Lac Estate in Lake Tahoe, originally built in 1934 as a summer retreat for industrialist Henry J. Kaiser. The boathouse was originally used to store Kaiser's private fleet of hydroplanes.

Gordon Willis's lighting is another integral part of why the scene is so striking. It's an interior, but with the actors next to the floor to ceiling windows of the boathouse there's an exterior right next to it.

'It was an aesthetic choice to make it look the way it does,' Willis told *American Cinematographer* in 1978. 'My choices are always aesthetic, but after you've made that choice, then you have to decide how you're going to spend money – what's best, what's fastest.'

In his 2001 DVD commentary of the movie Coppola said that by this point of filming he was feeling more confident, fuelled largely by his having made *The Conversation*. He felt this scene closely related to that film, it being a quiet personal scene that focused on strong acting.

Sidney Lumet who would direct Pacino and Cazale in *Dog Day Afternoon (1975)* said it was one of the best acted scenes he'd ever seen in the movies. 'It's basically John's scene,' he said in 2006.

The film closes with Pacino's Michael sitting alone with a blank stare upon his face. His enemies have been eliminated, his wife has left him and with his mother dead he has ordered the execution of his younger brother. Michael has nothing left but power.

It was a rare sequel that wasn't just as good as the original, it was even better.

Chapter 9

Dog Day Afternoon
(Film, 1975)

Directed by: Sidney Lumet
Screenplay by: Frank Pierson
Based on the *Life* magazine article *The Boys in the Bank* by P.F. Kluge and Thomas Moore
Produced by: Martin Bregman, Martin Elfand
Cast: Al Pacino, John Cazale, Charles Durning, Eugene Moretti, James Broderick, Lance Henriksen, Chris Sarandon, Penelope Allen, Sully Boyar, Susan Peretz, Carol Kane

On Tuesday, 22 August, 1972, around closing time at a bank in Brooklyn, Sal Naturile informed the bank manager Robert Barrett, 'This is a hold-up.' Naturile wasn't alone. John Wojtowicz, 27, began filling his attaché case with cash and traveller's cheques. The subsequent bungled twelve hours would be told in the pages of *Life* magazine's 22nd September 1972 edition by P.F. Kluge and Thomas Moore in a story headlined *The Boys in the Bank*.

An article in *Variety* on 17 January 1973 announced that producer Martin Elfand had purchased the life rights of Wojtowicz and his immediate family. Wojtowicz had yet to be convicted of the robbery.

In the *Life* article, Wojtowicz is described as having 'the broken-faced good looks of an Al Pacino or a Dustin Hoffman.'

Producer Martin Elfand hired P.F. Kluge and Thomas Moore to interview the bank robbers' families, as well as the bank employees who they held hostage, and the police and federal agents on the case. Bregman made sure that all involved had signed releases and they were convinced that the film would tell the story as it had happened. Elfand told *The Washington Post* that 'Everyone was suspicious.' He said he could understand their feelings. All bar one hostage took $600 for their story. The sole holdout for more money was written out of the film.

Frank Pierson used the *Life* authors' research as the basis for his script. He also did some additional research of his own, hiring Randolfe Wicker, a freelance journalist for LGBT newspapers who had written extensively about the robbery to take him to some of Manhattan's gay hangouts. Pierson attempted to get an interview with John Wojtowicz but was unsuccessful. They only met for the first time at a screening of the film at the 2003 Virginia Film Festival.

Rehearsals for the Theater Company of Boston production of Bertolt Brecht's *The Resistible Rise of Arturo Ui* with Al Pacino in the title role began in New York on 8th April 1975, the same day as the 47th Academy Awards ceremony, where Pacino was nominated as Best Actor for *The Godfather Part II*. Pacino was spotted that night in a Greenwich Village restaurant. The Oscar went to Art Carney, best known as Ed Norton in the sitcom *The Honeymooners*, for *Harry and Tonto (1974)*. Movie critics believed that Oscar voters were split between Pacino and Jack Nicholson in *Chinatown (1974)* which allowed dark horse Carney to steal in.

Martin Bregman was one of the producers of *Dog Day Afternoon* and approached Pacino who initially backed out of the project. Dustin Hoffman was mentioned as potentially interested, but Bregman felt only Pacino had what was required for the role and went to him again. Bregman told Pacino's biographer Andrew Yule that Pacino may have hesitated to take on a gay character.

Pacino's acting style was to *become* the character, and Bregman felt that it may be a place where the actor didn't want to go. There was also the concern that no major actor had played a gay character on screen. That was down mainly to the Hays Code which came into force in 1934. Homosexuality was banned under the banning of 'Any inference of sex perversion.' The Hays Code grew obsolete and was abandoned entirely in 1968 to be replaced by the Motion Picture Association of America's ratings system.

Bregman only wanted Pacino for the role and appeared to have him confirmed before Pacino changed his mind once again. He told Bregman that he would prefer to remain in theatre, and he wasn't comfortable in movies. He would admit later that his lifestyle had gotten the better of him. He was exhausted and had been drinking too much. But Pacino had feelings towards the character, and he loved Pierson's screenplay. He was finally in.

Pierson's screenplay was predicated on Pacino being involved. When he began to craft the script he thought about from whose perspective the movie would be told. Would it be from the cops' perspective? Or the robbers? Would the audience be inside the bank? Or outside? With Pacino involved it was a no-brainer the audience had to be inside the bank with Pacino.

Rehearsals for *Arturo Ui* were halted as Pacino went off to shoot the movie. He took some of the play's cast with him. Sully Boyar, Carol Kane and Penny Allen, were all cast in the film. 'Al tends to work with the same people,' Kane told the *Boston Globe*.

Charlie Laughton suggested John Cazale for the part of Sal Naturile. He was all wrong for Naturile, who was a teenager when the robbery took place; Cazale was in his late thirties. Lumet told Pacino that when Pacino insisted he have Cazale read. Lumet hadn't at that point watched either of the Godfather pictures. Reluctantly Lumet allowed Cazale to come in and read. Two sentences in Lumet stopped him. 'The part's yours.' The relationship between Sonny and Sal was there, it was real and it was touching. 'My heart broke,' Lumet said of Cazale's reading.

Speaking with the *Peninsula Times Tribune* in 1976, Cazale said that Naturile had lost contact with himself. 'His whole life seemed to be some kind of desperate attempt to find out who he was.' It was the first time Cazale played a real person in his film career, and he described the feeling as 'very eerie.' People who knew Naturile said he was extremely quiet. 'He was potentially a powder keg,' Cazale said, 'and I had a strong sense of what happened. In spite of what he said I don't think he would have killed anybody.'

Lumet was struggling to cast the role of Sonny's mother when Pacino suggested Judith Malina of The Living Theatre. The hardest part of the process after that for Lumet was tracking Malina down. He sent someone round to the last known address of the Living Theatre, and the elderly gentleman there found a phone number in Vermont which was where Malina was residing. Part of her fee for the film was a donation to the Living Theatre, which was working in Pittsburgh.

Before they began filming, Pacino and Cazale listened to the interview tapes that P.F. Kluge and Thomas Moore had recorded.

After the first day of shooting Pacino looked at the rushes. He wasn't happy, despite enjoying a three-week rehearsal period. He sat with Bregman and suggested to him that the first day might have to be shot over. Bregman looked incredulously at his star. He asked Pacino what he meant. Pacino didn't feel he had the character down. Lumet, though, felt that Pacino's instincts about the character were wrong, which shocked the director as he knew Pacino was normally spot-on about such things. Pacino was worried about how audiences would react to Sonny. In fact, Lumet thought Pacino was terrified.

He went home that night, and sat up with the script and a bottle of wine. When he came back to the set in the morning he felt he now had the character. He decided Sonny would be agitated and animated.

Early in shooting Lumet told Pacino and the rest of the cast that he wanted them to build the characters from themselves to use their own experiences, humour and emotions. They all earned an extra $2 a day for wearing their own clothes.

Although they had those weeks of rehearsals it was only when they got on set that moments revealed themselves. Sonny struggling to free his gun from the box was a moment that simply happened and wasn't planned and the fact that he and Cazale couldn't see each other for the pillars was another comedic moment that only occurred once they were on set.

Apart from the scenes at Kennedy Airport, the film was shot in one location in Brooklyn, on a quiet stretch of shop fronts on Prospect Park West between 17th and 18th Streets, just south of Park Slope, just a few blocks from where the real events had taken place. The mayor's office rerouted the bus line to ensure the production wasn't affected by the noise.

The production hired 400 to 500 extras, but at night, those numbers swelled when members of the public, back home from work, joined in. Lumet was an old hand at shooting in New York, and he knew that in the streets there, you didn't just get what you needed, you got a little more.

Having worked with Pacino previously, Lumet knew that the actor would be constantly moving, so he adapted his process to capture this energy. He employed similar techniques he had used in *Serpico* by putting cameramen on rollerskates and sitting them in wheelchairs to ensure they could follow Pacino wherever he felt like moving.

Dog Day was filmed with only naturally available light. Lumet was aware that the title card would say 'Based on a True Story' so he didn't want the set to be filled with movie lighting. The bank had fluorescent lights, so the crew added more fluorescents. For close ups, when more light was needed on an actor's face the lighting department rolled up a fluorescent of a smaller wattage to provide a fill light.

In rehearsal, Lumet became increasingly concerned about the conversation between Sonny and Leon, and in particular the line 'And to Ernie, who I love as no man has ever loved another man…' He feared the kind of reaction that might provoke in Saturday night movie audiences if it wasn't handled just right. Sex and death he felt could do strange things to people and here was one character dictating his wishes to his lover moments before he believed he was going to be shot to death.

For the first time in his career, he allowed actors to improvise lines. Lumet wasn't a great believer in improvisation but he felt it was right to allow the actors to explore the script in that way. 'It was a remarkable group,' Lumet wrote in his memoir *Making Movies*. He wrote that Pacino led his cast with a courage he had seen in only two actors in previous films Lumet had helmed – Katherine Hepburn in *Long Day's Journey Into Night (1962)* and Sean Connery in *The Offence (1973)*. Both Lumet said had also taken risks in those movies.

A crucial scene became a point of discussion when Al Pacino voiced concerns about a scripted kiss between him and Chris Sarandon. Pacino felt the scene was unnecessarily exploitative and argued that the script was too heavy-handed in emphasising the characters' homosexuality. He believed the audience would already understand the nature of their relationship and wanted to focus instead on portraying its breakdown. He wanted to show two people who loved each other but couldn't find a way to live together. Pierson came to agree with this perspective, especially after learning that the real-life couple had never kissed but had communicated primarily by phone. As a result, he rewrote the scene to feature a telephone conversation instead.

It comes around two-thirds of the way through the film, Sonny makes not one, but two crucial phone calls – one to his lover who sits at a barbershop across the street, having been brought there by the police, and another to his estranged wife at home.

Lumet recognised that Pacino would deliver his most powerful performance if they could capture the scene in a single, uninterrupted take. The sequence took place at night, with Sonny having been trapped in the bank for twelve hours, requiring Pacino to appear utterly spent and exhausted. As Lumet understood, when people are tired, emotions are more readily available, which was precisely the vulnerability he sought.

There was however a technical challenge. Standard film cameras held only a thousand feet of film which was approximately eleven minutes, while the two phone calls ran nearly fifteen minutes. Lumet's solution was ingenious: positioning two cameras side by side with their lenses as close together as physically possible, using identical lenses to ensure visual continuity. When the first camera reached 850 feet, his crew would start the second while the first continued rolling, knowing that cutaways to Angie, Sonny's wife, would allow seamless editing between the two cameras. This approach preserved Pacino's continuous performance, maintaining the emotional authenticity of a real-time experience.

To maximise Pacino's concentration, Lumet cleared the set of non-essential crew entirely, then erected black flats five feet behind the cameras to block out the physical set. The prop department rigged the phones so the off-camera actors – Chris Sarandon and Susan Peretz – could speak from across the street, allowing Pacino to hear their actual voices through his phone.

Lumet employed another technique for building emotional intensity: moving rapidly from take to take without allowing actors to cool down emotionally. He would often keep cameras rolling between takes, quietly directing, moving everyone back to starting positions. Even his call of 'Action' was calibrated to the scene's mood – gentle for intimate moments, sharp and commanding for high-energy sequences.

However, reloading film magazines typically required two to three minutes, enough time for an actor's emotional peak to dissipate. To prevent this disruption, Lumet erected a black tent around both cameras and their operators, cutting holes for the lenses. He stationed the second assistant cameraman inside with a spare film magazine ready.

When they began filming, the first take unfolded as planned. As camera one approached 850 feet, camera two began rolling. The take was wonderful, yet Lumet's instincts told him to attempt another. With camera two having used only 200 feet, he made a quick decision.

'Al, back to the top, I want to go again,' Lumet called out gently.

Pacino, having given everything to the first take, looked at his director in disbelief. 'What?! You're kidding!' he responded, clearly exhausted.

'Al, we have to. Roll camera,' Lumet insisted.

They proceeded with camera two, which had approximately 800 feet remaining. Behind the concealed tent, the crew reloaded camera one. By the time camera two had used 700 feet – eight minutes into the take – the reloaded first camera began rolling again.

The second take pushed Pacino beyond his limits. Upon finishing his lines, he appeared disoriented, looking around helplessly in sheer exhaustion. Then, by chance, his eyes found Lumet's. The director was visibly moved to tears by the performance he had just witnessed. When Pacino saw this genuine emotional response, their eyes locked, and he burst into tears himself before slumping over the desk.

'Cut! Print!' Lumet shouted, leaping into the air with excitement.

Lumet told Charlie Rose that Pacino didn't even know they had done a second take; he was so completely spent afterwards.

Peretz spoke lines from the script as Pacino improvised, while Pacino and Sarandon's conversation went through a lengthy process. Pierson knew that this conversation had to say everything about the lovers' relationship, so he went back to all he knew about their lives together, and decided he would write it as monologues. Pacino and Sarandon were given their monologues and they sat across a table. The pair delivered them while interrupting each other. Lumet had a tape recorder running. After twenty minutes the recording stopped and was given to an assistant to transcribe and become the basis for the scene. 'What makes those moments work is very often their banality,' Sarandon told *The Cincinnati Enquirer* in 1976.

Sarandon clutched the dressing gown his character wore around his chest, indicating his vulnerability. Sarandon had noticed from a photograph of the real Leon that he was doing this so he made a mental note to include it in his performance.

Although *Dog Day Afternoon* is a heist movie, it's very different from any other heist movie you would have seen: in the 1970s or any other era. The film reveals that Sonny's motivation to steal the money is for his lover's sex change operation. Not for a second does it take the viewer out of the movie or dilute the tension. It was such an unusual moment in what was a major motion picture, but it was perfectly in keeping with the sensitive, compassionate, hopelessly out of his depth character Pacino created.

Lumet reckoned that around 60% of the dialogue in the movie was improvised, although he stressed that they followed Pierson's scene by scene construction, and indeed Pierson was involved in some of the improvs. After being involved in rehearsals Pierson attended the set on day one wished everyone good luck and left, telling Lumet to call him if he was needed. Lumet didn't call. In *Making Movies* Lumet asserted that Pierson deserved his Academy Award for writing the screenplay, the actors speaking not his words but his intentions.

There's tragedy coming in the film, and while no one in the bank is shot or killed the audience fears that something bad is bound to happen, that surely not the robbers and all the hostages can get to the airport and have a happy ending.

When the FBI agent tells Sonny that if he just sits still they'll take out Sal but leave him unharmed, Sonny rejects the suggestion. When Sal asks him what they were talking about, Sonny lies. When the film was shown in Lewisburg PA federal prison, where Wojtowicz was being held, his fellow inmates took this to mean that he had double-crossed his partner. It led to Wojtowicz being sent to solitary confinement for his own protection.

'That's when they started trying to kill me,' Wojtowicz told *The Daily Progress* in 2003, 'and my cell was set on fire three times.' It was a part of the movie that Pierson had invented. The screenwriter wrote a letter explaining that the scene was his invention. It was printed in the prison newspaper.

Jim Murphy was the real-life FBI man, portrayed by Lance Henriksen, who shot Sal Naturile, much in the way it happened in the film, although Murphy fired his Smith and Wesson model 15 into Naturile's chest, instead of his head, as the film shows. When Dog Day was released in 1975, Murphy took his wife to see it in a packed movie theatre on the Upper East Side. He found that the cinema audience were rooting for Pacino and Cazale, not the cops, very much like the crowd were in the 1972 robbery. When Sal's shooting came the audience booed. Murphy couldn't wait to leave in case someone recognised him.

Filming the scene, Cazale and Henriksen, who had worked together on stage, couldn't stop laughing, as a way of dealing with the tension.

Lumet decided that there wouldn't be a score. As the events really happened, he didn't want an audience to have a score indicating to them how they should feel when watching. The only music in the film is the Elton John song *Amoreena* during the opening titles. Editor Dede Allen initially used it as a filler over the opening montage of scenes of a hot day in New York City, but she and Lumet grew attached to it, and the song plays over the would-be robbers' car radio.

When the Oscar nominations were announced on Tuesday 17th February 1976 *Dog Day Afternoon* landed six, with *One Flew Over the Cuckoo's Nest (1975)* receiving nine and Barry Lyndon (1975) getting seven.

In March, Pacino won the Best Actor in a Leading Role BAFTA jointly for *Dog Day Afternoon* and *The Godfather Part II*. He would give the award to Lee Strasberg.

The night of the Oscar ceremony Pacino was performing in a workshop performance of *The Local Stigmatic* at Joe Papp's Public Theater in New York, going out for dinner in the city afterwards. He didn't look for a television set to see the announcement and he refused to pose for photographers. Jack Nicholson took home the Best Actor Oscar for *One Flew Over the Cuckoo's Nest. Dog Day*'s only Oscar went to Frank Pierson.

It was an amazing run of roles in motion pictures for Pacino. Michael Corleone, Frank Serpico and Sonny Wojtowicz were all memorable characters, each one different from the next, each one intense, era defining and all of them have endured with cinema audiences and aspiring actors over the decades.

It was Pacino's performance that convinced a theatre minor at Central Michigan University called Jeff Daniels to move to New York and become a movie actor. He paid in to see the movie six times. Actor Oscar Isaac, star of *Inside Llewyn Davis (2013)* and *Ex Machina (2015)* told *Details* magazine in 2015, 'Dog Day Afternoon taught me just as much, if not more, about acting than going to Juilliard did. There was a period when I would watch it once a month. I've seen *Dog Day Afternoon* more than myself in the mirror.'

Surprisingly, after *Dog Day Afternoon*, Cazale didn't have an agent. 'I thought I'd get reaction from Godfather II but I was wrong. I could be wrong again,' he told the *Peninsula Times Tribune*.

Chapter 10

The Resistible Rise of Arturo Ui
(Stage, 1975)

Written by: Bertolt Brecht
Translated by: George Tabori
Directed by: David Wheeler
Produced by: Jerome Rosenfeld
Cast: Al Pacino, John Cazale, Taylor Mead, Brad Sullivan, Carol Kane, Jaime Sanchez, Paul Benedict, Penelope Allen, Sully Boyar, Garry Goodrow, Jack Hollander, Owen Hollander

Pacino was appearing at the Charles Playhouse, Boston for a reported salary of $250 per week. Tickets were $6.50, $7.50, and $8.50.

The Resistible Rise of Arturo Ui was written by Bertolt Brecht in Finland in March and April of 1941, a year after Charlie Chaplin's film *The Great Dictator (1940)*, which was an influence on him. Brecht had left his native Germany in 1933, the night after the German parliament building, the Reichstag, had been burnt down, moving initially to Prague. He was stripped of his German citizenship by the Nazis in 1935. It was in this year he had the idea for a play that satirised the rise of the Nazis.

For the model of his lead character, Brecht used Adolf Hitler, shaping him as a Chicago mobster. The character was ruthless, cunning and amoral, not unlike Richard III. Indeed, the play contains quotations from *Richard III* and *Julius Caesar*. The play was designed to show Hitler as absurd. Criminals, Brecht said, must be exposed and preferably to ridicule.

The other characters in the play were also analogous to senior members of the Nazi Party. Dogsborough stood in for Hindenburg, the President of Germany, from 1925 to 1933. Giri was analogous to Hermann Göring, head of the Nazi air force. Givola represented Joseph Goebbels, the Nazi propaganda minister. Ernesto Roma, Arturo's lieutenant was Ernst Röhm, head of the Nazi storm troopers.

Brecht had written the play while waiting for a visa to travel to America, where he had visited in 1935. He had a fascination with American gangsters. For research, he had read F.D. Pasley's 1930 book *Al Capone: The Biography of a Self-Made Man.* This was the fourth and final time Brecht used Chicago as a setting for one of his 36 plays. He saw the parallels between how organised crime had taken over Chicago with how Hitler had taken over Germany.

The play was never performed in Brecht's lifetime. He died in 1956. Its first performance was in Stuttgart, West Germany in 1958 where it was directed by Peter Palitzsch who had worked with Brecht in the Berliner Ensemble, the theatre company Brecht had formed with his wife, Helene Weigel in 1949. The Berliner Ensemble, taking six months to rehearse, staged *Arturo Ui* the following year, with Palitzsch co-directing with Manfred Wekwerth. Brecht's son-in-law Ekkehard Schall portrayed Ui.

The play came to Broadway in 1963 with George Tabori's 1961 translation, when David Merrick produced the show at the Lunt-Fontanne Theater with Tony Richardson directing. The lead role was played by Christopher Plummer. William Mootz of the Courier-Journal called it 'one of the great disasters of the 1963 Broadway season when it was gimmicked up outrageously in an attempt to make it palatable to the tired businessmen.'

In the UK, Leonard Rossiter had taken on the title role originally in September 1967 in a production at the Citizen's Theatre in Glasgow. The rehearsal period was just under three weeks. The production, directed by Michael Blakemore, went on to appear at the Lyceum in August of the following year as part of the Edinburgh Festival. There the *New York Times* wrote that 'Leonard Rossiter's performance stands comparison with Berlin's Ekkehard Schall; and one can not pay a bigger compliment than that.' It then moved on to Nottingham in April 1969 before arriving in London's West End at the Saville Theatre in July 1969.

Pacino had intended to do *Arturo Ui* in New York with Joseph Papp, who gave him $40,000 to develop it. A cast rehearsed with director Ted Cornell in the backroom of a storefront annex of the New York Shakespeare Festival Public Theater for six weeks in the summer of 1974.

The space was filled with rehearsal materials such as copies of *The Rise and Fall of the Third Reich* by William L. Shirer and films borrowed from the Museum of Modern Art depicting life in 1930s Europe and Chicago. They also watched movies from the 1930s. One they tried to get but couldn't find was *Scarface (1932)*.

Pacino fostered an ensemble approach to the production, and his intention was to have a lengthy rehearsal period. The cast was filled with actors he had known for years, and he trusted and believed in their talents. The rehearsal period Pacino said was for the cast to 'talk to the play.' The actors in rehearsals numbered around thirty, but everyone made a creative contribution. It was what Pacino called 'An actor's theatre.'

The play went on a sabbatical as Pacino, Cazale and a few others from the cast went off to make *Dog Day Afternoon*. Taylor Mead, star of Andy Warhol movies such as *Taylor Mead's Ass (1964)* and *Lonesome Cowboys (1968)* managed to exclude himself from the movie by walking out of the New York rehearsals. For Pacino the process was an exploration and investigation of the play and its characters. The cast were discussing the play one day, in what Mead described to the *Globe* as 'an intellectual manner,' when the conversation paused, Mead stood up from his seat and announced, 'Excuse me, before you continue, I think you had better find a new Young Dogsborough.' He walked out of the theatre. 'There was too much theorising going on,' Mead said. 'It was getting too heady. Then I regretted it before I got to the door, but I had too much pride to turn back. So I'm not in Dog Day, but I begged my way back into Ui.' He added, 'We do what we believe in.'

Rehearsals resumed in January of 1975 but without any theatre commitment at that stage. The play at this point was just for the actors and not an audience. Pacino wasn't the only actor in the cast who could choose to spend their time more lucratively making movies and not theatre. Carol Kane had just completed *Hester Street (1975)*, for which she would earn an Oscar nomination, Cazale starred opposite Gene Hackman in *The Conversation (1974)*, while Brad Sullivan had been in *The Sting (1973)*. Mead, an original beat poet who was friends with Allen Ginsberg and Jack Kerouac, said, 'This is dedication. We all have a love of Al Pacino. He's a very human person. A very beautiful person. For the time of this project a lot of us have not been exploring other possibilities because this is an all-consuming venture.'

Mead told *Gay Sunshine* that the cast was 'the most brilliant cast of thirty people I've ever seen assembled at once.' He noted that Pacino's part must amount to a couple of hours of lines. In the interview Mead warmed to talking about Pacino, although he said that the ethos of the cast was that it was a family and none of them should go talking about the family outside. But Mead clearly had a lot of warmth for Pacino, saying 'I tried to put the make on him after rehearsal' and suggesting Pacino enjoyed the attention.

John Cazale played one of Ui's chief henchmen with Jaime Sánchez playing the other. Sánchez had appeared in *The Wild Bunch (1969)* and would feature alongside Pacino in several movies including *Carlito's Way (1993)* and *Looking For Richard (1996)*.

Pacino felt that they hadn't quite got the play right during that development period, but that the time away from it helped a lot. That way of working led to Pacino suggesting that his movies would benefit from a similar approach, reviewing everything that was shot after a two-week break and then reshooting as required. None of his directors took Pacino up on that idea.

Pacino was aware that although he was working as an actor and doing what he loved every day as a film star he wasn't visible, so the movie-going public would assume he was out of work. Around this time he read in the press that his movie career was on the wane so he had been forced back onto the stage. It was disappointing for Pacino that was the way his beloved theatre was perceived, as a lesser form of work. He was always aware though that while he was attempting to ride both horses perhaps his focus on each one wasn't as sharp as it could be.

After a week of previews, the show opened on May 14th 1975 and played until 29th June. At the same time downstairs at the Charles in the Cabaret was the Madhouse Company of London. They were billed as 'Five British lunatics certified by the New York Times as INSANE.' The cast included Jim Carter who would become a well-known actor in films and TV, appearing in *Brassed Off (1996)*, *Shakespeare in Love (1998)* and *Downton Abbey*.

Pacino wouldn't perform in the Wednesday and Saturday matinees from 17th May as the producers said that the heavy vocal demands of the strenuous role had left Pacino with a 'scratchy throat.' His doctor had ordered him to limit himself to one performance per day. The role would instead be performed by David Clennon.

Pacino's Michael Corleone the war hero at his sister's wedding with James Caan's Sonny.

Pacino with Francis Ford Coppola discussing the scene in the Italian restaurant that perhaps saved both of them.

Pacino as Michael now showing a little of the swagger as he becomes comfortable in the role as Godfather.

On location in New York for Serpico with director Sidney Lumet.

Although they didn't share a scene in the movie Pacino and Robert De Niro pose here in character for The Godfather Part II.

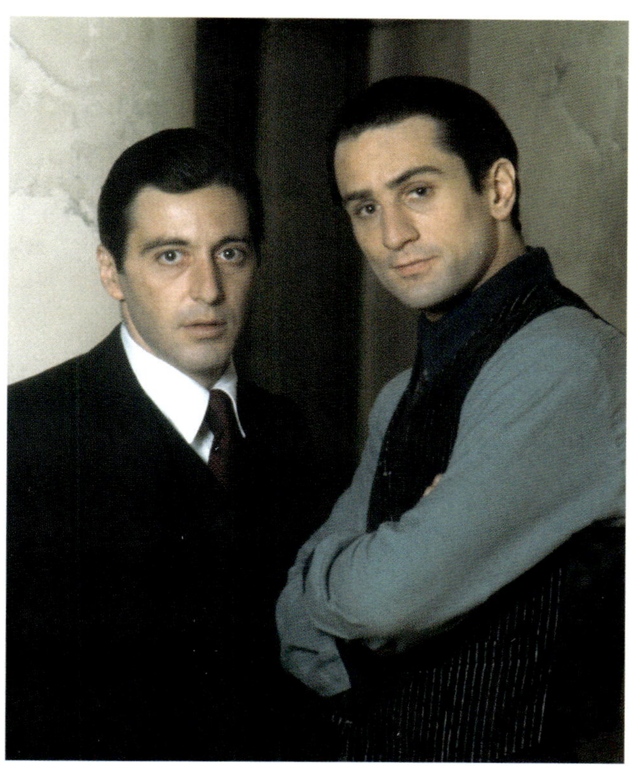

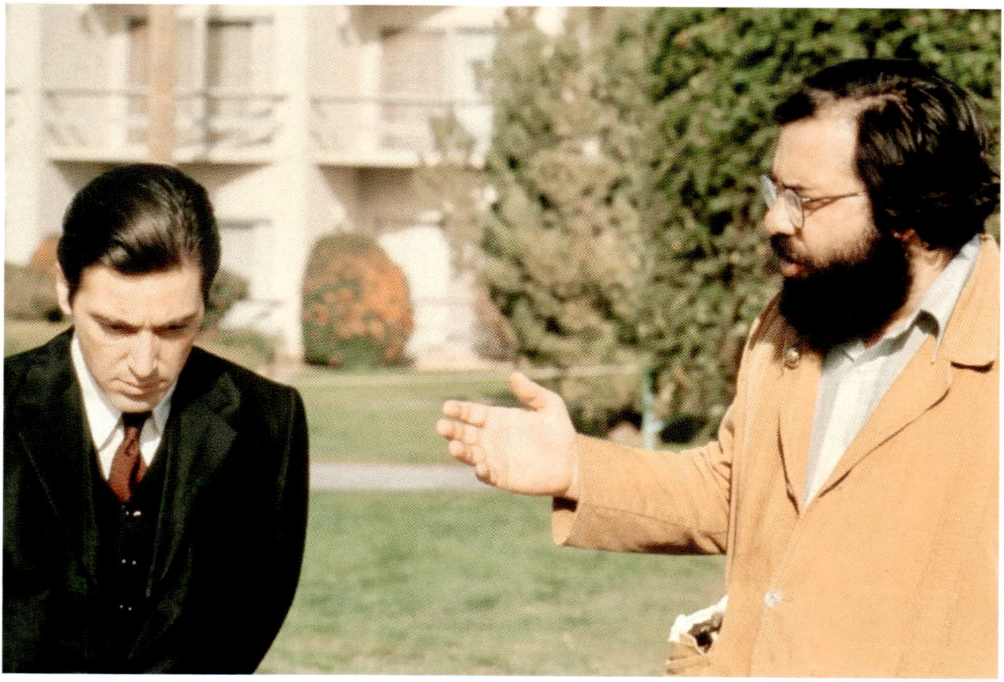

On the set of The Godfather Part II with director Francis Ford Coppola.

Hyman Roth implores Michael to invest with him in Cuba. Pacino was partly responsible for his mentor Lee Strasberg landing the role.

John Cazale's Fredo attempts to salvage his ruined relationship with his brother.

The transformation of Michael from war hero to Godfather is complete.

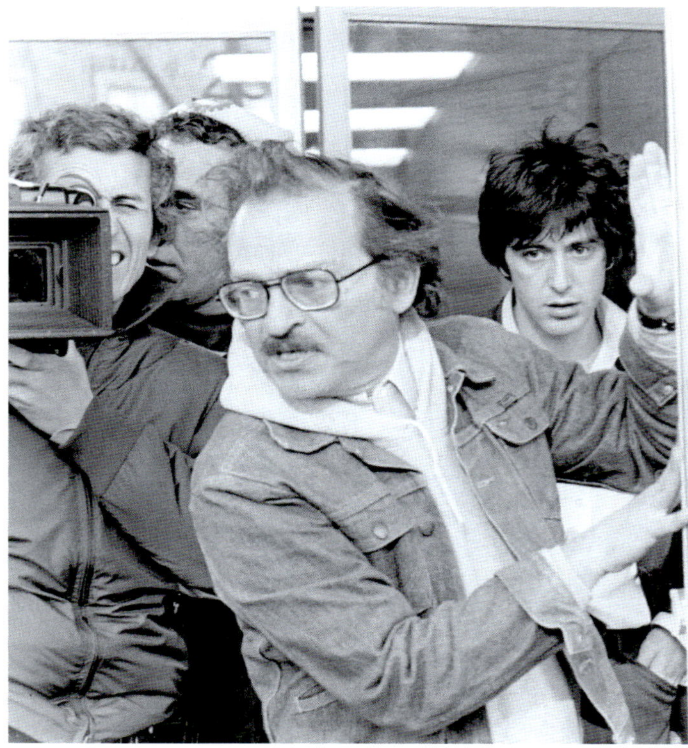

Pacino looks on as Sidney Lumet sets up a shot on Dog Day Afternoon.

John Cazale as Sal and Pacino as Sonny in Dog Day Afternoon.

Sully Boyar and Penelope Allen watch on as Pacino's Sonny takes a call from the police.

Pacino looks every inch the movie star as Sonny begins to lose control of the situation.

John Cazale was a big influence on the way Pacino approached roles and was an actor he collaborated with often.

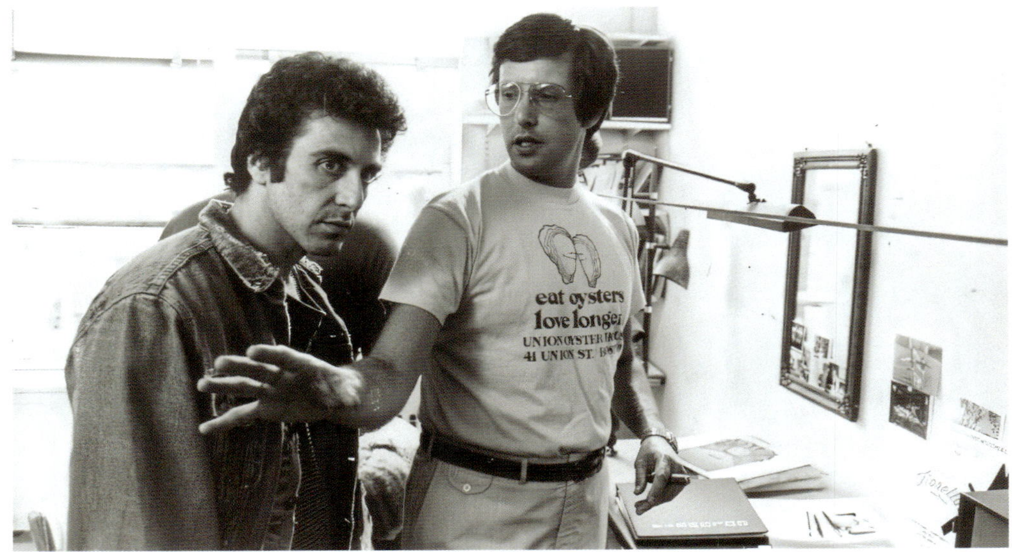

Pacino on the set of Cruising with director William Friedkin.

Pacino as undercover cop Steve
Burns in Cruising.

Cruising turned out to be a misstep for Pacino's career.

Pacino as Tony Montana in Scarface. The scar over his eyebrow Pacino said was to suggest chaos.

Montana dripping in blood after a memorable scene from Scarface.

It's hard to believe now that even several years after its release Scarface was considered a flop. It's now widely acknowledged as a classic.

Ellen Barkin and Pacino in a publicity still for Sea of Love, the film that would mark his comeback.

Scent of a Woman's Lt. Col. Frank Slade was the role that finally landed Pacino the Oscar.

On the set of Carlito's Way with director Brian De Palma.

Pacino consults with Heat director Michael Mann.

During filming of Heat's famous coffee shop scene Michael Mann directs Pacino and De Niro.

Pacino as Vincent Hanna in Heat.

James Russo, Pacino, Michael Madsen, Bruno Kirby and Johnny Depp in a publicity shot for Donnie Brasco.

Pacino as Roy Cohn in Angels in America.

Pacino as Dr. Jack Kevorkian in You Don't Know Jack.

Pacino as Danny Collins.

Pacino as Jimmy Hoffa with Robert De Niro and Ray Romano in The Irishman.

Pacino with Logan Lerman in Hunters.

Paul Benedict was now appearing regularly on television in the sitcom *The Jeffersons*. He appeared in the play as a sodden Shakespearean actor, an old-time ham, hired to teach Ui how to command an audience.

Writing in the *Los Angeles Times*, William Glover said, 'Pacino evokes a highly personalised caricature of the Nazi Atilla. Probably unintentionally, the portrait also caricatures the basic Pacino performance. Every twitch, shuffle and slur used before seems to have been flamboyantly allowed the star by Director David Wheeler.'

In the *Boston Globe*, Kevin Kelly wrote, 'Al Pacino plays Arturo in a perceptive spinoff from his brilliant characterisation of Richard III with a harsh element of ironic humour. In his tent-like suit, his worn thin shoes and his 5 o'clock shadow, he looks like a James Cagney henchman on the make.'

'Al loves the town and Boston audiences,' producer Jerome Rosenfeld said after Pacino's final performance. 'There were standing ovations at every performance of Arturo Ui and we did capacity for the full eight weeks.' The show was the biggest in the history of the Warrenton Street theatre, with people turned away each night. It was clear Rosenfeld wanted Pacino to return. 'I've been talking with Al and he really wants to do Hamlet,' Rosenfeld said to the Boston Globe, 'but isn't able to make a definite decision yet.' Pacino was heading for Italy to pick up some film awards, on his return Rosenfeld was hoping to meet him in New York. There had been suggestions that Arturo Ui would move to Broadway under Joseph Papp, but the chance had now receded.

The following year John Cazale played as Angelo opposite Meryl Streep's Isabella in Shakespeare's *Measure For Measure* in Central Park. The pair became a real life couple. His final film role was *The Deer Hunter (1978)*, which just like every other film he appeared in was nominated for Best Picture at the Academy Awards. John Cazale died of cancer on Sunday, 12th March 1978, at Memorial Sloan-Kettering Cancer Center, aged only 42. Memorial services were held on Wednesday 15th March on both coasts, with the New York memorial at Joseph Papp's Public Theatre. Papp and Pacino had attended tests at hospital with Cazale all through his illness.

Chapter 11

Cruising
(Film, 1980)

Written and directed by: William Friedkin
Based on the novel by Gerald Walker
Produced by: Jerry Weintraub
Cast: Al Pacino, Paul Sorvino, Karen Allen, Richard Cox, Stuart Richards, Don Scardino, Ted Bailey, Joe Spinell, Jay Acovone, Gene Davis, Randy Jurgensen, Barton Heyman

Cruising had been in gestation for some time. Gerald Walker began adapting his 1970 novel about a serial killer targeting New York City's gay community in 1971 for a proposed movie for producers Phil D'Antoni and Robert Weiner.

In 1972, *Variety* wrote that Paul Morrissey would direct. Morrissey was a former 'Warhol Superstar' and had directed a number of films centred around the gay scene such as *Flesh (1968)* and *Trash (1970)*.

By 1973, the producers had backed out, and the industry press cited a 'Supreme Court ruling on obscenity,' making the project difficult to finance. Around 1974, Brian De Palma wrote a screenplay adaptation of the novel, but when he couldn't obtain the rights, he made *Dressed to Kill (1980)* instead.

D'Antoni, producer of William Friedkin's *The French Connection (1971)*, approached Friedkin about the project. Friedkin read the book, and although he found it interesting, it didn't compel him to turn it into a movie. D'Antoni moved on to Steven Spielberg, and the pair attempted to set up the project, but no studio would take it on.

The project was revived when Jerry Weintraub, a man Friedkin described as 'a very persuasive guy', approached him. Weintraub was a music promoter who had worked with everyone from Frank Sinatra to Elvis Presley. He wanted to get into the movie business and purchased the rights to the book. At the time, Friedkin still wasn't interested in turning it into a movie, but soon, his interest in the gay world had been piqued by several things.

AIDS had begun to ravage the gay community, although the illness was yet to have a name, and there was a poor understanding of what it was. There was also Friedkin's friend Randy Jurgensen, a New York cop, who, just like Pacino's character, was assigned to go undercover into gay nightclubs. To further intrigue Friedkin there were a series of real-life unsolved murders in the S & M clubs in the Meatpacking District on the Lower West Side during the 1970s, which were reported on by *Village Voice* journalist Arthur Bell. Friedkin thought Bell's work was 'great reportage.' Ironically, Bell would lead the protests to have the filming of *Cruising* shut down and referred to the film in the pages of the *Voice* as a 'vile piece of trash.' Paul Bateson was a doctor's assistant who had appeared in Friedkin's film *The Exorcist (1973)*. He had been arrested on suspicion of some of the killings. Friedkin contacted his lawyer and visited him at Rikers Island Penitentiary. At the time Friedkin had been planning to direct a 10-hour television adaptation of *Blood and Money*, a 1976 true crime novel by Thomas Thompson, but when that hit a snag he found himself free. All these elements were a perfect storm for the director, and he contacted Weintraub, telling him he now knew what to do with *Cruising*.

Friedkin's script, the first one he had written on his own, contained elements of Walker's novel, Jurgensen's story, Bateson's case and Arthur Bell's reporting.

Jurgensen and Bateson served as consultants alongside Sonny Grosso, Friedkin's previous collaborator from *The French Connection*. Jurgensen and Grosso were childhood friends and had been partners in the New York Police Department. They both also made cameo appearances in the film.

The production company Lorimar signed on to finance the film in 1979, with Jerry Weintraub producing and Friedkin directing, with a reported budget of $11M, although Friedkin recounts in his autobiography the budget was only $7M.

Friedkin's first choice for the role of police officer Steve Burns was Richard Gere, whose most recent starring roles were *Days of Heaven (1978)* and *Yanks (1979)*. He had the toughness Friedkin sought but also possessed an androgynous quality. Gere agreed to take on the role. Just as an offer was about to be made, Friedkin received a call from Stan Kamen, the head of the William Morris Picture Department, who told him that Al Pacino had read the script and loved it. Pacino thought that the script had a little of Harold Pinter and a little of Alfred Hitchcock. Friedkin knew Pacino from working with him on Oliver Stone's script *Born on the Fourth of July* in 1978. That project looked like it was set to go ahead, and rehearsals had started, when the German co-financing dropped out and no other money could be found. Lorimar and United Artists offered Pacino $3M to star in *Cruising*.

Several years later, Pacino would be offered the role of Edward Lewis in *Pretty Woman (1990)*, only to turn it down and see the part go to Richard Gere. 'Richard was perfect for it,' Pacino said in an interview with the BBC in 2024. 'It fit him so well. I love Richard Gere. I think he's a great actor, and I've seen him do such great stuff.'

Paul Sorvino, who played Captain Edelson, had worked with Friedkin previously in *The Brink's Job (1978)*. Ed O'Neill was appearing on Broadway as a boxer in a play called *Knockout*. Friedkin saw him and cast him as one of the detectives. O'Neill continued to perform in the show during filming. Don Scardino who played the playwright who rooms with Pacino's undercover cop was a stage actor who had played Jesus in *Godspell* for more than 1000 performances.

Production began in July 1979, with 80 filming locations in the Greenwich Village neighbourhood of New York City over ten weeks.

The film's production faced several challenges, particularly regarding locations. While the story was meant to depict cruising at the Mineshaft bar, filming restrictions forced the production to recreate the environment at another club, people's memory of which doesn't pin down the exact location, the Hellfire Club and J's being mentioned. The production did manage to incorporate Mineshaft regulars as extras and film in nearby locations.

The film was shot in the actual New York gay bars, which Friedkin said in his autobiography were 'off-limits to all but the devotees of hard-core male sex.' Friedkin had done research in the bars, speaking to managers, bartenders, and customers. He found the level of energy and the patrons' dedication to that world exciting. When Friedkin went, he would adhere to the themed dress codes of the bars, for example stripping down to his jockstrap and socks for Jockstrap Night.

Most of the bars in the area were run by the Mafia at that time, but Friedkin found them very cooperative. The Genovese crime family member Matty 'The Horse' Ianniello made introductions and provided protection.

There were no Screen Guild members as extras; all the supporting actors were the bars' own clientele. Friedkin didn't offer them any direction. He asked that they 'do their thing' and allow him to film it. Around twenty extras dropped out when the protests started and some who remained passed information on to the protesters so they could organise protests at locations more effectively. There was no art direction in the clubs either; the decor was all as it was.

When the film was announced, the protests began. Although Friedkin said that people had taken exception to his films since *The Boys in the Band (1970)*, he didn't expect there to be protests. Gay groups protested to Mayor Koch, requesting that the film be denied a filming permit, as they felt it would inspire a 'potentially inflammatory and explosive' reaction to the homosexual community. The director of the Mayor's Office of Motion Pictures and Television, Nancy Littlefield, agreed to take the request to the Mayor, but said she knew of no precedent for permission to film being denied to a company that met all legal and safety guidelines. Their appeal was rejected.

Bootleg copies of the script's third draft circulated, focusing on the most controversial aspects of the movie. One scene the National Gay Task Force objected to concerned a man whipping another man. Weintraub pointed out the script they had was not the shooting script.

One of the leaflets that was handed around in protest read, 'Gay people will die because of this film.' Arthur Bell wrote that the movie would set gay life back years. Bell later compared his clarion call in the *Village Voice* that encouraged the gay community to protest the filming as like the Declaration of Independence to Jefferson. On a later interview with an ABC morning show he had advocated gays use violence against the picture. He later backtracked, telling the *New York Times*, that he had only had two or three hours' sleep before the interview and hadn't thought through his comments appropriately. Throughout the filming, pickets followed the crew to many of the approximately 80 locations that were used. Protesters employed various tactics to disrupt filming, including using mirrors to interfere with lighting and creating noise that required extensive audio overdubbing.

In the film's commentary track, Friedkin acknowledged that he could understand why the protests had taken place and that members of the gay rights movement 'felt that Cruising was not the best foot forward for gay rights.' However, he asserted that the murders taking place around the leather bars in the late 70s made for a unique setting for a murder mystery, and *Cruising* made no attempt to comment on gay life.

In July 1979 Jerry Weintraub told the New York Times in the wake of the protests, 'We're not making a gay film. We're making a murder mystery set in the gay community.'

The apartment scenes were shot in actual apartments, however adjacent residents played their music loud, and it obliterated the dialogue causing the need for it to be added in post.

On 26th July, three weeks into filming, 800 protesters marched from a rally in Sheridan Square in Greenwich Village to a filming location on West Street around a mile away. They blew whistles and stopped traffic, walking 15 abreast across Christopher Street. The protest picked up more numbers as people came out of bars along the way. A group splintered off to get close to the camera, only to be dispersed by police on horseback. Protesters grabbed a camera cable as one attempted to set it alight. Again, the police repelled them.

The protest ended with a sit-in and the protesters dispersed around midnight.

'When I looked into that mob that night, I saw a gang of unruly fanatics, blowing whistles, throwing bottles and cans at the trucks, at the actors and at me,' Friedkin told the *New York Times*. 'So how could I believe that this group of people was representing the legitimate interests of a very significant minority in this country?'

One of the protesters, Scott Tucker, wrote in *The Body Politic*, 'Tugging on that cable – knowing I wanted to destroy that camera, stop the filming – I suddenly saw how it had crystalised for me. I knew exactly what I was doing.'

In the *Village Voice* Richard Goldstein wrote that the film had provided the gay community its strongest organising tool since the November 1978 assassination of politician Harvey Milk.

In the gay magazine *Mandate* editor in chief John Devere offered an opposing view. He had applied to be an extra and wrote an article based on his experience. He observed that more than 1600 gay men participated in the film, while the protesters numbered far lower. The day-by-day number was usually around the same 25 people augmented by several others each day. He wrote that the gay patrons of the bars the movie was based in – the Eagle, the Spike, the Mineshaft and the Anvil – were in the movie and were quite happy with how their world was depicted.

The protests surprised Pacino. He told the *Village Voice* in 2018 that he went in to the project thinking about what the role meant, he didn't look at its place in the wider community. The controversy did teach Pacino to be more aware of what he was representing when he took on roles, and how the world around him was affected by that.

Karen Allen who played Nancy Gates, Pacino's character's girlfriend recalled that Pacino had to be ushered to locations to protect him from people throwing things at him. Allen didn't think Pacino would have wanted to be in that situation if he had an inkling that the movie would cause so much controversy.

Pacino had decided to have his hair styled by a gay barber in the West Village. What he got was something like a crew cut, and he was outraged. He now no longer looked like the movie star Al Pacino. He didn't want to look like that in front of the camera. Weintraub called for hair stylists in New York and Los Angeles. They tried wigs, but nothing would placate Pacino. The start date was postponed until his hair could grow back. Eventually, a personal stylist and hair extensions did the trick, and the production could begin.

Pacino didn't want to see the shooting locations ahead of time as he wanted to experience the environment exactly as his character would. Friedkin said that Pacino was uncomfortable while filming in the gay clubs, but Jurgensen had told him that was exactly how he felt, so he was confident that Pacino's visceral reaction was perfect for the part. The film was about the character's crisis of identity so the unfamiliarity Pacino experienced suited the role.

Speaking to Cindy Heller Adams for her 1980 biography of him, Lee Strasberg said of Pacino, 'It's not right that he carries an identity with him long after a role is over. It isn't healthy. Al has not absorbed all the steps in the system.'

Pacino was a great collaborator with his co-stars. In an interview with Arrow Video for the 2025 Blu-Ray release Karen Allen talked about her audition. She was reading with Pacino, who she knew slightly socially, in front of Friedkin. 'Al was about as kind as an actor can be in a situation like that,' Allen said. The actress, who had recently appeared in *The Wanderers (1979)* was nervous, but Pacino sought to calm her. Allen recalled him saying to her, 'The point of a compass always shakes before it finds its true point.' 'It was making something positive out of the fact I was nervous,' Allen said.

Richard Cox, who played Stuart Richards, one of the suspects, said that Pacino stayed after his filming had finished in order to act off camera while Cox filmed his lines, a gesture that many leading men would have considered beneath them. Cox would later appear in Pacino's documentary *Looking For Richard.*

All of the murder scenes that take place in the film are based on actual murders that took place at that time and were widely reported in the newspapers. Friedkin took the details and fictionalised them for his script.

After finishing filming in September Friedkin told the *New York Times* his reasons for making a film were neither because he was for something nor against something. He was of the opinion that all the films he'd made were hugely ambiguous.

As the film was being edited Pacino went out to Los Angeles to sit in with Friedkin. When he got there though Friedkin wouldn't let him into the editing room and had no interest in any suggestions Pacino had. The disagreement ended their relationship.

The film faced significant post-production hurdles with the Motion Picture Association of America (MPAA) rating system. Friedkin reportedly submitted the film fifty times, at a cost of $50,000 and removed 40 minutes of explicit footage before securing an R rating. Friedkin acknowledged that the material being cut was justified in order to secure an R rating as, 'it really was pornography.' An extra, Ted Heaney, said in 2024 that one of the scenes filmed was so extreme that the cameraman fainted and refused to continue filming. Friedkin looked for the deleted material years later in order to reinsert it into a new cut or add it to a DVD as extra material, but he couldn't find it, assuming that United Artists had it destroyed, as many studios did at the time with cut material.

This was confirmed by James Pearcey and James White of the Arrow Restoration team, who in 2024, searched every probable element in Warner's archives (Warner having acquired producer Lorimar's collection of film materials when that company folded) before accepting that the footage was just not available.

Prior to release, Friedkin sought input from gay novelist John Rechy, author of *City of Night*, leading to minor editorial changes and the addition of a disclaimer stating the film was not meant to represent the entire gay community. However, this disclaimer became a point of contention, with Friedkin later claiming it was imposed by the MPAA and United Artists, while gay film historian Vito Russo viewed it as an admission of the film's problematic nature. Rechy had written an article in the *Village Voice* dated 6th August 1979 in support of *Cruising*'s right to be made.

Friedkin has said that *Cruising* is more about raising questions than providing answers, which would seem to be the film's defining legacy. The film appears to have multiple killers – the first killer becomes the second victim, for example – and there seems to be a suggestion that Pacino's Steve Burns might be one of them. Friedkin felt, however, that although ambiguous the story was clear.

While Pacino initially defended the film against accusations of anti-gay sentiment, comparing its portrayal of leather bars to *The Godfather*'s depiction of the Italian-American mafia, that being just a fragment of the community represented. He later revised his position. In his 2024 memoir *Sonny Boy*, he acknowledged viewing the finished film as exploitative and declined to participate in its promotion.

Cruising opened in Los Angeles and New York on 15th February 1980. It would earn $19.8 million at the box office. Though initially receiving largely negative reviews and continued protests from gay activist groups, critical opinion of the film has somewhat improved over time through reassessment. By the time the DVD was released in 2007 the representation of gay people on the screen was viewed as a positive by film critics.

At the time though it was certainly viewed as a mis-step in Pacino's career.

Pacino took half a million dollars from his pay check and he set up a trust fund. The money went to AIDS research, support for the homeless, feeding children and other charitable pursuits. With the interest it lasted for more than twenty years.

Chapter 12

American Buffalo
(Stage, 1980–84)

Written by: David Mamet
Directed by: Arvin Brown
Cast: Al Pacino, Clifton James, Tom Waites

American Buffalo began life as a work-in-progress show in October 1975 at the Goodman Theatre Stage II by the St. Nicholas Theater Company of Chicago, directed by Gregory Mosher with a cast of JJ Johnston, Bernard Erhard and William H. Macy. Mamet had walked into Mosher's office at the theatre, having complained about the terrible play he had been hired to direct, handed him a manuscript and said, 'Do this play. Just do it.'

It cost $200 to put on and it played for twelve performances. One review in the *Chicago Tribune* suggested that Mamet wrote his dialogue first, then found characters to fit and only at that point looked for meaning. It was a work-in-progress, so the fact that the reviewer felt there were only twenty usable minutes from a largely directionless whole is perhaps understandable. Johnston remembered asking Mamet of the ending, 'Where's the payoff?'

'As much as people hated it, people loved it,' Macy said in 1989. The play underwent several revisions before it opened in the 226-seat main theatre on 23rd November, playing Fridays through Sundays for nine weeks. Mike Nussbaum replaced Erhard as Teach.

Mamet was at the time beginning to develop a reputation as a playwright to watch. His plays *The Duck Variations* and *Sexual Perversity in Chicago* had played Off-Broadway at St Clements in 1974, having previously played Off-Loop, Chicago's version of Off-Broadway.

As a teenager, Mamet worked backstage at the Hull House Theater, Chicago. His father, a lawyer, Mamet once described as 'hopelessly stage-struck.' He majored in English Literature at Goddard College in Vermont, he said, simply to stay out of the Army. In his junior year, he studied acting at the Neighborhood Playhouse in New York, going on to work as an actor in Chicago. In 1970, Mamet returned to Vermont to work as a teacher. He founded the St. Nicholas Theater, which initially operated between Goddard and Marlboro Theater before relocating to Chicago. Mamet began writing plays as exercises for his students to develop specific acting techniques. His playwriting style was influenced by reading Samuel Beckett and Harold Pinter, when in the mid-1960s he would enter Oak Street Book Shop in Chicago and pick out one of their plays and sit down to read. Mamet would say that it was his first exposure to drama as literature. In particular Pinter's *A Night Out* and *The Birthday Party* were strong influences on him. Jack Lemmon would say that Mamet's brilliance lay not in what words he put on the page, but the words he didn't. It was here studying Beckett, Pinter and later Chekhov that he began to learn to cut his writing down to what was absolutely necessary. 'Chekhov removed the plot,' Mamet would say, 'Pinter removed the history and narrative, Beckett the characterisation.'

In 1974, along with Steven Schacter, Patricia Cox and William H. Macy he founded the St. Nicholas Theater in Chicago. Their artistic statement said the company tried 'to provide the most relevant and stimulating theatre we are capable of.' They originally set out to produce mostly premieres, with one classic per season.

The production moved to Broadway in February 1977 for a run that lasted 133 performances. That was deemed to be a modest run. The role of Teach was played by Robert Duvall, with John Savage as Bobby and Kenneth McMillan as Donny. The play cost $270,000 to mount this time.

When Jack Shepherd played Teach in London he said it took him weeks of rehearsal to work out that Mamet didn't write subtext. People in the play said what they meant. It was required, Shepherd noted, to play it at about ten times the equivalent speed as a play by Pinter or Trevor Griffiths.

Pacino had tested some plays quietly during 1979. He worked with Romanian director Liviu Ciulei on some staged readings of Bertolt Brecht's *In the Jungle of Cities*. He then organised a group of actors, including Emmy winner Ron Leibman, to workshop *Othello* in a rehearsal hall at Lincoln Center's Vivian Beaumont Theater for several weeks.

In the summer of 1980, Pacino called Arvin Brown, the artistic director of the Long Wharf Theatre in New Haven and told him he was interested in doing *American Buffalo*. The pair had spoken about working together for several years, but this was the first time their schedules aligned.

American Buffalo was set in Don's Resale Shop, a junkyard on Chicago's southside. It takes place over one day, the first act plays out on a Friday morning, with act two late that evening. Donny has only one employee, Bobby, a young man struggling with a drug habit. They conspire to rob a local resident of his valuable coin collection which includes an old Indian head buffalo tail nickel called an American Buffalo. But Teach, a player at Donny's poker game, gets wind of the plan and decides to muscle in.

The production had four weeks of rehearsal, not the longest period in theatre but a decent length of time to achieve Pacino and Mamet's aim which was to have the show 'play like jazz, fresh every night.' Pacino had grown frustrated with making something happen before it was ready, so he was pleased to indulge in an extended rehearsal period.

American Buffalo opened at New Haven's 484-seater Long Wharf Theatre on 2nd October 1980. The advert the theatre took out in the New York Times to announce the production omitted Pacino's name. Edgar Rosenblum, Long Wharf's executive director, told *Variety* that it was against the theatre's policy to mention individual performers in its advertising, no matter what their potential box office draw might be. Around 80% of the theatre's capacity was taken up by subscriptions. 'If we were to move the show to Broadway, then Al Pacino's name would be quite prominent,' Rosenblum said. 'We're not naive commercially.'

Tom Waites, not to be confused with the singer, whose surname omits the 'e' appeared with Pacino in *...And Justice For All (1979)* playing a young victim of the law. He was another actor who appreciated Pacino's looking out for him. In 2007, he spoke about working with Pacino on the film. 'We were doing a scene, and I just wasn't doing very well,' he said on the Movie Geeks United podcast. 'Al took me aside and counselled me until my nerves about the scene went away.'

After the play opened the cast continued to rehearse. The cast talked about the characters' relationships. For Pacino a Mamet play meant you had to learn the words and then you had to learn the acting.

In the *Hartford Courant*, Malcolm L Johnson wrote that the 1980 version differed from the 1977 production. 'It is less furious, somehow less abstract and considerably funnier.'

Johnson wrote of Pacino's performance that he made no attempt to make the character of Teach sympathetic. 'His Teach is detestable and pitiable but he is also completely compelling.'

In June 1981 it transferred from New Haven's Long Wharf Theatre where it played for a limited run to the 299-seater Circle in the Square on Bleecker Street off-Broadway. It was produced by Elliot Martin who had been the production stage manager of the original 1956 Broadway production of Eugene O'Neill's *Long Day's Journey Into Night*. He was now into his twentieth year as a producer. Martin had gone to see the production at Long Wharf and felt that in Brown's direction he had found the humour that was lacking in the Broadway production. He opted to take the production from Connecticut to London's West End. However, it took Equity so long to approve Pacino's appearance on the London stage that by the time approval came through Pacino had changed his mind. The decision was then taken to transfer to off-Broadway providing Pacino with a return after 15 years.

The top weekday tickets were $16.50 rising to $18.50 at weekends. The prices went up to $20 and then to $24. The tickets all sold. The run gave Pacino some of the best notices of his career.

Richard Christiansen of the *Chicago Tribune* called it 'a triumph for Pacino.' Variety's 17th June review inevitably compared Pacino to Robert Duvall's Broadway performance. Pacino was noted as being less menacing but far funnier. The review highlights Pacino's growth as an actor stating that although Teach is a similar lowlife to that Pacino had played on stage previously, there were subtle shadings to his characterisation. Pacino showed that he had his own route into the character, and critics came to accept that Pacino was doing something different with a part that they had largely thought was definitive in Duvall's hands.

'Pacino makes it all fall into place with his richly expressive funny, only slightly scary picture of Teach,' wrote Douglas Watt in the *Daily News*. 'With a mind as cunning as, but no more so than a wharf's rat. He is simply marvellous, at times hilarious, in a perfectly coordinated performance.'

Jay Sharbutt the Associated Press drama critic noted that Waites's 'deft – and risky – underplaying [is] a fine contrast to the commanding, always powerful stage presence of Pacino.'

The rest of the cast, the direction and the set were all also universally praised, as was Mamet's writing.

Elliot Martin praised Pacino's feeling for and attitude towards theatre when speaking with Ernest Albrecht of the *Central New Jersey Home News*. Martin was also impressed that Pacino frequently returned to the stage when there was more lucrative work on offer in cinema. 'It's a credit to him as a person and an actor that he does so.' It was heartening for Martin to note that the production was getting a new audience into the theatre. Young people who were fans of Pacino on screen were now eager to take this chance to see him live.

After that production Pacino went back to the movies to star in Author! Author! written by Israel Horovitz and directed by Arthur Hiller. Filming began on 2nd November 1981. By the time Hiller needed him to loop dialogue for the soundtrack in the spring of 1982 Pacino was back in New York and back in *American Buffalo* at Circle in the Square.

JJ Johnston rejoined the cast taking over his original role. Mamet was such a fan of Johnston's work that the play was dedicated to him, and the printed copies carry this dedication at the front. Johnston had to relearn the part as there was now a different ending from when he had originally played it, along with some other significant changes.

Johnston had been an amateur boxer fighting 56 middleweight bouts, between the ages of 16 and 25, losing only 8 and winning 34 by knockout. He was working as a bartender when the owner put in a dinner theatre and needed a Big Julie for his production of Guys and Dolls. Johnston then 32 had never acted before. He discovered he was pretty good. It led him to Second City and a children's repertory group in Chicago. It was there he met a 20-year-old actor named David Mamet. The pair played sailors in *Mr Roberts* and appeared in plays such as *Pinocchio*. Johnston remembered that Mamet was always writing things down in a notebook, but his fellow cast members had no idea he was about to become a heavyweight playwright.

In the afternoons Pacino was rehearsing with his fellow actors, scenes from *The Hairy Ape*, a 1922 play by Eugene O'Neill. Pacino had performed it at the Actors Studio with Allen Garfield in May 1967. He was hoping to mount it as a stage production.

In an April 1982 syndicated theatre gossip column written by Robin Adams Sloan – a pseudonym for journalists Liz Smith and Roberta Ashley – it was suggested that before each performance of *American Buffalo* Pacino insisted on an 'arduous full cast rehearsal.' The column quoted an anonymous cast member saying, 'With any other actor the constant rehearsing would be gruelling and get to be a drag. With Pacino it's a genuine privilege and he helps to develop new insights at every turn.'

In New Jersey's *Daily Record* newspaper Scott Fosdick suggested that this staging of American Buffalo suffered from commercial pressure. This revival only exists Fosdick said because Pacino wanted to play the role of Teach again. Fosdick acknowledged that Pacino gave a 'searing performance' but criticised him for drawing focus from the rest of the cast. The production set high ticket prices and sold out well in advance, it was successful Fosdick noted of identifying its most commercial aspect and squeezing it for all it was worth.

Jamie Portman in *Southam News* had a similar observation writing 'Pacino comes close to doing a travesty of all his most celebrated film mannerisms. But that seemingly is enough to make his live appearance a stellar occasion for audiences. The play is secondary.'

The play moved in August to the small Terrace Theater at the Kennedy Center for the Performing Arts in Washington. Pacino's co-stars were now JJ Johnston and James Hayden. Hayden was thrilled to be working alongside Pacino. He would hang around outside the theatre when Pacino did *Pavlo Hummel*. He was eventually invited in to work backstage, swapping up and doing odd jobs. He shared Pacino's method for observing the traits and mannerisms of people on the street in order to use for parts. Hayden would prepare for an hour before he went on stage, getting into the part. The three prepared together and talked about how the show had gone afterwards.

Hayden's father went into the theatre in the afternoon one day to watch one of the daily two-hour rehearsals where the three experimented with small changes, sometimes it was blocking, sometimes it was tone or intonation. 'They were selling out every night, and you would think they would just take it easy,' he later told *New York Magazine*. 'But they were there every day trying to find something to make it more effective.'

In October 1983, *American Buffalo* returned to Broadway at the Booth Theatre on West 45th Street. The play went to the Booth because it had a proscenium theatre, like the venues in San Francisco, Washington DC, Boston and London where the play would be toured. In a proscenium theatre, the audience all sit facing the same way. The stage is raised and the audience usually sits in raked seating. They had previously been performing *Buffalo* in the round.

In conversation with Leslie Bennetts of the *New York Times*, Pacino explained the value of repeating a role for him, citing the great Shakespearean roles and suggesting that an actor can never just do them once and be content. He emphasised that although he was doing the same role again and again it was never the same.

The reviews were lukewarm, to begin with. In the *New York Times*, Frank Rich wrote of Pacino on the opening night, that although it was a star turn his fans would love he had now precisely thought out every single line and every single move. It was, Rich wrote a 'calculated display of technique' which had 'doused much of the play's fire.'

Rich had noted that Pacino now faced the auditorium and not his fellow actors on stage. Rich saw that as a decline in his performance, that he wasn't playing a sad man looking for respect from his cohorts but he was simply a movie star on stage courting his fan base.

Other reviewers had noted that Teach's outburst towards the end wasn't the violent spasm it had been previously, Pacino giving the part a little more control. Again, reviewers couldn't help but mention Duvall who played the same scene in 1977 by wrecking the scenery.

The show experienced walkouts with the language, gestures and subject matter being too much for some audience members. One night someone in the auditorium began shouting at the cast and had to be escorted out.

One night a woman came by Pacino's dressing room and asked if he could sign something. Pacino said, 'Sure' and took the pen. What the woman handed him was a newspaper with the headline 'Al Pacino Fails Miserably as Scarface.'

The show was now standing room only, even on Monday and Tuesday nights, a rarity for Broadway.

On 7th November, ten days after opening, the show came down to a standing ovation. James Hayden, who played the drug-addicted Bobby, returned home to his apartment on Broadway and 69th Street. He was speaking on the telephone to his ex-wife at 4.30am when he suddenly stopped talking. His ex-wife called his physician who dialled 911. When police entered the 14th-floor apartment, they discovered Hayden's body fully clothed, slumped over the kitchen sink, telephone in hand. On the kitchen floor, they found a hypodermic needle and three or four glassine envelopes that they believed contained heroin.

Hayden had been a paramedic with the Army during the Vietnam War, although he had joined just as President Nixon signed the Paris Peace Accord. Reassigned to Fort Sam Houston in Texas he spent his days with men who had returned from Southeast Asia now addicted to heroin. 'I've always believed the real casualty of war was increased drug abuse here,' he said in an interview with the *Daily News* just a few weeks before his death. In preparation for the role he attended Narcotics Anonymous meetings and spoke with what would later become apparent were *other* drug users, about how they became dependent on drugs. It was also reported that he went down to Alphabetland, Ave A and Ave B of the lower East Side which was known for its wide-open drug sales. At the time the press was reporting his detailed research no one knew that he was a drug user himself.

A graduate of the American Academy of Dramatic Arts Hayden had recently filmed a part in *Once Upon a Time in America (1984)* alongside Robert De Niro. Arvin Brown, American Buffalo's director, who had also directed Hayden in Arthur Miller's *A View From the Bridge* told the Associated Press the 29-year-old 'Was about to become a big star.' He continued, 'I'm as convinced of that as I've been convinced of anything since I directed Meryl Streep some years ago and had the same feeling about her for many of the same reasons. You get a sense about an acting temperament, and when you hit it, that's what you mean by talent.'

'He wasn't trying to kill himself,' Johnston told *Newsday*. 'He knew what he was doing. He wasn't a mainliner. A mainliner builds up an immunity. But Jimmy had no immunity. He overdosed.'

The play didn't miss a performance as understudy John Shepard went on the next night. Before the show began Arvin Brown came onstage after the lights were dimmed and raised three times, and made an announcement. 'Early this morning we at American Buffalo lost an extraordinary friend and a most gifted actor, James Hayden. We are going on with the show tonight because there really isn't anything else we can do. Surely you will all understand and realise to whom this performance is dedicated.' It was noted in the press that a clearly tense and nervous Shepard had acquitted himself well in the circumstances. 'The audience knew they had experienced something special and gave them a long standing ovation,' Lawrence Grobel wrote in *Rolling Stone*. 'The actors took their bows, but they didn't smile.'

Bruce MacVittie, who had played the role previously came in as a permanent replacement. The play was his Broadway debut.

Pacino told reporters outside the theatre that Hayden's death was 'A great loss to me personally, to the play, and the world and the theatre.' Pacino and Hayden had worked together on the play for three years, and Pacino's representatives were keen to assert their client had no knowledge Mr. Hayden had resumed using the drugs he had claimed he'd left in his past.

Over 300 people attended Hayden's funeral at St Sebastian Catholic Church on 57th St, Woodside, Queens. It was the same church where a few years earlier Hayden's father had lit a candle for him before he went up for the role in *American Buffalo*. Pacino and Johnston sat together as Father James Michael, who had grown up with Hayden officiated. The priest had been counselling Hayden weekly for the past year over his drug issues.

The show extended beyond its 17th December scheduled ending and went into January 1984. By March it had begun previews in San Francisco at the Curran Theater.

Elliot Martin agreed to produce Mamet's latest play Glengarry Glen Ross, which was premiering in London in 1983. It would have its US Premiere on 27 January at the Goodman Theater in Chicago and then move to Broadway.

Pacino would earn a Drama Desk nomination for Best Actor, losing out to Dustin Hoffman for *Death of a Salesman*.

American Buffalo and Pacino came to London in August 1984 to play a limited run at the Duke of York's. Inevitably English critics lined up to mark Pacino and the show down. Jack Tinker in the *Daily Mail* wrote that there was a great divide between 'what the British believe to be fine acting and what passes for the same in the more undisciplined area of Broadway.'

In the *Financial Times* Michael Coveney criticised Pacino's reliance on the method as taught by Lee Strasberg and wrote that the play was much more successful with a British cast at the National Theatre. Milton Shulman in the *Evening Standard* called Pacino 'both hypnotic and tiring to watch.' In the Daily Mirror Arthur Thirkell's brief review spent three paragraphs being outraged by Pacino's 'foul-mouthed' character. 'The play went down well in New York. I wish it had stayed there.' In *The Observer* JC Trewin counted 'well over' 100 obscenities and referred to it as a 'tediously involved story.' The Sunday Telegraph's review by Francis King offered, 'Though the story has irony and pathos it is far too slim to provide a whole evening in the theatre.' 'How can such illiterate inconsequential chatter sustain our interest for two hours?' asked Eric Shorter in the *Daily Telegraph*. 'Nothing happens. Much of the talk is of people we never meet and most of it is unprintable.'

Arvin Brown though was always impressed by Pacino's performance, his sense of ensemble and his absorption into the show. 'His ID as a star has been submerged entirely,' Brown said to the *Sacramento Bee*. 'My experience is that the "star" feels more vulnerable, more exposed in the theatre than the performers without such a large identity.'

In London the 14-year-old Martin McDonagh went to the theatre for the first time as he wanted to see Pacino on stage. Although his influences were mainly rooted in cinema Mamet's work had an impact on him and he later wrote provocative plays of his own in *The Lieutenant of Inishmore* and *The Beauty Queen of Leenane*.

Rumours were that Pacino would soon begin filming the movie of American Buffalo with Sidney Lumet directing. There was a point Pacino was asked to direct but after doing it onstage for four years he didn't feel he could. Pacino's understanding of the project was that Jerry Tokofsky, who would later produce *Glengarry Glen Ross (1992)* would produce with John McNaughton directing.

The film would eventually be made in 1996 with Michael Corrente directing. In the fall of 1994 Pacino was offered the role, but also given a firm deadline of when he had to accept it. When the deadline passed without Pacino signing Corrente moved on. Pacino said he felt an allegiance to Tokofsky. Dustin Hoffman would take the part.

Chapter 13

Scarface
(Film, 1983)

Directed by: Brian De Palma
Written by: Oliver Stone
Based on the novel *Scarface* by Armitage Trail
Cast: Al Pacino, Steven Bauer, Michelle Pfeiffer, Mary Elizabeth Mastrantonio, Robert Loggia, Míriam Colón, F. Murray Abraham, Paul Shenar, Harris Yulin, Ángel Salazar

Pacino had heard of *Scarface (1932)* his entire life; his mother would talk about it, particularly the iconic sequence of George Raft flipping a half-dollar coin, which became shorthand for movie toughness. While working on *Arturo Ui*, Pacino knew that Paul Muni's performance had been a reference for the character. He had, however, never had a chance to see the picture.

One day, Pacino was out with friends, and they were walking along Sunset Boulevard, where they passed the Tiffany Theatre. *Scarface* played at the Tiffany in December 1979 and January 1980 in a double bill with Howard Hughes's *Hell's Angels (1930)*, a film about British First World War pilots, which was Jean Harlow's first starring role. It was the first public screening in 30 years for both films. Pacino suggested to his friends that they go in and have a look.

Paul Muni's performance completely mesmerised Pacino. Becoming almost that kid who performed as Ray Milland for his relatives, he wanted to be Paul Muni. He wanted to act like that. He found the nearest phone box, and he called Martin Bregman. Pacino asked his manager if he had ever heard of the film. He told him it was a movie they should remake.

Martin Bregman, however, had a different memory of how the project came about. 'I know Al thinks it was his idea to remake *Scarface*,' Bregman told Stephen Rebello in a feature for *Playboy*, 'and somebody at Universal also thinks it was his idea, but it was mine.' Bregman's consistent story through the years has been that he was watching TV at home in New York late one night in 1980 when he caught the Howard Hawks original. He felt that Pacino could bring something extraordinary to it. Bregman felt that in a remake Pacino's early theatre skills would serve him well. In *The Godfather*, he played a rich man's son, not someone from the street; this was the chance to bring out the streetwise character he had done so well on stage in *The Indian Wants the Bronx* and *Does a Tiger Wear a Necktie?*. Bregman had been a nightclub agent in New York, in an era where many clubs were mob-controlled, so he felt he knew the world.

In 1980, Brian De Palma spoke to Pacino about taking on the lead role in *Blow Out (1981)*, a part that would ultimately go to John Travolta. During their discussions, Pacino told De Palma of his interest in remaking *Scarface* and sent him a videotape of the film.

De Palma joined up with David Rabe to write a script. They began with the original movie's concept of Italians in Chicago. By August 1981, the film press reported that there was disagreement between the writers and the producers over the direction the script should take. De Palma and Rabe left the project when it couldn't be resolved.

Sidney Lumet was then approached to direct, an obvious choice since Pacino had enjoyed a great working relationship with him on *Serpico* and *Dog Day Afternoon*. Lumet's lasting legacy to *Scarface* was his identification that the film had to examine the immigrant experience. Paul Muni's Tony Camonte was an Italian immigrant and he felt Pacino's character should also be an immigrant looking for a new life in America. In the spring of 1980, Cuba opened its port at Mariel Harbor, and thousands of Cubans set sail for America. In January 1982, as the US moved to tighten immigration from Cuba, there were 800,000 Cuban exiles in the USA, and 5,000 were in Miami. Lumet felt that was a rich vein to tap into, so Pacino's character would be a Cuban immigrant. Pacino wanted Lumet to direct, although Bregman felt he needed a director with more edge, someone more contemporary.

Bregman approached Oliver Stone to write the script. Although Stone had won an Oscar for writing *Midnight Express (1978)*, his most recent directing project, *The Hand (1981)* with Michael Caine, disappointed him.

However, when Bregman asked him to do *Scarface*, he turned the project down, saying he wasn't interested in doing remakes. When Bregman told him Lumet's idea to begin the film with the Mariel boatlift, it lit something under Stone. He recognised that the film could now be a modern gangster movie with the 1930s prohibition against alcohol being replaced by the 1980s war on drugs, the former creating the Mafia and the latter creating a new criminal class.

Stone began to research in Miami and in South America, where he spoke to people on both sides: drug dealers, lawyers and law enforcement. Bregman joined him in Miami and was stunned by how huge the drug world was. When the US attorney put a monetary figure on how big the industry was, Stone had to ask him to repeat it. The figure wasn't the $100 million Bregman and Stone thought they'd heard – it was $100 billion.

Stone had been doing cocaine during his research, but he knew he had to break his habit to write the script. He felt he couldn't do that in America, so he moved to Paris to write. Having poured so much of his energy and money into the drug, Stone felt the film was his revenge on cocaine. He kept his writing room very dark to give him separation and concentration.

The original story was based on Al Capone. Howard Hughes had bought a book called *Scarface* by Armitage Trail. He took it to Howard Hawks, even though, at the time, Hughes was suing Hawks for similarities between Hawks' *The Dawn Patrol (1930)* and Hughes's *Hell's Angels*. Hughes agreed to call the lawsuit off if Hawks would discuss working on the picture with him.

Scarface was set in Chicago. 'The Borgia family live today in Chicago and Cesare Borgia is Al Capone' was how Hawks recalled pitching the film to screenwriter Ben Hecht when he spoke with Muni's biographer Jerome Lawrence in 1973. 'I never make a picture that's supposed to be a big one,' Hawks said, 'I like to take a little picture and make it big.' The film centred around the world of bootlegging and the liquor industry. In the 1980s, the obvious change to make was to centre the story around the drug trade.

Stone brought his script back to his director but found that Lumet didn't like it. Lumet thought it had too much gratuitous violence and was over the top. He left the project. Stone wanted to direct the film, but his track record wasn't strong enough as a director to helm a big picture starring Al Pacino. Stone worked with Pacino briefly in 1978, during which there was a full cast rehearsal of Stone's script *Born on the Fourth of July*. Pacino's performance was so good Stone said it lived with him for ten years.

Armed with a new screenplay, Bregman went back to De Palma. When De Palma read the script, he immediately saw that it differed greatly from what he and Rabe had been doing. It was a whole new way of approaching the material, which resonated with De Palma, and he eagerly agreed to direct.

Bregman scheduled the film to begin shooting largely in Florida in the summer of 1982, and New York casting sessions began primarily at the West 47th Street Puerto Rican Traveling Theater.

Although De Palma wanted John Travolta for the role of Manny, casting director Alixe Gordin, who had cast *Klute (1971)* and Sophie's Choice (1982), said the only choice was Steven Bauer. Bregman and De Palma liked Bauer when he first came in. Bregman, very familiar with Pacino's work, was aware, though, that when Pacino was on screen, it was hard to watch another actor, and as the character of Manny shared most of his scenes with Pacino's Montana, it needed a strong personality to play opposite him. After Bauer had done a reading for them, Bregman was convinced he was the right actor. He could see Bauer had life experience, and the reading showed what a strong actor he was.

De Palma had seen *Grease II (1982)* and hated the film, so he wasn't interested in seeing Michelle Pfeiffer for the role of Elvira. However, Gordin persuaded him, so he let Pfeiffer read for him. Pfeiffer, a former Miss Orange County, had hoped *Grease II* would be her big break, but some of the poor reviews shocked her. Bregman told Pfeiffer's agent that if she flew herself in, she would get a reading. The production would eventually compensate her for her fare, but to Bregman, paying her own way showed her commitment to wanting the role. Many young actresses, including Courteney Cox, Jamie Lee Curtis, Isabelle Adjani, Sharon Stone and Debra Winger, were tested. When Pfeiffer read for Bregman, he realised she would be perfect. Pacino's choice was Glenn Close, but he ultimately deferred to Bregman. The part was re-written by Stone from an affluent New York girl who was slumming in the drug world to a typical American girl from Miami.

Pacino rented a house in Malibu, and he and Steven Bauer would work on their parts. Martin Sheen would sometimes come by. They didn't work on the script; for a month, they talked about their characters' lives in Cuba, which preceded the film's opening shot. Bauer felt that this work was an enormous help when it came time to shoot.

While Pacino initially wanted to mimic Paul Muni, he began to do what he regularly did to create a character. He found the look and worked on the gestures. Pacino worked intensively with Charlie Laughton and Robert Easton, a famed dialect coach. Bauer, who was Cuban, helped Pacino with the language. Pacino also trained with an expert in knife combat and worked with a trainer to shape his body. He also had two wildly diverse influences. One was the Panamanian boxer Roberto Durán, who exuded confidence and had a swagger in the ring. The other was Meryl Streep in *Sophie's Choice*. Pacino felt that her performance in that film was courageous. Pacino would later talk about the fearlessness he felt when he inhabited Tony Montana.

Once the production arrived in Miami in June 1982, some issues needed to be ironed out. The local Cuban community had a feeling that the film was going to be insulting to Cuban Americans. There was nothing publicly available about the story except that Pacino was playing a Cuban gangster, but the community feared it would heighten stereotyping and result in discrimination. Miami City Commissioner Demetrio Perez Jr, a Cuban immigrant himself, drafted a city council resolution denying the production the necessary permits to film on city property and on city streets. However, it didn't come to a vote. To ease concerns, production officials met with several minority groups, including the Spanish American League Against Discrimination and the Cuban National Planning Council.

Bregman outlined that the film was not about Cubans in Miami but about one gangster. He insisted that the film wouldn't depict Cuban-Americans poorly. Nothing Bregman could say would dissuade them that the film had bad intentions towards their community. Although executive producer Louis Stroller agreed to include a disclaimer in the credits noting that the film was 'not meant as an indictment of Miami's Cuban refugee population.' 'If they don't want us there, we'll move,' Bregman told the *Miami Herald*. 'Believe me, this is not going to give Miami or that area a bad image. It already has that image.'

Governor Bob Graham's office and the Greater Miami Chamber of Commerce lobbied Bregman to keep the production in Miami. The producer was amenable to their suggestions, but the *Miami Herald* published two opinion columns. One by Guillermo Martinez, writing in the paper's editorial pages, said that making the protagonist a Mariel refugee would perpetuate the refugees' image as criminals. The other, written by Roberto Fabricio, editor of the paper's Spanish edition, called Bregman 'an idiot.'

Fabricio responded that although he agreed with Perez that the film could damage the community, he felt the Commissioner had taken a course of action that amounted to 'irresponsible overkill.' Fabricio had suggested that Bregman had been an idiot for first calling Perez an idiot and threatening to move the production.

Another *Miami Herald* editorial on 21st August felt that to run the production company out of town would be detrimental to Miami as a whole and in particular to the burgeoning local film industry. Letters both for and against the filming of *Scarface* flooded into the newspaper.

The issue, though, had spooked Bregman, and by the end of August 1982, he wanted to take the production out of Miami, saying that he was afraid of demonstrations.

The production opted to cut their losses and make the film in Los Angeles, using Santa Barbara for some exteriors and doing just 10 days of shooting in Miami at the end of the film. Bregman suggested that the decision added almost $5 million to the budget.

The production returned to Miami in April 1983 to film at Brickell Avenue, Biscayne Boulevard, and the Mutiny Hotel. De Palma's shooting pace was slow, and he and Pacino would discuss things at length in Pacino's trailer before they began each set-up. After 24 weeks of filming, *Scarface* completed principal photography on May 6, 1983.

Primarily due to violence and language deemed to be obscene, in October, Scarface was awarded an 'X' rating by the MPAA. The 'X' rating was usually only awarded to pornographic films, and many movie theatres simply refused to show films with an 'X' rating. The film was edited and re-submitted to the MPAA three times. De Palma described MPAA chief Richard Heffner as overly demanding, claiming in a 9 Nov 1983 LAHExam brief that Heffner harboured resentment toward him ever since they fought over the rating of *Dressed to Kill (1980)*.

Despite De Palma's cuts, the MPAA's decision was upheld. That was the final straw for De Palma who refused to remove another frame. Bregman supported his decision and told him that they would 'go to war.' The filmmakers appealed to the MPAA's Classification and Rating Administration (CARA). De Palma submitted not the third edit but his original cut.

Bregman organised a presentation in front of the whole board. At the appeal, movie critics Jay Cocks and Roger Ebert spoke on the film's behalf alongside Nick Navarro, a Cuban Florida-based law-enforcement officer specialising in narcotics, who worked on the film as a technical advisor. Navarro claimed that young people should see *Scarface* because it accurately portrayed the 'ugliness behind the drug trade.' The appeal was successful, and *Scarface* was awarded an R rating. De Palma was overjoyed. Howard Hawks fought a similar battle with the Hays Office in the 1930s. After filing a series of lawsuits, he, too, eventually won.

Bregman told the *LA Times*, 'Wait until you see Pacino's performance. It's the best thing he's ever done. By far.'

'The book will shock you – the movie will blow you away,' read the posters all over Los Angeles.

On 1st December 1983, Scarface was shown in a private screening in a theatre in Times Square to a celebrity audience. Eddie Murphy, Raquel Welch, Cher, and Lucille Ball were among the celebrities in attendance. Novelist Kurt Vonnegut left after 30 minutes, claiming the film was 'too gory.' John Irving wasn't long behind him. Model Cheryl Tiegs, draped in chinchilla, called it 'the most violent film I've ever seen. It makes you never want to hear the word "cocaine" again.' Lucille Ball bristled at the copious swearing, 'We thought the performances were excellent,' she said, 'but we got awful sick of that word.'

After the screening, Bregman hosted a party for 130 at Sardi's, the famous celebrity eatery in Manhattan. Pacino missed the screening as he was on stage in *American Buffalo*. He arrived at the party just before midnight, staying an hour with his girlfriend, Kathleen Quinlan. 'The crowd looking at me coming into Sardi's was a lot like that audience watching "Springtime for Hitler" in Mel Brooks's movie *The Producers*,' Pacino told *Playboy*. The one person Pacino recalled approaching him to say he loved the film was Eddie Murphy.

The film had 226 instances of the word 'fuck' being uttered. 'The Time magazine critic, I remember, Richard Schickel…he made a point of it,' Bauer said in 2018. 'He counted. And that was part of his review really.'

At the LA premiere Joan Collins, while miscounting the number, provided the best quip when she said, 'I hear there are 183 "fucks" in the movie, which is more than most people get in a lifetime.'

In an interview with *Creative Screenwriting* in 2015, Stone explained that the word was used deliberately for rhythm but that Pacino had inserted more in it as he found his natural rhythm to speak the lines.

Bauer recalled the initial reactions to the film for *Playboy*. 'When the movie opened, most reviews said it was a piece of shit, an insult, an outrage with an over-the-top performance from Al. We were devastated.'

'We didn't get reviewed, we got eviscerated,' recalled Pacino.

On 4th December, in the *Miami Herald*, movie critic Bill Cosford awarded *Scarface* two and a half stars. 'Scarface is one of Brian De Palma's B movies, neither as haunting as Carrie not as fully realised as Dressed to Kill.' Its success, Cosford would suggest, is that it liberated De Palma from being a Hitchcock clone. What Cosford does nail in his review is his summary of the film's denouement. 'Scarface does contain one scene that seems destined to be a screen classic: crazy Tony behind his big desk in the mansion, burying his nose in a mound of coke and rooting in it like a hog, then lifting his head up to reveal a hilarious white-tipped nose.'

Pauline Kael's review in *The New Yorker* was particularly unkind to Pacino. 'After a while, Pacino is a lump at the centre of the movie,' Kael wrote. 'Nothing develops in Pacino's performance. This is a two-hour-and-forty-nine-minute picture with a star whose imagination seems impaired.'

Years later Pacino would say to his biographer Lawrence Grobel that he felt *Scarface* wasn't understood at the time of release. Pacino believed the movie was about avarice, excess and everything in the character's world being out of proportion, The critics just didn't get the joke.

Gradually, however, *Scarface* grew to become a cult film, and one of the places its reputation grew was in the rap world. Stone recalled hearing some of his dialogue when he was walking the New York streets a year or so after the film was released. 'Black kids were getting it, the future rap kids. There were also all these white professional working men who'd get together for a drink and quote the dialogue. I'd often go places and hear that.'

'I did have a feeling,' Pacino said about the film in 2018. 'With Scarface, I must say, there was something about the preparation, there was something about the text and Brian working together with everybody that I found that channel in myself, that I felt this is about something that I really wanna say in some way.'

In the years following Scarface would be looked on within a handful of movies around the time that flopped for Pacino. Now, however, it may be his most popular and iconic role. Lines like 'Say hello to my leetle friend,' have become part of the everyday language and Scarface has become a must-see movie for every new generation of film fans.

Chapter 14

Revolution
(Film, 1985)

Directed by: Hugh Hudson
Written by: Robert Dillon
Produced by: Irwin Winkler
Cast: Al Pacino, Donald Sutherland, Nastassja Kinski, Dexter Fletcher, Sid Owen, Joan Plowright, Dave King, Steven Berkoff, John Wells, Annie Lennox, Richard O'Brien, Paul Brooke, Frank Windsor, Jesse Birdsall, Larry Sellers, Graham Greene, Robbie Coltrane

On the BBC's *Film 93* programme, first broadcast on BBC One on 8th March 1993, Barry Norman, the UK's most respected film critic, sat down with a contented Al Pacino, recently Oscar-nominated for *Scent of a Woman (1993)*. While the two discussed Pacino's latest film and his chances of finally landing an Academy Award, Norman, never one to pander to stars, took a breath and prefaced his next question. 'Everybody says, "Look, for God's sake, don't ask him about Revolution."' So Norman did. 'It was a flop,' Norman said. 'You must admit that, but everybody's entitled to a flop, surely.'

Pacino, by now quite media savvy, responded thoughtfully, explaining that some flops are quiet disappointments while others carry significant expectations. He admitted uncertainty about whether he should have made the film, but noted that the experience of filming *Revolution* and living through that period remained one of his most memorable moviemaking experiences.

Pacino reflected on the paradox of filmmaking: sometimes a painful production experience results in a pleasant outcome when the film is released, while other times a wonderful filming experience produces a movie that doesn't succeed. When Norman suggested that the disappointment from

Revolution had caused Pacino to retreat from movies for four years and return to theatre, Pacino acknowledged this likely played a role, though he wasn't certain it was a conscious decision.

He explained that the film was completed in September but had to be released in December, leaving him feeling it wasn't as finished as it could have been. While he couldn't say definitively whether more time would have improved the final product, he confirmed that he did have a reaction to the film's outcome and his subsequent career choices. 'No doubt I did.'

In the early 1980s, producer Irwin Winkler envisioned creating a film about the American War of Independence, believing the period would make compelling cinema. Fresh from his success with *The Right Stuff (1983)*, Winkler opted to tell the story through the lens of a fictional father and son rather than historical figures, saying that he'd had enough of those after *The Right Stuff*, where almost every character was based on a real person. Winkler thought the subject was ripe as he couldn't recall a film based on the American Revolution since D.W. Griffith's *America (1924)*. Robert Dillon was commissioned to write the script under a development deal with Warner Bros. The script found its way to *Chariots of Fire* director Hugh Hudson who was attracted by the subject matter. He met with Winkler after the 1984 Cannes Film Festival and agreed to work on the film. Though the studio ultimately passed on financing the project, Winkler retained the rights and through Hudson's suggestion found an enthusiastic partner in Sandy Lieberson of Goldcrest Films, who agreed to back the production provided a U.S. studio would co-produce. Warner Bros. eventually returned as co-producer.

Within Goldcrest there was a lot of hesitation over the script. Script readers and executives alike had suggested there was no real story, the battle scenes were there in lieu of any drama, and there were too many coincidental meetings of characters throughout the movie. But the project moved ahead.

Goldcrest had recent success with *Chariots of Fire (1981)* and *Gandhi (1982)* both of which triumphed without big stars in the leading roles – *Gandhi* being the film that made Ben Kingsley's international reputation. *The Killing Fields (1984)* while still making a decent profit and garnering Academy Awards wasn't as successful at the box office and one factor was thought to be the casting of an actor who wasn't a star name in Sam

Waterston. So when it came to *Revolution* movie stars were a must. It was a move that would buckle Goldcrest financially as they offered inflated fees and profit shares.

Pacino, who joined the project relatively late after Sam Shepard, Michael Douglas, Sylvester Stallone and Robert Duvall were considered, was chosen for his ability to bring realism to the role of Tom Dobb, a New York frontiersman who becomes unwittingly embroiled in the Revolutionary War. Now 45, Pacino saw the film as an opportunity to pay tribute to his South Bronx roots and America's origin story. He asked for $3M plus expenses, plus 10 percent of the gross. The board at Goldcrest met to discuss this request, as it was way over what they had budgeted for. Hudson went to bat for his chosen star. David Norris at Goldcrest negotiated with Pacino's agent and eventually the deal was done at $3M paid weekly over the film's production, expenses and 20 percent of the net profits. In the contract Pacino would also have rights to rehearsal time and approval of any changes to the script.

At the time Winkler acknowledged that Pacino's fee was seven figures. 'But lower seven figures than Sly Stallone or Robert Redford,' he said.

Sandy Lieberson would advise the production that adding a star of Pacino's calibre was great in the sense that it would lift the scale of the project, but that would also change the mindset of everyone working on it, leading inevitably to an increase in the budget.

Hudson didn't meet Nastassja Kinski until the first day of shooting. Later he believed she was the wrong choice for the role. The pair didn't get along on set. Pacino wouldn't start filming until he and Kinski had time to rehearse. Hudson wanted to bring in Colin Welland, *Chariots of Fire*'s Oscar winning screenwriter to do some work on the script, but Lieberson, formerly president of the 20th Century Fox Film Corporation, refused, stating that there wasn't enough time or budget.

Despite Winkler's preference to film in America, Goldcrest pushed for shooting in England. Lieberson felt all the appropriate locations were in England and the film could be shot cheaply there. The move took the budget before stars' pay cheques were taken into account from $13M to $10M. The thought was that *Revolution* could be a movie with similar heft to *Gandhi*. It would, Lieberson hoped, balance out the number of low budget movies they had on their slate. The production was primarily based in King's Lynn,

Norfolk, with key battle scenes filmed at Burrator Reservoir on Dartmoor and near Challaborough Bay in South Devon.

'They convinced me that England had a lot of hamlets, wide-open areas and houses that hadn't been changed in 200 years,' Winkler recalled in his autobiography.

Additional locations included Melton Constable Hall and the battle training area near Thetford, Norfolk. The production even included scenes shot in Norway due to partial financing from investors Norwegian Viking Film who put in $4M.

The film changed focus as the production went on. Initially it was to be a personal story set against the backdrop of the American Revolution. The battle scenes would be close up at ground level. Lieberson's inspiration was *Culloden*, Peter Watkins' groundbreaking 1964 BBC TV docudrama of the 1746 Battle of Culloden. That version would have had a modest budget, and probably no big-name stars.

As production rolled along however Hudson's vision grew more ambitious. While retaining the ground level idea Hudson wanted to open the film up to go into more period detail with extensive sets and props. It would push the budget up. The number of extras increased, so too did the costumes required for them, as did the meal budget. The calibre of supporting actors had to increase as the three leads, Pacino, Kinski and Donald Sutherland had to be acting opposite strong supporting actors.

The shoot proved extraordinarily challenging. Hudson wanted to authentically portray the squalid conditions of early America through wet and muddy scenes. He wanted to show 'how squalid a beginning America had,' he said to *The Guardian* in 2009.

The film was beset by problems. Early on Pacino developed pneumonia, conditions were so harsh that extras walked off the set in protest, and Nastassja Kinski went AWOL for several days after visiting her boyfriend in Rome. There was a fire, a crane costing £250,000 fell over a cliff and the weather wouldn't do what the production needed which caused the schedule to be changed. On her return, Kinski also fell ill.

Annie Lennox, one half of Eurythmics whose most recent album *Touch* went to number 1 in the UK and number 7 in the US, took on a role in *Revolution* after turning down numerous acting offers. She wished she hadn't bothered. She caught the flu on the set, while only appearing for around three minutes of total screen time as a character called Liberty Woman. Lennox reportedly found the experience so unpleasant it permanently discouraged her from pursuing an acting career.

Goldcrest's chairman and chief executive James Lee visited the set. Hudson took the opportunity to ask if Colin Welland could rewrite the script. Lee, unaware this request had already been made and turned down, agreed. The decision caused a row between Lee and Lieberson, while Pacino didn't want the script changed at all.

Line producer Chris Burt told Jake Eberts, Goldcrest's founder for Eberts's book *My Indecision is Final*, the problem with the way *Revolution* was shot. The film should have been tightly centred around Pacino, Burt noted, the way a director like John Ford who helmed films such as *Rio Grande (1950)* and *The Searchers (1956)* would have done. But Hudson used Pacino in some scenes as if he was an extra, being caught amongst battles, which Burt felt was more akin to a director like Gillo Pontecorvo who made the classic *Battle of Algiers (1966)*.

By early 1985, Goldcrest Films was simultaneously producing three expensive features: *Revolution, The Mission,* which again required star casting this time in the shape of Robert De Niro and Jeremy Irons and *Absolute Beginners,* with a combined budget of $53 million (equivalent to $130 million in 2025). Under financial pressure, Goldcrest promised Warner Brothers a Christmas Day release for *Revolution,* despite filming only wrapping in July. This was needed to qualify for the Academy Awards, and there was a feeling that *Revolution* and *The Mission* should not compete for the same awards, so should be released in separate years. This decision shocked Hudson, Pacino, and Winkler, who understood the film needed careful post-production attention.

Hudson realised during editing that the film required narration to bridge its dual ambitions of being both a historical epic and an art-house meditation on war's futility. However, the rushed release schedule left no time to bring Pacino back for voice-over work. The resulting theatrical cut was released on December 25, 1985, in an incomplete state that satisfied neither its commercial nor artistic aspirations.

The film was a commercial and critical disaster. With a production budget of $28 million, it earned only $346,761 in the United States. Goldcrest Films lost £9,616,000 on their £15,603,000 investment. Critics were merciless, with *Variety* comparing it to a lifeless museum exhibit. The film received four Golden Raspberry Award nominations and won the Stinkers Bad Movie Award for Worst Picture.

In *Newsweek*, David Ansen wrote, 'There may be a smashing movie on the cutting room floor, but what's on screen is a shambles.'

The experience proved particularly devastating for Pacino, as it drove him away from films for several years. He later described Revolution as a 'disorienting experience,' expressing shock that the studio would release what he considered only 'half a film.' He would say that it was more disappointing than *Cruising* as with *Revolution* there was a good film there that wouldn't come out. Hudson too turned away from movies, not making another film until *Lost Angels (1989)*.

In 2009, Hudson released *Revolution: Revisited*, a director's cut that finally incorporated Pacino's narration and trimmed the runtime by approximately 10 minutes. The narration allowed audiences to get more of a sense of who Dobbs was. Hudson would say on the 2012 Blu-Ray release that Dobbs was a movie character ahead of his time, being an anti-hero.

While *Variety* noted that some problems remained 'insurmountable,' the new version garnered more positive attention. The British Film Institute's 2012 Blu-ray/DVD release included both cuts and essays arguing that the original film had been unfairly maligned due to bad publicity and cultural misunderstandings, with critic Philip French declaring the revisited cut a 'masterpiece.'

Although contemporaneous accounts of the set suggested that Hudson and Pacino did not get on an interview with the pair on the 2012 Blu-Ray release shows that they had a lot of warmth and affection for one another in addition to professional respect. In fact, they had spent around twenty years meeting up periodically to discuss what changes they could make to the movie to one day establish their vision.

However, in 1986 *Revolution* was the latest of an increasing number of movies in which Pacino seemed miscast and didn't achieve what they set out to do. Pacino had taken on *Revolution* in the spirit of what he had learned at the Actors Studio to do roles that challenged him, and went against what he thought he was supposed to do. However, he was learning that now he was a film star, and the audiences expected him to do certain parts. There was a Pacino persona that the filmgoing public wanted to see, and Tom Dobb in Revolution was not it.

Chapter 15

Sea of Love
(Film, 1989)

Directed by: Harold Becker
Written by: Richard Price
Based on the novel *Ladies' Man* by Richard Price
Cast: Al Pacino, Ellen Barkin, John Goodman, Michael Rooker, William Hickey, Richard Jenkins, John Spencer, Michael O'Neill, Paul Calderón, Gene Canfield, Larry Joshua, Christine Estabrook, Barbara Baxley, Patricia Barry

There's no question that *Sea of Love* was seen as Pacino's comeback. To promote the movie Pacino went on a publicity tour, including a *Vanity Fair* cover story. Pacino, though, was reluctant to see it that way. His relationship with movies had changed as he took some time spending his money and making a film of Heathcote Williams play *The Local Stigmatic*.

Pacino intended to film the play with the Theater Company of Boston for archive purposes. It became something a little bigger and turned into an hour-long film that was shown at the Museum of Modern Art. The process brought Pacino closer to the intricacies of movies. Despite being in movies for twenty years, doing this film allowed him to really learn the mechanics. 'I had a kind of aloof relationship with what was happening in movies,' Pacino told the *Citizen Register*. 'It wasn't that I was aloof, it was really a precaution because I was worried about being taken up in them. It's only recently that I've started to come closer to movies. That's why I've decided to make more.'

Once the hottest movie star in the world Pacino now hadn't made a commercial film in four years and hadn't had a hit movie in 14 years.

In the Spring of 1988, Pacino played Mark Antony on stage in the New York Shakespeare Festival's production of *Julius Caesar*. It was a role played on screen by Marlon Brando, who was cast by John Houseman, the artistic director of the Acting Company and the producer of the 1953 film. 'Everyone thought I was crazy,' Houseman told the *New York Times* in 1988. 'People thought of Brando as the mumbler of Streetcar, but I had seen him on stage in a production with Paul Muni and I knew he had perfectly good speech.'

'The image, the idea that Brando had done it, was an encouragement to me to think that I could do it too,' Pacino said. Joseph Papp cast Pacino when, at a meeting at Papp's Manhattan apartment, the producer asked him what Shakespearean role he would play if given the chance. An interesting question given that Papp had fired him from the role of Hamlet some years earlier.

Martin Sheen played Brutus in the production, which performed to a sell-out 299-seater audience each night. Papp ensured Pacino shared a dressing room with two other actors to prevent him from brooding. John McMartin, who played opposite Shirley MacLaine in *Sweet Charity (1969)* took on the role of Caesar.

For his movie return Pacino was playing Frank Keller, a 46-year-old hard-drinking detective who was resisting calls to retire, holding on to his job, and the bottle; the two pursuits he's confident he still knows how to do. His wife has left him for another detective, something that, when the film opens, Keller is keen to remind everyone of.

When two men who placed personal ads are found murdered, Keller and his partner, Detective Sherman, place personal ads of their own to collect fingerprints of potential suspects. Along the way, Keller begins an affair with Helen Cruger, but suspicion arises that he may be sleeping with the killer.

Sea of Love was based on Richard Price's 1978 novel *Ladies' Man*. It was released the same week as *Fools Die*, Mario Puzo's first novel since *The Godfather*. There was interest in turning *Ladies' Man* into a movie from its early days, but the story of the lead character, Kenny Becker, who was a door-to-door salesman of household products journeying around single bars suggested any movie would be labelled with an R rating. Price had written the novel in three weeks.

Price wrote the screenplay of *Sea of Love* originally for Dustin Hoffman. After the success of Price's first script, *The Color of Money (1986)*, for which he received an Academy Award nomination, Hoffman approached him and said he'd love to work with him. Price presented his idea for *Sea of Love* about how an urban male deals with sexual longing and loneliness.

If it seems like a leap from the salesman Kenny Becker to the cop Frank Keller the jump came in this moment when Price realised the way to turn his novel into a screenplay was to give the lead character a gun. Price hung out with cops and put some of his observations into his script.

By the time Price finished his first draft, *Rain Man (1988)* had come along, and Hoffman moved away from *Sea of Love* to take on what would become one of his most notable roles. Price worked on *Rain Man* for six weeks, writing, by his own count, around thirty pages, but he didn't have any control over the project so he left. His relationship with Hoffman cooled. Price took his *Sea of Love* script and hand-delivered it to Pacino[3].

'When Dustin was involved with Sea of Love, everybody loved it,' Price told the *East Hampton Star* in 1997. 'When he cooled, so did everybody. Then, when Al Pacino took it up, everybody loved it again. It's got nothing to do with the writing. It's like, who's attached to this?'

The film wasn't intended by its writer to be a thriller. Price said he wanted it to be 'two hours of high mopery.' Price's first draft didn't introduce Helen until two-thirds of the way through. Price wanted it to be a character study. The finished movie's central element is the fear that she's our killer. Price had to bring this into the script through several rewrites. The studio insisted that Helen be introduced much earlier, and Price didn't know what to do with the character for 60 pages, so he invented the 'Is she?/Isn't she?' dilemma.

Pacino had made a number of poor financial investments, and was broke by movie star standards. He had to make a return to film. He would acknowledge years later that he thought he could return to movies whenever he felt like it and was shocked by how quickly the movie business carried on without him. However, *Sea of Love* seemed like the perfect comeback. Pacino called Martin Bregman, and suggested that they rekindle their partnership which had lain dormant since they made *Scarface*. Bregman read the script, knew it was good for Pacino and came on board.

---

3. In Sonny Boy, Pacino writes that it was Diane Keaton who gave him the script, which at that time had 'another actor' attached.

Gregory Hoblit was initially signed up to direct, leaving his role on the TV series *LA Law* to do so. In his 2024 autobiography Pacino writes of a 'director [the studio] had picked up from television' who came out to Pacino's house. They didn't get along. Ten days before filming was due to start, Hoblit was fired. 'It was painful, very painful,' Hoblit told the *New York Times* in 1996. 'Still is.'

Harold Becker, director of *The Onion Field (1979)* and *Taps (1981)*, signed on. When Tom Pollock, the head of Universal, called Becker about the movie, he got on a plane the next day. Becker had previously met with Pacino to talk about doing a film called *Johnny Handsome* about a bank robber with a grotesque face who gets plastic surgery in prison. Pacino did makeup tests, but the pair felt they couldn't make the ending work as it centred around revenge. Pacino felt that if the character had changed externally, he would have changed internally, too, so his lust for revenge didn't ring true to him. The film was eventually made with Mickey Rourke in the lead, and Ellen Barkin as one of the criminals he swears revenge against. It was released two weeks after *Sea of Love.*

John Goodman came on board as Pacino's partner. Pacino got him into the Actors Studio. When Becker was cutting the movie, Goodman went to see him to tell him that he had been offered a TV show. Becker attempted to talk him out of accepting, telling him he was on the verge of a great movie career. The show was *Roseanne,* which cemented Goodman's reputation as a great comic actor.

Ellen Barkin had seen Pacino do *American Buffalo* five times. She felt like it was going to acting class. 'I took Sea of Love because of Al and only because of Al,' Barkin told *Variety.* 'I knew that acting with him would make me a better actor, and it did. Really all I wanted was to be pushed forward by him.'

Sea of Love went into production on 22nd May 1988 in Toronto. All the interiors were filmed in Canada, but Becker, as a New Yorker, insisted that the exteriors be shot in New York.

In the opening scene, Keller and Sherman lead a sting to snare criminals with outstanding warrants to a ballroom, where they arrive thinking they are about to have breakfast with players from the New York Yankees. This was based on a real police sting operation named Operation Flagship which took place on 15th December 1985.

Several weeks beforehand, a fictitious company called Flagship International Sports Television Inc. sent invitations to 3000 wanted criminals in Washington. The invitations were to a Washington Redskins game with the Cincinnati Bengals, before which they would enjoy a pre-game brunch at the Washington Convention Center.

As the 101 people who turned up waited to collect their free tickets, an MC came onto the stage and announced a surprise for them. They were all about to be arrested. The numbers in the room then swelled with 28 flak-jacketed US Marshals and DC police. They executed 170 outstanding warrants on the individuals.

Becker loved working with Pacino as he knew that he would get something a little different with each take, giving him more options in the cutting room. After each set-up was over, Pacino and Becker generally agreed on which was the best take. Becker saw the movie as not a crime story but a love story. Getting a convincing love story from the script and finding the emotional impact would be the hard part for him and the key to making the movie work. He and Pacino would meet in a motel room in the evenings during the shoot to work on the script.

Pacino suggested they do what he and Chris Sarandon had done so well in the pivotal telephone conversation scene in Dog Day Afternoon and do some improvisations[4]. The improvisations would be recorded and then transcribed. Becker would then read the transcripts, and from that, they would construct a scene.

The film opened the week after Labor Day, generally considered a dead week for releases, but *Sea of Love* opened strongly.

When the film was reviewed, it may be interesting to note that *Scarface* was still grouped amongst Pacino's recent disasters along with *Author! Author!*, *Cruising* and *Revolution*.

In his review, Roger Ebert wrote that what impressed him most was the personal chemistry between Pacino and Barkin. He called Barkin 'One of the most intense and passionately convincing actresses now at work in

---

4. While at a live Q & A after a Sea of Love screening in 2018 Pacino and Becker described their improvisation techniques, screenwriter Richard Price has indicated that the words in the film were all in the script.

American movies.' What let the film down the legendary critic thought was the way the plot 'had played fast and loose with the rules of whodunnits.'

In a 2023 interview with HuffPost, Barkin outlined some of the misogynistic experiences she had suffered as an actress in Hollywood in the 80s, one of which she alleged was on the set of *Sea of Love*.

'What was I going to do when Harold Becker on *Sea of Love* walks over and literally rips my merkin off, taking some pubic hair with him and saying, "What do you need this for? Nobody's looking at you."?'

Sea of Love was a big hit, taking in over $100M at the box office. Pacino didn't have a back-end deal, so didn't cash in on its success. Being out of the movie business for a few years he wasn't in the position to negotiate the way he could previously. However, he was now back in the movie business. In November of 1989, Pacino returned to his most famous role, that of Michael Corleone, in Francis Ford Coppola's *The Godfather Part III*.

Pacino would say that both he and Coppola were broke so were happy to take on a third instalment. The original script centred around Robert Duvall's character Tom Hagen, but when Duvall refused to return the script was rewritten. Despite being successful at the box office, the film would turn out to be a disappointing final chapter certainly considering how well regarded the first two films were.

There wouldn't be an Oscar nomination from his return to Michael Corleone, but Pacino's next movie would see him earn another nomination. His turn as Big Boy Caprice in Warren Beatty's *Dick Tracy (1990)* which he said contained elements of the character he played in *Arturo Ui*, landed Pacino a Best Supporting Actor nomination. Joe Pesci would take the award for his role in *Goodfellas (1990)*. But Pacino was at the start of another run of Academy Award nominations.

Chapter 16

Glengarry Glen Ross
(Film, 1992)

Directed by: James Foley
Screenplay by: David Mamet
Based on the play *Glengarry Glen Ross* by David Mamet
Cast: Al Pacino, Jack Lemmon, Alan Arkin, Ed Harris, Kevin Spacey, Jonathan Pryce, Alec Baldwin

Glengarry Glen Ross was the story of seven salesmen in Chicago selling Florida land developments called Glengarry Highlands and Glen Ross Farms. Much like *American Buffalo*, *Glengarry Glen Ross*'s central maxim is that one can only succeed at the cost of the failure of another.

It was Mamet's 17th play, and it premiered when he was 36. It was based on his experiences in his 20s working as an assistant office manager at a Chicago real estate office. It was what Mamet would describe as a 'fly by night operation' which sold tracts of undeveloped land in Arizona and Florida to what could only be described as gullible Chicagoans. He began to admire the salesmen there, calling them 'a force of nature.' They were men who didn't work for a salary, they were on commission only so they worked on their charm, wits and guile.

Portland Repertory Theatre held the rights to the play for a few years before ultimately deciding that Mamet's language and by extension the play was probably not appropriate for their audience.

Mamet had found writing *Glengarry Glen Ross* more challenging than his previous plays, and he found that no one was interested in producing it. He hit upon the idea of sending it to Harold Pinter with a note saying 'What's wrong with this play? What does it need?' Pinter wrote him back, 'It needs a production. Be here in six months.' Pinter forwarded it straight to Peter Hall at the National Theatre in London, who immediately arranged for it to be staged at the Cottesloe in the autumn of 1983. The Stage called Mamet, 'The leading dramatic chronicler of the futility of much of American life.'

Pacino was offered the role of Ricky Roma, it would have been perfect casting but at the time Pacino was on stage in *American Buffalo*. After London Glengarry went on in Chicago at the Goodman Theatre before transferring to Broadway with a no-star cast.

In April 1984, Mamet was awarded the Pulitzer Prize for drama for Glengarry Glen Ross. It was the eighth year in a row where the winner originated in non-profit theatre as opposed to Broadway.

Mamet later commented that the play resonated more with American audiences than the London audiences of its initial run because it depicted people they recognised from their own lives, while London theatre audiences saw it as something Americans did.

In an interview with Matthew C. Roudané in 1984, David Mamet said of *Glengarry* 'Although it has aspects of tragedy in it, [it's] basically a melodrama – or a drama.' Mamet noted that while tragedies are resolved at the ending and the protagonists generally undergo a reversal of the situation they found themselves in, Glengarry has none of that.

Producer Jerry Tokofsky, formerly the head of production at Columbia Pictures, had read the play in 1985 at the suggestion of Irvin Kershner, director of *The Empire Strikes Back (1980)*, as Kershner was keen to direct a movie adaptation. After reading the text, Tokofsky went to see the play on Broadway. Now committed, he got on the phone to Mamet. The playwright wanted $500,000 for the rights to the play and a further $500,000 to write the adaptation. Tokofsky said yes.

It would take a persistent Tokofsky around five years to get it off the ground. Jack Lemmon identified why the big studios had shown a lack of interest. 'It's got no women, it's got no sex, it's got no violence and it's got no special effects.'

It was a powerful play, but Tokofsky thought that the way to get a movie audience in to see the film was to turn it into 'a happening.' The strategy for casting was to go out to A-list stars who would like to appear in a David Mamet play. With A-list stars, though, came A-list salaries. Initially, both

Al Pacino and Robert De Niro showed interest, with De Niro originally wanting to play Ricky Roma. When Pacino was also considered for the same role, De Niro indicated he would consider another part.

Despite having both Pacino and De Niro attached at one point, Tokofsky couldn't secure studio interest, and eventually De Niro dropped out. Irvin Kershner then left the project to focus on other work.

James Foley, director of *At Close Range (1986)* and Madonna's *Who's That Girl? (1987)*, had seen *Glengarry Glen Ross* on Broadway. He enjoyed it, but that was it for him, until his agent called. He told Foley that he also represented Al Pacino, and Al wanted to discuss a few ideas he had. Foley agreed to meet and began to look for his diary to find a free date. 'He's outside your house,' Foley was told.

Pacino had met Foley a few years previously through Diane Keaton, and he felt the pair quickly developed a shorthand. At Foley's kitchen table, Pacino spread out the four scripts he brought with him. When he mentioned *Glengarry*, Foley told him he'd liked it on stage, but it wasn't anything he wanted to make into a movie. He remembered it as being a short play, which was one of the things he liked about it. Pacino explained that Mamet had opened the story out a bit and added some things to the script that made it far more practical as a movie. 'I read it and totally agreed,' Foley told *Vanity Fair* in 2022. 'I loved the script compared to what I saw on Broadway.' Foley thought that the adaptation was much more profound than he remembered the stage play being. The culture had changed too in the few years since the 1985 production, dog-eat-dog real estate hustlers had become much more recognisable.

Foley came on board, but the money still didn't come in. Pacino organised a reading at his house one afternoon with Foley. He invited over Jack Lemmon and a number of other actors. Lemmon also had the same agent as Foley and Pacino. Foley was open to Lemmon coming in, but if he decided Lemmon wasn't right for the role, he asked his agent who would tell the Oscar winning movie legend. His agent said he would. As it was, Foley realised Lemmon was perfect for the part of Shelley 'the Machine' Levene. 'I was convinced to do it by Al's enthusiasm for the project,' Lemmon told the *Windsor Star*, 'and he helped put together the best damn cast I ever worked with.' Lemmon later said that he would have auditioned for the role if he had been asked to.

Getting friends together to read scripts was something Pacino did regularly throughout his career. 'I don't trust reading the scripts that much,' Pacino told the *Daily News* in 1992. 'Sometimes I read scripts and record them and play them back and see if there's a movie. It's very evocative.'

However, years went by and Tokofsky still couldn't get financing in place. Pacino departed to make *Frankie and Johnny (1991)* at his regular fee. Alec Baldwin withdrew when the producer couldn't provide a letter of credit guaranteeing his payment. James Foley also departed as the cast disintegrated.

All along, Tokofsky would point out several other plays that went on to become successful movies such as *Who's Afraid of Virginia Woolf? (1966)*, *A Man For All Seasons (1966)* and *Driving Miss Daisy (1989)*. Other recent financial successes like *Rain Man* and *Dead Poets Society (1989)* were also touchstones for Tokofsky's belief that Glengarry could be commercially successful.

By March 1991, Tokofsky was nearly back at square one. He approached Baldwin again, who expressed that the script was better than anything he had recently read and agreed to join if the film received the green light. This commitment helped bring Foley and Lemmon back to the project, and Pacino also returned.

At a certain point, Tokofsky decided it was time to bring out the big guns. Hollywood attorney Jake Bloom organised a meeting at Creative Artists Agency (CAA), which represented many of the performers, and insisted that the agency support the project. Like other agencies, CAA had not placed Glengarry on its high-priority list. Following this intervention, CAA clients Ed Harris and Kevin Spacey joined the cast.

Casting director Bonnie Timmerman told *Vanity Fair*, 'When people ask me, what is your favorite movie that you cast, I'm going to say Glengarry Glen Ross. Every time.'

Kevin Spacey had in June 1991 won a Tony award for Neil Simon's *Lost in Yonkers*, in which he was still appearing as filming began. Bruno Kirby would take over from him. Jonathan Pryce also won at the same awards ceremony for Best Performance by a Leading Actor in a Musical for *Miss Saigon*.

The actors would need to take pay cuts if the project were to be realised. Pacino came down from his usual $6M salary to $1.5M. Jack Lemmon was paid around $1M, while Alec Baldwin's two-day cameo earned him around \$250,000. The actors also received a share of the film's profits. The total budget was \$16M.

The package that was put together in order to get the cameras rolling included commitments from cable and video companies, a German television station, an Australian movie theatre chain, several banks and New Line Cinema, which distributed the movie. The deal was completed on 17th July 1991, just a few weeks before shooting was due to commence.

Movies were now in the era of video rentals. Financial return wasn't just limited to runs in the cinemas, but business was now extending to post cinema release, where films would have a further lease of life on home video.

Foley and his actors had three weeks of rehearsal for the film, which was something Pacino loved, as this was the way he really liked to work. Shooting began on Tuesday 6th August 1991, at the China Bowl on 44th Street off Broadway. The film was made in New York because, as Tokofsky said, to *Newsday*, 'Al Pacino lives here.' There had been a recent six-month boycott of New York over labour costs. It had been resolved, but there were fewer films being made in the city at that time. Production ended two months later. The set was joyful, with the actors all getting on and working well with each other.

Pacino played Ricky Roma, a role originated by Jack Shepherd on stage in London. On Broadway the part was played by Joe Mantegna who went on to win a Tony award. Roma is a swaggering hot shot, good looking, cocky, self-assured, effortlessly good at his job.

The most memorable scene, and now in the YouTube age the most clippable, is where Alec Baldwin's motivational speaker, lays it down to the salesmen in no uncertain terms. The part only existed as Baldwin couldn't get out of a contract for a movie to be on-call in case the director needed to do reshoots while *Glengarry Glen Ross* was shooting. When he was free the film had wrapped. Baldwin asked Mamet to write him a scene, so he could be in the film. Mamet did. The scene has become iconic. 'Always Be Closing,' 'coffee is for closers only' and 'third prize is you're fired,' have all become lines that people throw into regular conversation.

Baldwin asked Mamet why he felt the need to add that scene. The play won a Pulitzer after all. Mamet said he needed to increase the pressure on the salesmen, to incentivise them, to make them go so far out a limb they'd commit a crime.

While all the salesmen's desks looked forward to the office Ricky Roma's faced in a different direction. Pacino told Jane Musky, the production designer, that Roma's desk would have locks on it. He wouldn't trust anyone else in the office.

Glengarry Glen Ross received its world premiere in September 1992 at the 49th Venice Film Festival, the oldest film festival in the world. In *The Guardian* Derek Malcolm suggested that if Jack Lemmon didn't win the Volpi Cup for Best Actor he would be surprised. Lemmon did.

The film was a box office disappointment, earning only $10.7 million.

Joanna Connors, the film critic of the *Plain Dealer*, Ohio's largest newspaper, wrote that Mamet's script, 'is little more than a series of long, repetitive speeches delivered like rabbit punches by actors who treat Mamet's numbing profanity as though it were Shakespearean verse.'

While not a criticism Pacino called Mamet's writing 'restrictive' meaning that you couldn't deviate even for a word or two as the syntax would be lost. Pacino actually found that style of writing helpful, and it allowed his mind to build a picture to go alongside the words.

At the end of filming Pacino announced to the cast and crew that it was the best work experience of his career. Lemmon called it 'The best all round cast I've ever worked with – of any film.'

At a roundtable interview with journalists in 2004 to promote his film *Spartan (2004)*, Mamet was asked what he would have changed with the film of *Glengarry Glen Ross*. 'Oh, nothing. I wouldn't have changed anything. I love that one.'

Pacino enjoyed working with Foley and felt that *Glengarry* was superbly crafted. It led him to work with Foley on a low budget movie a few years later called *Two Bits (1995)*, where he aged up to play an old man he modelled on his grandfather. It didn't make an impact and Pacino would say later that it 'missed its mark.'

Despite many of the reviews suggesting that Jack Lemmon was a safe bet for an Oscar nod, *Glengarry* only received one Academy Award nomination, for Al Pacino for Best Supporting Actor. The award would be won by Gene Hackman for his role in *Unforgiven (1992)*.

Pacino looked at Jack Lemmon and recognised that his latest work was his best work. Lemmon kept fresh on screen, he was never an old actor, and that was something Pacino took into his own later work.

When Pacino came back to *Glengarry* on stage, he stepped into the shoes of Shelley 'the Machine' Levene, a formerly great salesman now on the decline, the role Lemmon played in the movie. In the script, Roma is listed as in his forties while Levene is written as being in his fifties. Pacino was 72 when he took on the part.

Derek Newark was the original Shelley Levene in London. When it transferred to Broadway Robert Prosky took on the role.

Levene is on the downslide, a salesman who once was on the top of the board, but his heat has gone. He's still in the game, though, and he's now grown desperate and borderline pathetic.

The character was the inspiration for Gil Gunderson in *The Simpsons*, who first appeared in a 1997 episode called *Realty Bites*, where the whole episode was inspired by *Glengarry Glen Ross*.

Director Daniel Sullivan had worked with Pacino on stage two years earlier in *The Merchant of Venice*, Pacino receiving a Tony nomination for his Shylock.

The 2012 revival played at the Gerald Schoenfeld Theatre for 48 previews and 45 performances. While the movie was a disappointment at the box office, that wasn't the case for this stage revival. Glengarry made $6M in advance sales before opening.

The cast featured a number of well-known names from television and movies. Bobby Cannavale played Ricky Roma with David Harbour, Richard Schiff in his Broadway debut, Murphy Guyer, John C. McGinley and Jeremy Shamos made up the rest of the cast.

Critics weren't invited to attend until the first week of December more than six weeks after the show began previews. It was scheduled to open on 11th November. The norm for play revivals was three weeks of previews. In the *New York Times*, Ben Brantley wrote it was 'an indecently extended preview period.' Brantley wrote of 'a grizzled Al Pacino with the exaggerated pantomiming of a boozy player in a late-night charades game.'

Reviews of the production suggested that the ensemble drama had been weighted more heavily in favour of Pacino, knocking the things off balance. Glengarry was a commercial smash nonetheless and easily recouped its investment.

Mamet had two plays on Broadway, but his newest *The Anarchist* had posted its closing notice two doors along from the Schoenfeld at the Golden Theater after only a week. He wasn't the first Pulitzer winner to suffer a quick Broadway failure as Tennessee Williams, Arthur Miller and Edward Albee had all experienced this in the 1980s.

Later, Pacino would admit he was miscast in the part of Shelley Levene, and that he struggled with his lines, sometimes improvising, which would occasionally throw his castmates off. In a 2014 interview with John Lahr of *The New Yorker*, Mamet compared Pacino to jazz trumpeter Louis Armstrong, saying, 'He's incapable of doing it the same way twice.'

Chapter 17

Scent of a Woman
(Film, 1992)

Directed by: Martin Brest
Screenplay by: Bo Goldman
Suggested by a character from *Profumo di Donna* by Dino Risi, based on the novel *Il Buio e il Miele* by Giovanni Arpino
Cast: Al Pacino, Chris O'Donnell, James Rebhorn, Gabrielle Anwar, Philip S. Hoffman, Sally Murphy, Michael Santoro, Nicholas Sadler, Todd Louiso, Bradley Whitford, Rochelle Oliver, Ron Eldard, June Squibb

Scent of a Woman has become best known as the film that finally landed Pacino an Oscar. The common perception is it's not the film that he should have won for; it was to make up for missing out on *The Godfather, Serpico, Dog Day Afternoon* etc. Screenwriter William Goldman, wrote in February 1994 that although Pacino deserved a Best Actor Oscar, *Scent of a Woman* was his worst nominated performance. The win, he said, was down to history being on his side.

Pacino plays a blind former Army officer, Lieutenant Frank Slade, who is angry and volatile. He leaves for New York on a Thanksgiving weekend accompanied by Charlie, a sweet-natured teenager who attends a snobbish prep school and is hired as his companion. Their adventures are raucous and poignant and irrevocably change them both. Charlie is a working-class kid who attends the school on a scholarship, so while his peers are all on skiing trips for Thanksgiving, Charlie takes on a job to earn money for a plane trip home to Oregon for Christmas.

Scent of a Woman was based on an Italian movie, *Profumo di Donna (1974)* which itself was based on a novel titled *Il Buio e il Miele* by Giovanni Arpino.

It was a solid commercial movie produced for the Italian domestic market, and it premiered in Italy on 20th December 1974. It was seen in New York

City and other parts of the world during 1976. Martin Brest had aspirations for several years to remake it.

Bo Goldman won two screenwriting Oscars: a Best Adapted Screenplay award for *One Flew Over the Cuckoo's Nest (1975)*, which he shared with Lawrence Hauben, and a Best Original Screenplay award for *Melvin and Howard (1980)*. One day, he went to Universal to watch the movie in a screening room.

Alessandro Momo, who played the role of the young army private, was killed in a motorcycle accident shortly after filming. Vittorio Gassman played Captain Fausto. He won the Best Actor award at Cannes for his portrayal. While watching the film, Captain Fausto began to remind Goldman of his oldest brother, Chester.

Goldman based Lt. Col. Frank Slade on a combination of his father, his brother and a sergeant under whom he had served while in the 442nd Regimental Combat Team. 'He just terrified me,' Goldman said of the sergeant to the *New York Times* in 1993. 'He was the first man I ever met in my life who was living his life exactly the way he wanted. He was a soldier. That's what it was all about.'

An incident when his brother Douglas got drunk while at the boarding school, Phillips Exeter Academy, was also woven into Goldman's script.

Martin Brest and Bo Goldman began working on the script by having long, meandering chats. Eventually Brest suggested that they had talked for two weeks, and while they were having a great time they should surely be starting work. Goldman though told him a lesson he had learned from director Mike Nichols who had said that digressions are part of the work. Sure enough, much of what they had talked about – childhood memories, people they'd known – was reflected in the script.

Both Brest and Goldman discouraged Pacino from seeing the Italian movie before making *Scent of a Woman* as they assured him their version wasn't related to the original.

Pacino said he enjoyed playing blind as he relished the opportunity to use the obstacle and take the focus off himself.

It was during his preparation that Pacino stumbled on something that would define him to an audience for the rest of his career. He worked with a military officer on disassembling and reassembling a .45 caliber gun.

Whenever Pacino would get the moves correct the officer would say, 'Hoo-ah.' Pacino asked him what that was and the officer said it was something they said in the military as an affirmation. Immediately Pacino knew he would use it for his character.

It's a phrase that has been used in the military for a long time. Its etymology is unclear. Some theories suggest it was a toast in the Indian wars of the 1840s, while some people say it is an abridged version of 'heard, understood and acknowledged.' It may even go back to the British 'Huzzah!' of the 1700s. After *Scent of a Woman* though it was ubiquitous.

'It started out as kind of an exclamation point, and that was just fine,' retired Brig. Gen. Creighton Abrams, told the *Los Angeles Times* in 2003. 'Then it became something almost perfunctory, as in saying "Hoo-ah!" instead of saying "goodbye." Unfortunately, it's become a bit much.'

Paul Pellicoro was chosen to teach Pacino and Gabrielle Anwar to dance the tango. He also choreographed their famous routine. Anwar told Pellicoro she felt like she had been on a carousel. 'I told her to save that feeling,' Pellicoro said in his 2002 book, 'use it for her scene in the film.' Anwar probably makes the most impact with the least screen time in any Pacino film. She went through a year-long audition process for what would be just two days on set. She called Pacino 'A true gentleman.'

The scene was filmed at New York's Pierre Hotel in their balconied Cotillion Room after it was transformed into a restaurant. Anwar never actually rehearsed with Pacino. 'I always thought that was really odd until quite recently when Chris [O'Donnell] told me that it was because [Pacino] wanted to keep a spontaneity and a freshness to the dance,' Anwar told *Entertainment Weekly* in 2018.

In the part of the prep school student who betrays his roommate was a 24-year-old Philip Seymour Hoffman (billed as Philip S. Hoffman). He had auditioned five times for the part. When I catch *Scent of a Woman* on television now, Hoffman told the *New York Times* in 2008, 'I'll watch it, and I say, "Do less, Phil, less, less!" Now, I'm a little mortified by parts of my performance. But back then, it was huge! It was pure joy to get to do the work.' His future directors Mike Nichols and Paul Thomas Anderson both first noted Hoffman in the role.

In the *New York Times*, Janet Maslin wrote, 'Mr. Pacino roars through this story with show-stopping intensity. Bo Goldman's screenplay provides him with a string of indelible wisecracks, and Martin Brest's direction allows room for the character to be developed at great length. Mr. Pacino's contribution, in the sort of role for which Oscar nominations were made, is to remind viewers that a great American actor is too seldom on the screen.'

Pacino would be nominated for Best Actor at the Academy Awards. He was also nominated for Best Supporting Actor for his role in *Glengarry Glen Ross*. Pacino's double nomination was the first time an actor had been nominated for different performances in two categories in the same year. In a strange anomaly Barry Fitzgerald was nominated for best actor and best supporting actor for the same performance in *Going My Way (1944)*.

'I think I've been really lucky this year to have two scripts that you can say are literary and afford the actor that kind of an opportunity, which is akin to the stage,' Pacino said in a press interview with Paul Willistein. 'That's a rarity in movies.'

On 24th January 1993, at the Golden Globes Awards, *Scent of a Woman* won Best Dramatic Picture, Pacino took home the Best Actor in a Dramatic Role, and Goldman received the Screenplay award. It was a shock as *Unforgiven*, *A Few Good Men (1992)*, which failed to win in any of the five categories it was nominated in, *Howards End (1992)* and *The Crying Game (1992)* were all rated as much more likely successes.

In *Newsday*, film critic John Anderson wondered if the Academy would 'redeem itself' by awarding Pacino an Oscar. He wrote, however, that with *Scent of a Woman* it was a film that was 'a virtual betrayal of his best work, of the stuff that makes him Al Pacino.'

The ceremony was held on Monday 29th March 1993 at the Dorothy Chandler Pavilion, Los Angeles. Jodie Foster presented Pacino with his award. It was his first win from eight nominations. It was met by a standing ovation. He would jokingly say afterwards 'You broke my streak.' In his speech Pacino looked back on people who had encouraged him to act when he was younger.

'You know, it's not about deserving it, it really isn't,' Pacino said about his Oscar success to *The Independent*. 'It just was my turn, and it was wonderful. The feeling you have afterwards is hard to describe because people keep coming up and congratulating you so that keeps it afloat. I have never experienced anything like that ever.'

Pacino went straight from the ceremony to a private plane laid on by Bregman. He had to get back to New York to shoot his latest project *Carlito's Way*.

Chapter 18

Carlito's Way
(Film, 1993)

Directed by: Brian De Palma
Screenplay by: David Koepp
Based on the novels *Carlito's Way* and *After Hours* by Edwin Torres
Cast: Al Pacino, Sean Penn, Penelope Ann Miller, Luis Guzman, John Leguizamo, Ingrid Rogers, Viggo Mortensen, James Rebhorn, Paul Mazursky

Judge Edwin Torres wrote *Carlito's Way* in 1975, its sequel *After Hours* was published four years later. Pacino had been shown the books by Judge Torres in 1979. The pair worked out together in the gym at the YMCA in Chelsea. Pacino informally consulted Torres over his role as Arthur Kirkland in *...And Justice For All*.

Torres was a trial judge who sat in New York's Supreme Court. Once, when sentencing a defendant, Torres told him, 'Your parole officer hasn't been born yet.' Torres was born into poverty in Spanish Harlem in 1931. He attended Stuyvesant High School, one of New York's premier public secondary schools. Going on to study at City College of the City University of New York, followed at his father's insistence by the Brooklyn College School of Law. He was admitted to the New York State Bar Association in 1958. He transformed himself from a teenage member of the street gang The Eagles to the first Puerto Rican assistant D.A. in the Manhattan District Attorney's office in 1958. He worked as a defence lawyer from 1961 to 1977, during which his wife Vickie, tired of listening to him complain about books and movies that weren't depicting crime realistically, dared him to go and write a book himself. Torres worked on his novels at night after a day in the courts. He was appointed to the bench in 1977. His 1977 novel Q & A had been made into a 1990 film by Sidney Lumet.

The project was another project Pacino would be involved in that was a long time in the making. The 16 Aug 1988 HR production chart noted that Al Pacino would star in the Elliott Kastner Productions project, and listed a January 1989 start date. It was rumoured that Marlon Brando would co-star.

In October 1988, it was reported in the *Miami Herald* that Pacino was about to begin filming *Carlito's Way* with *Miami Vice* and *Crime Story* director Leon Ichaso, starting in March 1989. Ichaso and Jesse Graham had written a script.

'We started to prepare the movie,' Ichaso said to *The Morning Call* in 1994. 'And during pre-production, Al Pacino walked out of the project. He's notorious for doing that in the past, only this time, he walked out of the project *with* the project.'

By April 1989 *Variety* reported Sydney Pollack would be directing, and Martin Bregman was set to produce for Universal Pictures.

The following month, the *Los Angeles Times* reported that Elliott Kastner producer of *Where Eagles Dare (1968)* and *The Long Goodbye (1973)* had filed a lawsuit in an LA Court for $6M from Pacino for reneging on an agreement to star in the film, which he claimed Pacino signed in April 1988 agreeing to star for a fee of $4M plus a percentage of the profits. The lawsuit claimed that Pacino had worked with Kastner and co-plaintiff Cinema Corp. of America for over a year, writing the screenplay, selecting co-stars and rehearsing. 'Nonetheless, at the 11th hour Pacino announced he did not intend to fulfill his promises,' read the breach of contract and bad faith complaint, which sought $1M in costs spent on the project and $5M in punitive damages.

Variety reported that Pacino allegedly denied that a verbal agreement made through his agent, Rick Nicita, for Pacino to star in the picture was legally binding.

By October 1990 The Hollywood Reporter reported that David Koepp was writing a script of *Carlito's Way* for Pacino in a Martin Bregman produced $25M vehicle. By the summer of 1992 Brian De Palma was reported to be planning to shoot the film in the Fall.

De Palma was coming off the back of two commercial failures – *Casualties of War (1989)* and *Bonfire of the Vanities (1990)* and one film that had been a personal disappointment to him in *Raising Cain (1992)*, but Martin Bregman trusted De Palma to deliver on this picture.

Torres had sold and resold the development rights 10 times. 'When the producer told me they were going to finally make it, I told him I'm losing money here!' Torres said to the *New York Times* in 2008. 'I just as soon kept selling the options.'

Pacino made several trips with Judge Torres into Spanish Harlem, getting a feel of the neighbourhood, going to Salsa clubs and hanging out with some of the people there. He found that the guys there weren't much different from the crowd he grew up with in the South Bronx.

Pacino patterned his cadences and speech patterns from Torres although he admitted that he 'threw in a little bit of Scarface to keep the voice from being the exact same.'

Just like Pacino, casting director Bonnie Timmerman also toured Spanish Harlem with Judge Torres. When she approached a man in a club who she wanted to cast in the film he screamed at her when she tried to take his picture. Torres laughed and told her, 'He probably had four warrants out for his arrest.'

Torres was delighted that Pacino was playing Carlito despite grumblings from certain quarters that the actor wasn't the right ethnicity. 'Al Pacino – the greatest actor in the world – deigns to be my guy. Who would not be honoured?' he told the *LA Times*. De Palma said that Torres was always available for consultation on any aspect of the movie.

After several delays, principal photography finally began in New York on 22 March 1993.

Sean Penn hadn't acted in three years since *State of Grace (1990)*, and had in fact announced his retirement. In that time, he had directed *The Indian Runner (1991)*, a financial disaster, and was now looking to set up his second film *The Crossing Guard*. 'You can never say never,' Penn said to *Newsday* in September 1991, about his retirement from acting, saying that any future movie roles 'would only be for financial considerations,' to bankroll his own films. The money was a big incentive to return to acting, but so was working with Pacino. Penn had worked with De Palma previously on *Casualties of War*.

He put in arguably the best performance of his career as Carlito's lawyer David Kleinfeld, a man who is seduced by the money and glamour that a life of crime can bring him. Torres personally knew three lawyers who were killed after becoming mixed up with the criminals they were defending.

Penn based his unusual look on a photograph of a young law student he saw in *Life Magazine*. 'He's just all actor,' Pacino said of Penn after the film was released. 'He's all movie.'

The picture was set in 1975, where after serving five years of a 30-year prison sentence, Carlito Brigante is released from jail thanks to his dogged lawyer Kleinfeld uncovering illegal wiretaps. The debt that Carlito feels he owes his lawyer will get him dragged into a life he wanted out of. As Kleinfeld has climbed the legal ranks, his attraction to the people from the criminal underworld he represented grew. His legitimate and lucrative income as a mob lawyer isn't enough any more and Brigante will find that his friend has entered the world of criminality himself. A world where his legal nous is no substitute for street smarts.

While he returns to his old neighbourhood of Spanish Harlem, Carlito is intent on putting his drug dealing days behind him, although his former associates don't believe him. He wants to raise $75,000 legitimately and pursue his dream of buying a share in a Bahamian car rental agency. However, he can't escape his legend, and soon, he's attracting unwanted attention. His cousin Guajiro is thrilled by the idea of the legendary Carlito Brigante accompanying him on a routine drug deal at a bar. Guajiro, though, has been set up and is killed, and Carlito has to shoot his way out. But he can't resist the leftover bag of money and uses it to buy into a Latino disco called El Paradiso. He intends to leave as soon as he's raised enough money to pursue his dream and retire to the Caribbean.

'The character has passion, internal conflict,' Pacino said in an interview with *The Tennessean*. 'He wants to do things different, but he is driven along by his past and his warped sense of honour. What a challenge for an actor.'

The opening recalls Billy Wilder's *Sunset Boulevard (1950)* as in both cases the lead character lies dying and takes the viewer on a journey as to how they arrived at this point. Screenwriter David Koepp wrestled with the idea of using a voiceover, but ultimately decided that there was no way to tell the story without it. The script was revised 33 times, until the director and star were happy with it.

There was a natural comparison to be made with *Scarface*, but Pacino highlighted the fact that Tony Montana never repented the way Carlito had, Scarface just kept living the life until it was too late. Ángel Salazar, who played Chi Chi in *Scarface*, took on the role of Walberto, one of Carlito's friends from the old days.

Penelope Ann Miller played Gail, Carlito's love interest from before he went to prison who he attempts to reconnect with. At the time Miller was best known for *Kindergarten Cop (1990)*. 'Al brought out the woman in me,' Miller said at a New York press conference just after the film's release. 'He really brought out the fire.' The fact that there was stripping involved in her role initially put Miller off taking the part. She decided however to at least go in to meet with Pacino and De Palma. 'I realised that this was a great, meaty role and that the stripping was a very small part of it,' she told the *Baltimore Sun*.

In his 2006 autobiography, John Leguizamo wrote that one of his attractions to playing the part of Benny Blanco from the Bronx was that 'the part was so badly underwritten I figured I'd have a lot of leeway to change it, to make him more real.'

In an interview with *Business Insider* in 2022 Leguizamo was asked if it was strange playing opposite Pacino as a Puerto Rican. 'I know he's trying and he's a great actor, so brilliant, he was my hero,' Leguizamo replied. 'But it was odd, man. It's an odd experience to be a Latin man in a Latin story written by a Latin man, and the lead guy's a white guy pretending to be Puerto Rican. I turned the part down a few times and then eventually I decided to do it.' According to Leguizamo, heroin was known as Benny Blanco for a year after the film came out.

Viggo Mortensen excels in a small role in the movie, as a former associate, now in a wheelchair, who tries to set Carlito up by going in to see him while wearing a wire. Mortensen enjoyed working with Pacino, saying that he just loved to act. Mortensen told the All About Al podcast that in the scene he throws a diaper at Carlito, and in one take it hit Pacino in the face, but Pacino didn't break and continued acting, which impressed Mortensen.

In July 1993 *Daily Variety* reported that Penn refused to appear on set for one day after learning that the teaser trailer for *Carlito's Way* did not include him. The teaser was reportedly filmed before Penn was cast in the picture. Penn's actions were rumoured to have caused Universal to consider suing or replacing him, but filmmakers finally agreed to re-cut the trailer at a cost of $400,000. De Palma told the *Daily News* that Penn was justified in his actions.

As the movie reaches its pulsating climax, it sees Carlito pursued by mobsters through New York's Grand Central Station in a scene widely acclaimed as one of cinema's greatest-ever chase sequences. De Palma told Quentin Tarantino when they met for a BBC *Omnibus* documentary in 1994 that the sequence, which runs for eight minutes, was not rehearsed. The director shouted instructions to Pacino, 'Duck, look left, look right,' and Pacino responded instinctively.

It was the first time Pacino had done a complicated Steadicam sequence. The Steadicam would be intercut with crane, dolly and tripod shots using the train station's architectural elements as points to conceal the camera. The Steadicam moves with Pacino, alternating between tracking Carlito and offering the character's perspectives, particularly when he has eyes on his pursuers. Larry McConkey would be the man operating the Steadicam. He had also been behind another widely heralded Steadicam shot which wound through the Copacabana club in *Goodfellas*.

Carlito's Way opened on 10th November, 1993. On its opening weekend, it took in $9,116,675, which was 25.0% of its total gross. Its domestic box office was $36,516,012.

The film received two Golden Globes nominations for Sean Penn as Best Supporting Actor and Penelope Ann Miller as Best Supporting Actress.

At the end of 1993, Pacino went back on stage. He appeared from 3rd December to 2nd January 1994 at the Stamford Center for the Arts' Pacino Festival. He would star in two plays. Pacino portrayed Harry Levine, a struggling New York novelist in Ira Lewis' *Chinese Coffee*. In the second play, *Salome*, Oscar Wilde's interpretation of the biblical story, which Pacino fell in love with years earlier, he played Herod. Arvin Brown directed both productions.

The last time Pacino saw Marty Bregman was in April 2018 at the thirty-fifth anniversary screening of *Scarface* at the Beacon Theatre. Bregman died, aged 92 in June that year.

Chapter 19

Heat
(Film, 1995)

Written and directed by: Michael Mann
Produced by: Michael Mann, Art Linson
Cast: Al Pacino, Robert De Niro, Val Kilmer, Tom Sizemore, Diane Venora, Amy Brenneman, Ashley Judd, Mykelti Williamson, Wes Studi, Ted Levine, Jon Voight, Dennis Haysbert, William Fichtner, Natalie Portman, Tom Noonan, Kevin Gage, Hank Azaria, Danny Trejo

When Pacino and Robert De Niro came out together at the 1995 Oscars to present the best Picture award to *Forrest Gump (1994)*, there was anticipation in the air. This publicly confirmed that they were working on their first film together.

Heat follows the intense cat-and-mouse game between Pacino's LAPD Lieutenant Vincent Hanna and De Niro's professional thief Neil McCauley played out across Los Angeles. Hanna is a relentless, Marine-trained detective whose obsessive dedication to his work has led to a crumbling third marriage and a troubled relationship with his stepdaughter, Lauren.

As Hanna pursues McCauley's crew following a deadly armoured car heist, the film explores the parallel lives of the two dedicated professionals on opposite sides of the law. In a pivotal scene – the first onscreen meeting between Pacino and his contemporary De Niro – Hanna and McCauley sit down for coffee, acknowledging their mutual respect while recognising they're destined to face off. Both men are consumed by their vocations, leading isolated personal lives despite their surface-level relationships.

This was another film that was a long time in gestation. Mann wrote the screenplay in the late 1970s, inspired by the real-life relationship between his friend Chicago cop Chuck Adamson and Adamson's adversary, a thief called Neil McCauley.

McCauley, whose first conviction came in 1934, was released from Alcatraz Penitentiary in 1962 after serving nine years for robbing savings and loan association offices. Detective Adamson tracked McCauley's crew, and their real-life coffee meeting is recreated in the film with the original dialogue.

The story culminated historically on March 25, 1964, when McCauley's crew robbed a Chicago National Tea grocery store of $13,137 (equivalent to $136,669 in 2025) minutes after an armoured express truck had made a delivery. The crew pulled off the robbery without incident. However, police had set up an ambush for them on account of their wave of robberies of that chain of stores. Adamson and his fellow cops had tracked the gang for nine weeks. A gunfight ensued outside the grocery store. McCauley was killed along with crew members Russell Bredon and Michael Parille, while Miklos Polesti – who inspired *Heat*'s Chris Shiherlis character – temporarily escaped before later capture. Around $6,000 was recovered.

Born and raised in Chicago, Adamson worked Vice before working in robbery and homicide for 14 years, where he worked on cases including Richard Speck, who murdered eight nurses in July 1966 and Valerie Percy, who was murdered during her father Charles Percy's senatorial campaign in September 1966.

When he retired Adamson went into television, where he started writing on the mid-1970s TV series *Baretta* before writing for *Starsky and Hutch*, *Kojak* and *Police Story*. He would go on to co-create *Crime Story*, which Mann produced.

Mann had first heard of Adamson in 1962 when home in Chicago from college during the summer; he heard what he described as 'a major shoot-out down the street.' Adamson and his squad had captured a gang of home invaders who had burgled around 200 homes, torturing the residents. The story was turned into a book called *The Home Invaders* by Frank Hohimer, which Mann adapted into the movie *Thief (1981)*.

Mann's script for what would become *Heat* totalled 180 pages, and it was so ambitious that Mann wasn't sure he could handle it. He had been friends with director Walter Hill since 1972, and knowing his work and him personally, Mann felt that Hill would have been a terrific choice to direct. Hill declined.

After Mann had completed *Thief,* he wrote the script again. Mann continued tinkering with the script through the years, and when *Miami Vice, which* Mann produced, was nearing its end, NBC asked Mann if he had anything he wanted to work on. He turned the epic script into a TV pilot. 'I abridged it severely,' he told the BBC in 1997. 'I extracted probably 110 pages from the 180 pages.'

Casting disagreements led to the project's transformation into a television film, *LA Takedown.* Scott Plank played Hanna, while Alex McArthur portrayed Patrick McLaren, the renamed McCauley character. The film was shot in just nineteen days, unusually quick for Mann, and aired on August 27, 1989.

Mann came to regard the film as a prototype. 'What's terrific about doing LA Takedown was being able to do what people do in theatre all the time, which is open a play for four weeks at the Long Wharf in New Haven before you take it to New York City. You learn things about it. You get deeper into character. You see where the shortfalls were. I didn't plan it to be that way. It just happened to serve as a prototype in a way.'

After he directed *Last of the Mohicans (1992),* Mann went back to read the script he had written in 1986 and decided he wanted to make it. He felt that the structure looked like verses and choruses.

Mann revisited the script in 1994, he met his friend the producer Art Linson for lunch. Linson asked to read the script. When he read it Linson said it felt just like winning the lottery. He couldn't believe Mann had a script as good as that just sat around in a drawer. He insisted it was ready to be made into a feature film.

Mann was introduced to Pacino by James Caan not long after they had finished work on *Thief.* The two became friends and soon were looking around for a project to do together.

Linson took the script to Robert De Niro first, while Mann approached Pacino. On reading De Niro didn't think it was something Pacino would do. When Linson told him Pacino would play Vincent Hanna, De Niro thought it was a great idea. He went back to look at the coffee shop scene with renewed relish, knowing that Pacino would be doing it with him. The pair were the ideal choices for the two leading roles, and the two actors responded to the script's authenticity and realism and their respective characters and had no hesitation in signing on.

Keanu Reeves was initially offered the Chris Shiherlis role but declined in order to perform *Hamlet* at the Manitoba Theatre Centre in Winnipeg, leading to Val Kilmer's casting.

Heat would have six months of pre-production. Principal photography lasted 107 days during the summer of 1995 in Los Angeles, with Mann insisting on location shooting rather than soundstages. Location manager Janice Polley and scout Lori Balton secured 85 locations, with fewer than 10 previously seen on film.

Pacino liked Mann's directing. He felt Mann's sense of control. There was a real sense that it was Michael Mann's set and Pacino found that comfortable. He could just be the character.

Mann found that De Niro and Pacino had different ways of working. De Niro would build his character up bit by bit. Mann compared this approach to the architect I. M. Pei who was responsible for The Louvre Pyramid in Paris. 'The way Al acquires insight into character is different,' Mann told the *New York Times* in July 1995. 'It's more like Picasso staring at an empty canvas for many hours in intense concentration. And then there's a series of brush strokes. And a piece of the character is alive.'

The characters were a contrast to one another. De Niro put in a quiet intense performance. He played a man who was driven but who was a loner. Pacino knew that what he was going to do with his part was at the opposite end of the scale from that.

The gun Pacino's Vincent Hanna has would have a pearl-white handle, just like the gun he remembered his father had when he served in the military police during World War II.

Cinematographer Dante Spinotti combined natural and practical lighting to achieve realism, using wide shots and long takes to capture Los Angeles's vastness and the characters' isolation within the urban landscape.

For technical accuracy, British ex-SAS sergeant Andy McNab trained the actors in weapons handling for three months, using live ammunition before switching to blanks for filming.

Some locations, like Los Angeles International Airport, proved challenging to secure, with filming nearly disrupted by a Unabomber threat. Mann later noted that post-9/11 security changes would make filming the airport climax impossible today.

In a film full of memorable scenes and moments the one perhaps most famous is the meeting between Hanna and McCauley in the coffee shop. While Pacino was making his way through the industry so too was De Niro, although he didn't take to the stage very often. After parts in small independent movies De Niro had risen to prominence with *Mean Streets (1973)* which led to his Academy Award winning turn in *The Godfather Part II*. He further cemented his reputation with *Taxi Driver (1976)*, *The Deer Hunter (1978)* and a second Academy Award win for *Raging Bull (1980)*. For many years film fans talked about the pair acting in a movie together. Now it was finally happening.

The scene filmed at Kate Mantilini restaurant was shot with minimal rehearsal to maintain authenticity, using multiple cameras to capture the nuances of both performances.

Pacino went away to think about the scene and to learn it inside out. That way, he felt he could be in the moment, looking and listening, and if De Niro did something unexpected, Pacino could react to it.

De Niro and Pacino spoke about the scene together when interviewed by the *LA Times* in 2020. 'We didn't rehearse that scene in Heat,' De Niro said. 'I didn't want to.'

'And that was wise,' Pacino replied. 'Because these two guys have never spoken to each other. And when we finally meet for the first time, there's an energy in that wariness.'

'It's one of the favourite scenes I've ever done,' De Niro said.

'We talked about the scene, we analyzed the scene, but we didn't go too deeply into the scene,' Michael Mann told *Variety*. 'I wanted the full immersion to wait until they were in front of the camera. Al, Bob and I wanted to protect that.'

In his December 1995 review, Roger Ebert wrote, 'There is always talk about how actors study people to base their characters on. At this point in their careers, if Pacino and De Niro go out to study a cop or a robber, it's likely their subject will have modeled himself on their performances in old movies. There is absolute precision of effect here, the feeling of roles assumed instinctively.'

Pacino later revealed that he interpreted his character as being under the influence of cocaine throughout the film. It was the thing he based the whole part around. There was a scene shot where Hanna chipped cocaine just before he entered a nightclub. Mann explained in a 2017 interview with *Vulture* why he removed the scenes of Hanna taking cocaine. 'Al was edgy enough so that you didn't need to add that he was using coke, too. If I had done that, it would explain behaviour that I didn't want explained chemically. So it became a crutch we didn't need. You take the crutch away, and you're better, y'know what I mean?' Pacino thought that had the audience just seen the character take the drug then they would have been able to understand why some of his performance was memorably over the top.

Released by Warner Bros. Pictures on December 15, 1995, *Heat* succeeded both critically and commercially, earning $187 million against its $60 million budget. It eventually grossed $67.4 million domestically and $120 million internationally, ranking as 1995's 25th highest-grossing film. The film received widespread acclaim for Mann's direction and the performances of Pacino and De Niro, establishing itself as an influential crime genre film that has inspired numerous subsequent works.

Chapter 20

Hughie
(Stage, 1996–99)

Written by: Eugene O'Neill
Directed by: Al Pacino
Cast: Al Pacino, Paul Benedict

W.A. Darlington, the drama critic of the *Daily Telegraph*, once wrote, 'The paradox about Eugene O'Neill was, and is, that he was a writer of genius who couldn't write.' O'Neill's problem, Darlington said, was that although he had immense things to say about the world, the only way he could say them effectively was by saying an awful lot, and the length of time he took to say them diminished their message.

Hughie was a one-act play lasting around 55 minutes, and tickets for this production amounted to a dollar a minute. Hughie had its first performance at Long Wharf for three weeks. It then transferred to Broadway where it played at Gotham's Circle in the Square theatre with 604 seats. As the name suggests, the play was in the round. Previews began on 25th July 1996 and ran to sell-out houses each night. It was originally intended to run until 31st August but extended to 14th September. It extended again to October 9th.

The theatre filed for Chapter 11 bankruptcy in August of 1996 with debts of nearly $4M. Theodore Mann, who co-founded the theatre with Jose Quintero in 1951, resigned. Gregory Mosher stepped in as the new artistic director, immediately cancelling all the plays his predecessor had scheduled. Pacino's run continued to be extended.

Circle in the Square often staged O'Neill's work. Quintero directed 19 productions of O'Neill's plays between 1956 and 1996, including the four-hour and 45-minute Off-Broadway revival of *The Iceman Cometh*, with Jason Robards in May 1956. Quintero said that he believed O'Neill single-handedly elevated the American theatre from frivolity to seriousness.

Hughie was very rarely performed. O'Neill wrote it in 1942, at the age of 53; it was intended to be one in a series of eight one-act plays, titled *By Way of Obit*, in each of which a character would tell another about someone who had died. They were intended to utilise unconventional stage techniques. *Hughie* was the only one written.

O'Neill died in 1953 without *Hughie* ever being performed. It was first performed in translation in September 1958 at the Royal Dramatic Theatre in Stockholm, Sweden with Bengt Eklund and Allan Edwall in the cast and King Gustaf VI Adolf and Queen Louise in the audience. O'Neill's widow, Carlotta Monterey O'Neill, had presented the theatre with the play as a token of appreciation for the theatre producing several of O'Neill's plays in the past.

Carlotta had refused numerous requests from Broadway producers to stage the play. She believed the Europeans appreciated her late husband's work more than America did. As such, she permitted the first English language performance at the Royal Theatre, Brighton, in June 1963. 'Europe encouraged O'Neill. America neglected him,' Carlotta told *Guardian* journalist W.J. Weatherby. Burgess Meredith, who had just finished filming Otto Preminger's *The Cardinal (1963)*, would take on the role. Irish actor Jack MacGowran played the Night Clerk. The production, directed by Fred Sadoff, would also be staged at the Theatre Royal, Bath, before moving to the Duchess Theatre in London.

Hughie had two previous productions on Broadway first in 1964 directed by Quintero and starring Jason Robards and the 1975 production featuring Ben Gazzara and directed by Martin Fried. Like Pacino's production Quintero and Robards had decided to play *Hughie* on its own, as they felt, despite its length, it was powerful enough to sustain an audience for an evening on its own. However, in 1975 it was paired with David Scott Milton's play *Duet*.

Pacino cited O'Neill, along with Chekhov, as his favourite writer. This would be the first time he would perform an O'Neill play. He saw the character of Erie Smith as a prelude to Hickey in *The Iceman Cometh*.

Hughie is set in the summer of 1928 in a seedy Manhattan hotel between the hour of 3am and 4am. Pacino's character, Erie Smith, is a small-time gambler and occasional drug courier who struggles to overcome the death of Hughie, the former hotel night clerk. Paul Benedict played Charlie

Hughes, the new night clerk, whom Erie, just off a five-day bender, regales with tales of his predecessor. The play was a study of self-deception, and it becomes apparent that Hughie entertained Erie in his stories about how he would make it big.

The night clerk's asides were spoken by Paul Benedict through a mic effect that provided a sepulchral echo. Benedict began his acting career in the 1960s in the Theater Company of Boston. He was most famous for his role as the eccentric English neighbour on *The Jeffersons* on CBS from 1975 to 1985, which led to people assuming he was English. He was actually born in New Mexico.

Pacino decided to direct the production as he had formulated an idea of how he would like to do it. He reasoned that by the time he found a director and explained his vision to them he may as well just direct it himself.

Having a movie star in a small theatre performance surely attracted crowds, but it also had its drawbacks. As Pacino entered stage right to the sound of jazz music, it wasn't uncommon for the audience to react to his entrance much like the Paramount Studios Stage 19 audience did when Henry Winkler entered as The Fonz in *Happy Days*.

What was challenging and enjoyable for Pacino was that the weight of moving the plot forward fell to his character alone.

The run ended in November 1996 and earned the Circle $700,000. While money earned after the bankruptcy did not have to go towards any debts, much of the profits went to administrative and other costs.

In January 1998, Pacino held four excerpted readings of O'Neill's *The Iceman Cometh* at the Falcon Theatre, owned by TV and film director Garry Marshall and his daughter Kathleen. The assembled cast included Paul Benedict, Bruno Kirby, Harry Dean Stanton, Michael Jeter, and Peter Onorati, among others. Pacino read the role of Hickey, the part he had been so enraptured watching Jason Robards play. Arvin Brown directed. Pacino's plans to stage *Iceman*, though, would be derailed, as a London production had just opened with Kevin Spacey in the lead. That show would eventually transfer to Broadway in 1999.

Pacino would make his debut on the LA stage as *Hughie* opened at the Mark Taper Forum on 27th June 1999. Previews began on 19th June, and it ran until 25th July. By now critics could compare Pacino's Erie Smith with

Lefty, the low-level mobster he portrayed in *Donnie Brasco (1997)*. They both had the same understated yet full performance. Michael Phillips in the *LA Times* noted that while Erie was a minor O'Neill character Pacino's performance was far from minor. 'The acting's pretty damned good,' he wrote.

With *Hughie* Pacino would say that he enjoyed the journey, the feeling that once he stepped out onto the stage he couldn't turn back, that he had to keep moving forward.

Despite the success of *Hughie*, Gregory Mosher resigned in June 1997, with the non-profit Circle in the Square mired in $2M of IRS debt. With fears over back taxes and penalties, donors wouldn't step in to help. Their financial troubles couldn't be solved by the shows they put on their stage. The theatre got back up and running in February 1999.

Chapter 21

Donnie Brasco
(Film, 1997)

Directed by: Mike Newell
Screenplay by: Paul Attanasio
Based on the book *Donnie Brasco: My Undercover Life in the Mafia* by Joseph D. Pistone with Richard Woodley
Cast: Johnny Depp, Al Pacino, Michael Madsen, Bruno Kirby, James Russo, Anne Heche, Željko Ivanek, Gerry Becker, Robert Miano, Brian Tarantina, Rocco Sisto, Zach Grenier

The name Donnie Brasco first began appearing in the press in October 1981. Judge Edmund L. Palmieri in US District Court in Manhattan increased Benjamin 'Lefty' Ruggiero's bail from $150,000 to $350,000. Ruggiero, a reputed mobster, was accused of killing several men in a fight for control of the Bonanno crime family. It was alleged that in May 1981 he took part in the murders of Alphonse 'Sonny Red' Indelicato, a leader of a rival faction within the family, and of the slayings of two of his top captains Philip 'Phil Lucky' Giaccone and Dominic 'Big Trin' Trinchera. All three were listed as murdered by the FBI, although their bodies had not been recovered. The FBI's report was based on the information supplied by an agent who infiltrated the Bonanno crime organisation and worked undercover since 1976. He was known to mob figures as Donnie Brasco.

He was really Joseph Pistone who faced the world on Monday 2nd August 1982 when he was forced to give evidence in the case under his real name in open court. Brasco's cover was as a common jewel thief, known as Don the Jeweller who dreamed of becoming a man of honour. After a five-week trial, which largely rested on Pistone's evidence, Ruggiero and three associates were found guilty. Ruggiero received 15 years for his involvement in the murders and other racketeering crimes.

In the months that followed FBI agents put the word around Mafiosi, face-to-face when possible, that anyone who took up the reported $500,000 contract on Pistone's life would bring the Mafia nothing but trouble. Assistant Director Robert Young suggested that should their warning be ignored, and Pistone be murdered the FBI would retaliate with a high priority, and big budget, investigation of their activities on a nationwide scale.

Pistone retired from the FBI in August 1986, and in January 1988 his autobiography written with Richard Woodley was published. By February Pistone said that he had 'all kinds of offers,' from movies and TV to adapt the book. By March, the book was in its fifth printing.

In late 1990 it was reported that Barry Levinson and his producing partner Mark Johnson had Donnie Brasco on their slate of upcoming movies, which also included Wilder Napalm, a comedy written by Vince Gilligan. Filming was scheduled to begin in New York City in February 1991. 'Strictly speaking,' Johnson said to the *New York Times*, 'it's not a gangster movie. It's about a man's search for family.'

Casting director Louis DiGiaimo, who had cast *The Godfather* and *Rain Man*, among others, happened to have gone to High School with Pistone. He'd played basketball with him and met up with him socially, until the mid 70s when Pistone just disappeared. It was in August 1982, when reading the newspaper stories of Lefty's trial that DiGiaimo realised where Pistone had gone all those years. DiGiaimo met up with Pistone again and when *My Undercover Life in the Mafia* was written he took it to Johnson and Levinson while they were making *Rain Man*.

Levinson's take from the book was that mob life was similar to the lives he portrayed in movies like *Diner (1982)* and *Tin Men (1987)*. It was guys sitting around in coffee shops bullshitting and scheming.

Levinson brought in Paul Attanasio to write the screenplay. It was the writer's first time working with Levinson, a relationship that would lead him to create the TV series *Homicide: Life on the Streets*. Attanasio credited Levinson for allowing him to break free of the story structure he'd learned from screenwriting gurus Syd Field and Robert McKee. 'Barry, basically, if you wrote a funny scene—that's what he was looking for,' Attanasio told Mike De Luca for his series *The Dialogue*. 'It was really like the Howard Hawks' apophthegm that a good movie is five or six scenes and something in-between. If you have five or six scenes, the structure would announce itself. That was eye-opening for me.' Attanasio listened to hours of FBI wiretaps and honed in on Lefty. He understood that the movie's spine would be Donnie's relationship with Lefty and his decision to betray either himself or his friend.

Levinson didn't want to leave Los Angeles to direct, so Brit Stephen Frears was asked. Frears had just directed *The Grifters (1990)* and was in America on and off to promote the movie. *Goodfellas* had been a big hit, and there was a mood that *Donnie Brasco* crossed over in terms of subject matter. *Goodfellas'* director, Martin Scorsese had produced *The Grifters*. Frears spoke to him at director Michael Powell's memorial service. Scorsese had read *Donnie Brasco* and liked it. He pointed out the differences in the two films to Frears and indicated that he should make it.

Frears met with Attanasio, and the writer did another draft of the script. In discussions with actors, Frears told them they were making an FBI movie not a Mafia movie. Actors shuffled in and out, some worried that Goodfellas hung heavy over the project, *The Godfather Part III* was also now out and some people feared being swept up in a Mafia movie craze. Frears wasn't concerned, having decided that Mafia movies were just like Westerns – of their own kind and with their own rules. Frears listened to actors' concerns and requests for changes, but he couldn't find a cast. 'We have defended the script but have no stars,' he wrote in *The London Review of Books* in December 1990. 'I have told the producers to go ahead and cast the film. If the combination makes sense to me, I'll direct it.'

The movie would fail to begin shooting in 1991 and have several incarnations over the years, with Levinson's Baltimore Pictures producing. Throughout it all Pacino was committed to playing Lefty and vowed to make himself available whenever everything lined up. Unlike other projects in long term development like Modigliani the clock wasn't ticking on Pacino's suitability to play the ageing small-time mobster.

At one stage, Pacino was set to star with Tom Cruise as Donnie. Later, Christopher Menaul, a British TV director who had worked on *Homicide*, was attached to direct with Andy Garcia as the lead. Johnson and Levinson, who met while working for Mel Brooks in 1977, would break up their partnership in 1994 but would continue to develop *Donnie Brasco* together.

By February 1995, *Variety* reported that Frears would direct with Pacino and John Travolta starring. By this time, Attanasio had landed an Academy Award nomination for the screenplay of *Quiz Show (1994)*. Travolta, then hot due to the success of *Pulp Fiction (1994)*, was keen and hoped the movie would shoot in the Fall when he had a gap in his schedule. However, in June 1995, the *Daily News* reported that Travolta had asked for $8M and had been replaced by Johnny Depp, who had just finished filming *Nick of Time (1995)*. Director Mike Newell, who was enjoying international success with *Four Weddings and a Funeral (1994)*, was in final negotiations to direct. Newell said he was looking for an American movie to direct, and Attanasio's script was the best of the pile he was sent. 'It has a very classical shape with two very vivid characters who find themselves on a collision course,' he told Denis Hamill of the *Daily News* in April 1996. 'Both men are ambushed by their own feelings.'

Mickey Rourke was in consideration for the part of Sonny Black. He told the *Daily News* in January 1996 that he'd read for the producers and gave everything. Journalist AJ Benza suggested that Pacino wasn't keen on Rourke's reputation as being difficult. 'It really isn't Al's feelings, that's what I'm hearing,' Rourke replied. 'It's the *other guy* who doesn't like me. He never had since the one time we worked together on a film. Maybe the other guy spoke to him and said, "Stay away."' Rourke had worked with Robert De Niro on *Angel Heart (1987)*.

'The Al Pacinos of the world,' legendary writer Gay Talese said to the *New York Times* in 1997, 'they can do all the Hamlets they want, they can go upscale with Shakespeare, but where the money comes is the Mafia movie.'

Pacino, who had been honoured with a Lifetime Achievement Award by the Independent Feature Project in 1996, played Lefty, a small-time mobster who struggles to meet the mark his Capo asks of him, while gambling away any money that does come into his possession. Lefty begins to see he's on his way out, and perhaps his whole life in the mob has been for nothing. 'I think there are things in his struggle that civilians outside of the underworld can relate to,' Pacino told *The Independent* in April 1997. 'We can see a lot of his needs and frustrations in ourselves. That's what I latched on to, that and the subsequent sort of father-son relationship with Johnny, which I thought was an interesting element in this milieu.'

There's a lot of comedy in Pacino's performance. Lefty is a dangerous mobster, intimidating to those below him but fearful of those above. He and Depp play some scenes as a comedy double act with Depp as the straight man. Driving along in Donnie's car with Lefty smoking all the way Donnie lowers the windscreen to clear the air. 'You're gonna kill me with that draft!' Lefty suddenly snaps. After expressing his fears to Donnie that he's going to be whacked by Michael Madsen's Sonny Black after he's been called to a meeting, he discovers Sonny was giving him a present after being promoted to skipper. Hours later he's wining and complaining that he got passed over. 'Five hours ago you thought you were going get whacked,' Donnie says by way of consolation, 'Did I say I was going to get whacked?' Lefty says with incredulity after fearing of nothing else on the drive over.

In a tense moment Lefty lists all the things he's done for Donny. 'If I had any money I'd give it to you,' he says, quickly following it up with, 'I never had any money but….'. It's a moment that could easily be played for laughs, but like any great comedy actor Pacino plays it so straight it could almost be missed.

Lefty is also full of malapropisms which Pacino delivers brilliantly straight-faced. He says 'injected' when he means 'interjected' and 'pulled the wood over my eyes.'

At a press conference at LA's Four Seasons Hotel for the film's launch, Pacino admitted passing the script over at some point over the years of its development and its passing through the hands of various directors. He felt at the time that the territory was somewhere he'd gone before. However, as time passed, the distance gave it another perspective that Pacino appreciated, and he began to find the story a little more interesting. Pacino didn't see the film as being pushed by violence. For Pacino it was a relationship movie. He saw Lefty as a character pushed by his dreams.

Michael Madsen was asked to read for the part of Sonny Black. He refused. Madsen hated auditioning. He felt he had a mental block that meant he just couldn't read for anything. The producers felt he was perfect for the role, so they asked if he would come to New York to meet Al Pacino. Madsen was delighted to do so. 'It was like meeting some kind of diplomat,' Madsen told AV Club. 'I mean, he had guys with earplugs in and bodyguards walking up one hallway and down the other. It was a very secretive trail to get to Al.'

Pacino spoke with Madsen about the part. Madsen wanted Sonny Black to keep pigeons as the real mobster did in the book, but the script left the pigeons out. Pacino explained that showing Sonny Black looking after pigeons would elicit sympathy for him from the audience, and the movie couldn't have that. Madsen recalled that was about all they talked about and he was escorted back out of Pacino's room. Soon after, Madsen got the call that Pacino liked him and agreed with the producers that he was right for the role. When word of Madsen's casting was announced, Mickey Rourke spoke to the *Daily News*. 'Do you believe they chose Madsen? He's made a career doing a bad impression of me.'

Julia Ormond, Penelope Ann Miller and Marisa Tomei were all in the running for the role of Pistone's wife which ultimately went to Anne Heche.

Newell recognised that what made Joseph Pistone's undercover persona as Donnie Brasco a success in infiltrating the Mafia was that he developed a chemistry with the mob he was integrating himself with. He knew that chemistry was what his film needed to succeed too. Within a couple of scenes he was confident that Depp and Pacino had it. The pair had met for coffee before filming began and Pacino quickly warmed to Depp, someone he found made him laugh a lot.

Newell had spent time with the FBI guys through Pistone, but he also hung out and played cards with low level mobsters thanks to another of the film's advisers Rocco Musacchia, who made the transition from the streets to movies thanks to John Huston giving him an advisor role on *Prizzi's Honor (1985)*. Musacchia would introduce Marlon Brando to John Gotti while they worked on *The Freshman (1990)*. Pacino would later say that it was Newell who educated him on the world of the Mafia and not the other way around.

Donnie Brasco shot in Manhattan on Mulberry Street, Brooklyn, Fort Lauderdale, and Miami. The film shot for a while in Broward where Johnny Depp grew up. Newell enjoyed filming in Brooklyn as it reminded him of Manchester which had a similar energy and strong personality.

'Working with Al was everything and a whole lot more than I expected,' Depp told *The Times* in April 1997. 'It was a real treat and an honour. I learnt as much as I could. I expected him to be very serious, but he wasn't like that at all. He was constantly making jokes and making people laugh.'

Newell similarly found Pacino light and funny, but intense. 'Pacino…is an actor of big scale,' he told the *Daily News*, 'he seizes his point of view of a role very quickly and he's vivid, brilliant, insistent but never heavy.' Newell told author Christopher Heard, '[Pacino] gets along with anyone who shows up to work prepared and takes the work as seriously as he does.'

Pacino felt the strength of the movie was the relationship between Donnie and Lefty. It was real, tender and touching. Pacino credited Mike Newell for making the choice to focus on this relationship.

The production budget was $35,000,000. 'Great film, sure, but not a payday,' Madsen said to *The Guardian* of Donnie Brasco in 2004. 'Al and Johnny got all the money. There was none left for me.'

The film opened on 28th February 1997 in 1,503 theatres. On its opening weekend *Donnie Brasco* took in $11,660,216, which amounted to 27.8% of total gross. It remained in American cinemas for 16 weeks. Domestically the film took in $41,954,997, while its international box office was $23,348,055.

Pacino was beginning to promote his docu-drama *Looking For Richard (1996)*, which included a royal premiere in London which was a benefit for the Prince's Trust. Pacino and Prince Charles became friendly and Pacino even stayed at Sandringham. At the time Pacino was shooting *Devil's Advocate (1997)* and director Taylor Hackford allowed him some time off to fly over to England.

Chapter 22

Angels in America
(TV, 2003)

Written by: Tony Kushner
Based on the play *Angels in America* by Tony Kushner
Directed by: Mike Nichols
Cast: Al Pacino, Meryl Streep, Patrick Wilson, Mary-Louise Parker, Emma Thompson, Justin Kirk, Jeffrey Wright, Ben Shenkman, Brian Markinson, James Cromwell, Michael Gambon, Simon Callow, Robin Weigert

Tony Kushner's first major play was *A Bright Room Called Day*, first produced by the Heat and Light Company, which he had co-founded, in 1985. The play, strongly influenced by Bertolt Brecht, is set in 1930s Berlin during the rise of the Nazi Party but also includes scenes set in contemporary America. It explores the failure of progressives to stop Hitler's rise to power while drawing parallels to the Reagan era. It laid the groundwork for the more ambitious *Angels in America*.

Angels in America: A Gay Fantasia on National Themes made Kushner's reputation. It focuses on the AIDS crisis and gay experience in 1980s America during the Reagan era. The play interweaves the stories of two couples – Prior and Louis, a gay couple dealing with Prior's AIDS diagnosis, and Joe and Harper Pitt, a Mormon couple where Joe is a closeted gay man as they tackle issues of sexual, racial, and religious identity and the reality of the AIDS epidemic. Other key characters include Roy Cohn, the infamous lawyer, and Belize, a drag queen and Prior's nurse.

The play mixes realism with wild fantasy, featuring angelic visitations and surreal sequences. Through this, it explores themes of identity, moral responsibility, the failure of American ideals, and the possibility of redemption and progress even in dark times. Stylistically, it's epic in scope, with a

Brechtian use of direct address, a fragmented structure, and moments of campy excess.

Part One: Millennium Approaches, focuses on the various characters' struggles and culminates in a vision of an angel crashing through Prior's ceiling. *Part Two: Perestroika*, named after the reform movement in the USSR, depicts the characters finding their way forward, with Prior rejecting the angel's prophecies and choosing to embrace life.

Millennium Approaches was performed originally in a workshop production in May 1990. The play was first performed in its entirety in 1993, winning a Pulitzer Prize, a Drama Desk Award, and several Tony Awards, including Best Play.

The play ran over seven hours and was originally staged as two standalone works—*Millennium Approaches* and *Perestroika*—which opened on Broadway six months apart. 'That was sort of an accident,' Kushner said in a 2013 interview with the *National Endowment for the Arts*, 'It was also at a time when the only play that lasted two evenings that anybody had heard of was *Nicholas Nickleby*, and that was the Brits who were allowed to do anything because they had an accent. And it was Dickens, and it was this big event, and actually, *Nicholas Nickleby* almost failed, initially because nobody wanted to see it. So the idea of it being something that would last over two evenings, or a whole day was kind of unheard of.'

Both productions won Tony Awards for Best Play in 1993 and 1994, respectively. The ticket price in 1993 was a record $60.

In May 1994, *Variety* announced that Robert Altman was set to direct a motion picture adaptation of the play. Having recently completed *Short Cuts (1993)*, he seemed like the right director for the project, given that multi-character, multi-plot movies was what he excelled in. Kushner had hand-picked him, in fact he revealed in an interview with the *New Yorker* in December 1994 that the structure for *Angels in America* was lifted directly from *Nashville (1975)*. He had called playwright Christopher Durang to ask how Altman treated him when he filmed Durang's play *Beyond Therapy*, and Durang was effusive in his praise for the director.

Variety announced that Fine Line Features had agreed to produce back-to-back *Angels in America* movies. It was intended to be budgeted and shot as one movie, but be released as two separate pictures. Kushner wrote two screenplays, placing an emphasis on doing things on screen that he couldn't do on stage. He also tailored it for Altman's style, writing lots of overlapping dialogue.

Producer Cary Brokaw then approached Pacino about playing Roy Cohn and spoke to Meryl Streep's representatives about Streep playing Hannah Porter Pitt. The budget was then projected at around $25M. New Line baulked at the figure – Brokaw would tell Slate they were put off by the subject matter of AIDS and the controversy that would entail – and in August 1995 departed the project. Meanwhile, Altman made *Prêt-à-Porter (1994)* and *Kansas City (1996)*, both less successful than *The Player (1992)* and *Short Cuts*.

HBO became interested, but even though the budget was slashed in half they wouldn't commit. Kushner felt that Altman wasn't refining the script but adding more and more ideas to it. Eventually, around February 1996, Kushner and Altman parted ways amicably.

P. J. Hogan, who had an international hit with *Muriel's Wedding (1994)*, was briefly attached and attempted to condense the script into a two-hour movie, but soon he moved on. Neil LaBute was in talks with Kushner for a period, but he didn't feel he was the right person to make the film.

In 2000 Brokaw was producing *Wit* for HBO with Emma Thompson starring and Mike Nichols directing. During pre-production, Brokaw gave Nichols the scripts for him to read on a rainy weekend in London. Nichols loved what he read.

Brokaw pitched the package of *Angels in America* and Mike Nichols to Colin Callender, HBO's head of movies and miniseries, when he visited the *Wit* set. Callender thought that there was no better director for the piece. A budget of just over $37M was set. Calls were made to Pacino and Streep, while Emma Thompson on the *Wit* set was also enlisted. 'I read the script. It was incendiary,' Thompson told the BBC in 2004. 'The first page practically burst into flames in my hands.' The project was greenlit.

In 2001 movie stars like Pacino and Streep didn't do television. Pacino, though, told Callender that he thought HBO was an excellent place for the project, as he wasn't convinced it would work in the cinema and that he wouldn't have to worry about the opening weekend gross. Pacino likened acting with Kushner's script to musicians who get gratification from performing work by the great composers.

Pacino was still enjoying the process of acting, telling Douglas J. Rowe of the Associated Press that there was nothing like repeating the scene until he found a way to do it. He likened his process to top-class athletes who make winning performances look like they're doing very little. 'You can't be economic unless you know what you're doing,' Pacino said. 'It's called "being in the zone."'

While the top line cast were Oscar winning household names, Nichols decided that for the young male roles he wanted to go for actors who weren't so well known, but were connected to the theatre. Justin Kirk had appeared on television but had an impressive list of stage credits behind him, while Ben Shenkman had a Tony nomination for David Auburn's *Proof*. Brian Markinson followed Kevin Spacey and Bruno Kirby as Louie in *Lost in Yonkers* on Broadway. *Angels in America* opened just down the street. 'We were on different dark nights, and I got to see *Angels* when it opened,' Markinson told Vancouver is Awesome in 2017. 'My connection to it was very visceral. I put it in the same breath as *Death of a Salesman* or *A Streetcar Named Desire*.'

Jeffrey Wright was the only original Broadway cast member to appear in the HBO production. He had won a Tony Award for his role in *Perestroika*. Stephen Spinella, who won Tonys for both *Millennium Approaches* and *Perestroika* was considered to reprise his role as Prior Walter but after agonising over it Nichols and Brokaw came to the conclusion that, as Spinella said himself he was by now a decade too old.

Actors were doubled, for example Meryl Streep played four parts, the way they are in theatre which was unusual for television. The production began shooting in the spring of 2002 then broke at the end of July. Nichols was at the time 74 years old, so needed a break. Filming resumed in September and finished in the Fall.

The six-hour TV mini-series aired on HBO in two parts on 7th and 14th December 2003.

'When I did Angels in America, and I had Emma Thompson, Meryl Streep, Mary-Louise Parker and Al Pacino, it was like being in heaven a little early,' Mike Nichols said to *Variety* in 2013.

Streep and Pacino had known each other for 27 years, but this was the first time they had worked together. 'Al was the first famous person I ever met. Except for Richard Nixon,' Streep said to *Entertainment Weekly*, when the two sat down to promote the series. 'I remember the old Godfather days, walking around with you downtown. It was horrible. People would scream at you. I was determined I was never going to get famous.'

One of the scenes Pacino and Streep shared together was when Pacino's Roy Cohn was dying in a hospital bed. The two didn't know each other's way of working, but the trust was there between them from the beginning. Nichols and most of the crew were outside the room watching on a video monitor. 'It's a new thing,' Pacino said. 'In the old days, we didn't have that. You'd have the person in your face.'

The real life Cohn wasn't what anyone would call a nice guy. A lawyer who rose to prominence through his alliance with U.S. Senator Joseph McCarthy and his dogged legal representation of high-profile clients, including Fred Trump, his son Donald, shipping magnate Aristotle Onassis, and organised-crime leaders, such as Anthony 'Fat Tony' Salerno and John Gotti.

For Pacino, the chance to play a character who could wreak revenge on people just when he wanted to was too good to pass up. He told *Entertainment Weekly*, 'Like Scarface. Who wouldn't want to be the guy who can say to the guy who's about to cut your head off with a chainsaw, "Screw you."'

In 2013, Pacino told the Television Critics Association, 'When I did Roy Cohn, I don't think that Tony Kushner was writing about Roy Cohn. I think he was writing about this idea of the mythical Roy Cohn, in the same way Shakespeare wrote about Richard III. As has been proven, you know, this is not what probably was the real Richard III.'

In a disclaimer Kushner penned for the play's published edition in 2003, he wrote of Cohn, saying that for the most parts the acts attributed to him in the play were a matter of historical record. 'But this Roy is a work of dramatic fiction; his words are my invention, and liberties have been taken.'

Jeffrey Wright was thrilled to be working with Pacino, an actor he had looked up to throughout his career. He told *Entertainment Weekly*, '[Pacino] came of age in that era of filmmaking where films could say something, mean something about the world around. There was that stretch where it seemed every single film he did was a landmark. A career like his showed me what can be done. It's different now. Films are more measured as commodities. But he inspired me, and continues to inspire me.'

Ben Shenkman, who played Louis in the HBO series, didn't think Pacino was unusual casting. He thought that Roy Cohn was a powerful man on a continuum with characters like Michael Corleone and Tony Montana. He felt that the character was borrowing the size of Pacino's own persona.

Frank Rich called the film one of only three successful film adaptations of a major American play. He cited Elia Kazan's *A Streetcar Named Desire (1951)* and Nichols' *Who's Afraid of Virginia Woolf? (1966)* as the others.

Angels in America made Emmy Awards history as the first programme to win every major eligible category and all four acting categories.

At the Golden Globes, *Angels in America* won five of the seven awards it was nominated for, including Pacino's win for Best Performance by an Actor in a Limited Series, Anthology Series, or a Motion Picture Made for Television.

Chapter 23

You Don't Know Jack
(TV, 2010)

Written by: Adam Mazer
Directed by: Barry Levinson
Cast: Al Pacino, Danny Huston, Susan Sarandon, John Goodman, Brenda Vaccaro, James Urbaniak, Eric Lange, Richard E. Council, Sandra Seacat, Adam Driver

After Donnie Brasco Pacino had a good run of strong films, that still hold up well today. He played opposite Keanu Reeves in Taylor Hackford's *The Devil's Advocate (1997)* which allowed Pacino to play big. He had a much more subtle performance as TV producer Lowell Bergman when he returned to work with Michael Mann in *The Insider (1999)*. Pacino's turn as football coach Tony D'Amato in Oliver Stone's *Any Given Sunday (1999)* has led to countless coaches in many sports playing the motivational speech he gives his players late on in the movie to inspire many real-life teams when taking the field.

In 2002 Pacino worked with Christopher Nolan on a remake of *Insomnia (1997)* a Norwegian thriller about an accidental killing during the course of a murder investigation.

In June 2007, Pacino received the American Film Institute's Life Achievement Award. He was practically speechless when he accepted the honour at the Kodak Theatre in Los Angeles. 'I need a character,' he said. 'I don't think of myself as being able to do anything.' He was the 35th recipient of an award previously bestowed upon Sean Connery and Alfred Hitchcock. Watching a montage of clips from his career at the event, Pacino quipped, 'Seeing my life in the movies I have one question. Why aren't I in rehab?'

In 2003, Pacino worked again with his *Scent of a Woman* director Martin Brest, taking a small part in *Gigli (2003)*, a romantic crime drama with Ben

Affleck and Jennifer Lopez. He also made *The Recruit (2003)* with rising star Colin Farrell. He played Shylock on screen in *The Merchant of Venice (2004)*, directed by Michael Radford. The following year, he shared the screen with Matthew McConaughey in *Two for the Money (2005)*, a film centred around the world of sports gambling.

Pacino starred in the disappointing *88 Minutes (2007)* and played casino mogul Willy Bank in the third of Steven Soderbergh's Ocean's trilogy *Ocean's Thirteen (2007)*. He re-teamed here with Ellen Barkin, who played Willy's assistant.

What should have been an exciting project in 2008 turned out to be something far less worthy. Pacino teamed again with Robert De Niro, but this time in a lightweight movie called *Righteous Kill (2008)*, directed by John Avnet, who had also helmed *88 Minutes*.

Now Pacino was venturing back into television with *You Don't Know Jack*, a compelling examination of one of America's most controversial medical figures, Dr. Jack Kevorkian, whose crusade for physician-assisted death challenged both legal and ethical boundaries in the 1990s, and led him to being sentenced to ten to twenty-five years in prison. He was an eccentric who became the national focus for the assisted dying movement, a subject that is still emotionally charged and divisive today.

'There are not many people who would really go the last mile on something – very few throughout history,' Pacino said to the *Los Angeles Times*. 'A lot of people, I think, aspire to it, but very few actually do it.'

Barry Levinson's masterful direction, coupled with Adam Mazer's nuanced screenplay, created a narrative that delved deeply into the complexities of medical ethics, personal autonomy, and the right to die with dignity.

Levinson was drawn to the project by the character of Kevorkian, a man he found fascinating. He had known about the cause and what Kevorkian believed in, but he didn't know anything about the man. It was the man that intrigued him. The last thing he wanted to do was to make a drama about a cause, which he saw as being too polemical.

The screenplay, sensitively written, drawing extensively from Neal Nicol and Harry Wylie's 2006 book *Between the Dying and the Dead*, provides historical accuracy while maintaining dramatic tension. It chronicles Kevorkian's development of his death machine, a device allowing patients to self-administer lethal drugs and his methodical approach to documenting patient consent and medical necessity.

Once Kevorkian had been released from prison Mazer visited his home in Michigan several times to hear about the methods he used first hand. He also spoke to family members of patients Kevorkian had treated, his attorney Geoffrey Fieger, who would be played by Danny Huston and those on the other side of the fence who were against what Kevorkian had done.

The title came from executive producer Steve Lee Jones, who had grown up in Pikesville, Baltimore. In 2004 he read Nicol and Wylie's manuscript depicting Kevorkian as a visionary and a selfless crusader. 'You don't know Jack!' he pronounced, and the title stuck.

Pacino's portrayal of Kevorkian captured the physician's multifaceted personality – a man driven by unwavering conviction yet plagued by his own contradictions. The film carefully balanced Kevorkian's humanitarian mission with his often abrasive personality and growing obsession with challenging legal boundaries. Pacino's performance, which earned him multiple prestigious awards, captured both Kevorkian's intellectual passion and his social awkwardness, creating a character who is simultaneously sympathetic and frustrating.

The supporting cast adds crucial depth to the narrative. John Goodman as Neal Nicol, who assisted Kevorkian on many of the 130 assisted suicides he took credit for in the 90s and Brenda Vaccaro as Kevorkian's sister Margo Janus both supported Kevorkian's mission while occasionally questioning his methods. Susan Sarandon's portrayal of Janet Good, the Hemlock Society chapter founder, provided a powerful counterpoint to Kevorkian's clinical approach, offering a more emotionally connected perspective on the right-to-die movement.

The film's structure follows Kevorkian's escalating confrontations with the medical establishment and legal system, culminating in his fateful decision to personally administer euthanasia to 52-year-old Thomas Youk who had amyotrophic lateral sclerosis (ALS). This act, broadcast on *60 Minutes*, marked a crucial turning point that led to his imprisonment. The narrative skilfully weaves together Kevorkian's Armenian heritage – shaped by his parents' survival of genocide – with his militant dedication to patient autonomy, suggesting how personal history influenced his medical ethics.

Levinson's direction maintains a delicate balance between the film's heavy themes and moments of dark humour, often emerging from Kevorkian's eccentric personality. Kevorkian was a figure the American public were aware of, as he was often across the news media. The movie's visual approach, including cutting film of Pacino into real archival footage of Kevorkian's patients, grounds the narrative in stark reality while raising profound questions about medical ethics and human dignity. 'I thought it would be important to allow those faces and voices, to be, in fact, what they were,' Levinson said to the *Detroit Free Press*.

Filming began in August 2009 and was shot in New York and around Detroit.

What distinguishes *You Don't Know Jack* is its refusal to present Kevorkian as either hero or villain. Instead, it explores the complex intersection of personal conviction, medical ethics, and legal boundaries. The film examines how Kevorkian's initial mission to help terminal patients die with dignity became increasingly entangled with his personal crusade against the medical establishment.

Pacino enjoyed working in television as he said the speed that the medium worked in inspired spontaneity. At one point the production filmed 16 scenes in two days.

Pacino chose not to meet Kevorkian before playing him. He reflected in interviews about his two different approaches to playing real life characters where with *Serpico* he spent a lot of time with Frank Serpico while on *Dog Day Afternoon* he chose not to meet John Wojtowicz. 'I may have made a mistake,' Pacino said in a press junket promoting the HBO movie. 'I still think to this day, maybe I did. I probably made a mistake here too. That I didn't take advantage of access is a question I still can't answer. I don't know why I didn't.' Levinson did meet Kevorkian ahead of production and got a lot from the experience. Pacino did meet him after shooting ended[5].

In the *Boston Globe* Matthew Gilbert wrote, 'Pacino is extraordinary. It's a cliche but he disappears into the role, putting just enough – but never too much – of Kevorkian's cranky frumpled demeanour and Midwestern

---

5. Despite the contemporary interviews of the time where Pacino said he didn't meet Kevorkian before filming, in his 2024 autobiography he writes that he did meet Kevorkian 'in preparing to play him.'

accent into his portrayal.' Other reviews called Pacino 'barely recognisable' and 'mesmerising.'

The part is one of Pacino's most universally praised roles, and certainly one of his finest performances in the last couple of decades of his career. The fact though that it's perhaps been lost to the ephemeral nature of cable television at the time, being several years before streaming has managed to keep TV movies in constant rotation and spread them to a much wider audience is a great shame.

The film's critical success reflects its achievement in handling such sensitive subject matter with nuance and complexity. Rather than advocating for either side of the euthanasia debate, it presents the human stories and ethical dilemmas at the heart of this controversy.

Kevorkian was released from prison on parole in 2007 at the age of 79, and enjoyed attending the premiere of the movie in April 2010 at the Detroit Film Theatre where he received a standing ovation. He passed away in 2011.

You Don't Know Jack earned 15 Emmy nominations. Pacino won in the category of Outstanding Lead Actor in a Limited Series or Movie. Adam Mazer also won in the Outstanding Writing for a Miniseries, Movie or Dramatic Special category.

At the Beverly Hilton in Beverly Hills, CA, on Sunday, January 16, 2011, Pacino won the Golden Globe for Best Performance by an Actor in a Mini-Series or Motion Picture Made for Television.

Chapter 24

Danny Collins
(Film, 2015)

Written and directed: by Dan Fogelman
Produced by: Nimitt Mankad, Jessie Nelson
Cast: Al Pacino, Annette Bening, Jennifer Garner, Bobby Cannavale, Christopher Plummer, Nick Offerman, Cesar Evora, Josh Peck, Scott Lawrence

In an interview with Bob Thompson of Postmedia News in Canada, Pacino said it was thinking back to his early days doing two or three plays in repertory that led him to take a role he felt that was somewhat against type. 'Invariably I would not do as well in the play they wanted me to do, but better in the plays I didn't want to do. Sometimes we are not exactly aware of what we can do unless we try.'

The story of Danny Collins was loosely based on the tale of British folk singer Steve Tilston, who received an encouraging letter from John Lennon more than 30 years after Lennon wrote it. In 1971 Lennon had read an interview in *ZigZag* magazine with the 21-year-old Tilston where he had complained that financial success threatened to ruin his songwriting. Lennon wrote a letter telling Tilston not to worry about accumulating wealth because it would not change the important things in his life, like his emotions and relationships. Lennon signed it from him and his wife Yoko Ono and put his phone number at the bottom. He mailed it to the offices of the magazine. Once whoever collected it from the office realised it was from John Lennon it wasn't passed on to its intended recipient.

The first Tilston became aware of it was when a collector contacted him in 2005 to verify the letter's authenticity. Initially Tilston felt angry that someone had sold the letter instead of ensuring it was passed on to him. 'But you have to let these things go,' Tilston said to the *Daily Telegraph* in 2010. 'I feel it was a rather brotherly letter really. Not antagonistic, just offering words of advice. If I had received it all those years ago, my young self would definitely have rung him.'

That article went worldwide, and one of the people who was fascinated by the story was screenwriter Dan Fogelman. The writer of *Cars (2006)* and *Crazy, Stupid Love (2011)* got on the phone to Tilston and then began work on writing a screenplay.

'The film's not about me,' Tilston said to *The Herald*, 'I was a bit concerned at first that it might be and I didn't fancy that idea at all. But Dan assured me that the hero of the film would be a fictitious character and I think he turned it into a nice film that uses the device of that letter very well.'

Fogelman's only choice for the role of a delusional musician looking for a second chance was Pacino. He would say that Pacino reading his script was a career highlight, far less agreeing to be in his directorial debut. In the years while the project moved forward Fogelman, who had grown up in New Jersey and Pacino dined together a number of times. Fogelman noting that practically on every occasion someone would interrupt them to say to Pacino, 'Say hello to my leeetle friend.' The star of *Scarface* would always respond with good grace, acting like it was the first time it had ever happened and saying, 'Thank you.'

Speaking to the *Boston Globe* Fogelman, an Oxford University graduate, described Pacino as someone who, if he could be anywhere, would be on stage on Broadway. 'He's one of the world's greatest stage actors, who, because of his looks and charisma, became one of our biggest movie stars overnight.'

Pacino was involved in selecting the main co-starring roles. Bobby Cannavale had played Ricky Roma opposite Pacino's Shelley 'the Machine' Levene in the second Broadway revival of Glengarry Glen Ross in 2012/13. 'That was the preparation for the movie,' Cannavale told Postmedia News. 'We became close and tight and shared a lot of things, so we just continued the conversation into the movie.'

'I loved watching Al and Bobby together,' Jennifer Garner said. 'They're like an old married couple and very special together.' Pacino was Cannavale's inspiration to move from New Jersey to New York to become an actor. 'It was no secret I was obsessed with Al,' he said. 'My friends always made fun of me.' The pair first met when they were sat together at the 2011 Tony Awards. Cannavale was nominated for *The Motherfucker with the Hat* while Pacino was nominated for Shylock in *The Merchant of Venice*. Pacino went to see Cannavale in the Stephen Adly Guirgis play five days later. He went backstage afterwards and sat for an hour in the dressing room just asking Cannavale questions about him and his career. 'Al's always on the search and that's what makes him compelling,' Cannavale said. 'That's what makes him so watchable because he's searching for answers he's never going to get. This business is full of actors who love what they do and keep repeating it, and Al's not like that.'

Annette Bening plays Pacino's love interest and the pair create an entertaining and believable on-screen couple. Christopher Plummer has an entertaining turn as Collins' long-suffering manager.

Pacino was also responsible for securing the production the rights to songs by John Lennon by speaking with Lennon's widow, Yoko Ono. 'Yoko is very responsible for giving his songs to us,' Pacino said. 'She really is an advocate for the movie.' Pacino never got to meet Lennon, although they lived close to each other in New York. 'I saw John Lennon once in Central Park, and we smiled at each other. It was nice. And I was just so pleased and flattered that he recognised me.'

The signature song that Danny sings in the movie, the one he's trying to get away from, but keeps being forced to sign is called Hey Baby Doll. It was written for the movie by Australian Greg Agar and Ciaran Gribbin. Northern Irishman Gribbin briefly became the eighth lead singer of INXS when he fronted the band from 2011 to 2012. Pacino was coached to sing and play piano by Gerald White a session singer and producer, who regularly coached for the movies as well as private clients. Pacino performed the Danny Collins' hit Hey Baby Doll live on stage during a Chicago concert at the Greek Theatre in Los Angeles.

'When filming started Al got out of the way,' director Dan Fogelman told Postmedia News. 'But I would be pretty stupid if I didn't ask him questions and listen to what he had to say.'

'The early instincts are usually the ones you stay with,' Pacino said of his performance. 'And I had the instinct that he was a cross between Barry Manilow and Rod Stewart – the love child of those two.'

Pacino felt his experiences as a rising star in the 1970s could feed into his role as Collins. 'You know, you become this so-called movie star, and it's a different world. Then it's the combination of fame and being an actor, and then the loss of anonymity, which I so loved and cherished.'

Danny Collins is a highlight of Pacino's later work. There's a lot of charm in the character and Pacino is perfect casting, as the singer living a life outside the understanding of the normal family people he's trying hard in his own way to connect with. The movie is boosted by a strong supporting cast, who all gel well with Pacino. It's a movie Pacino says he is particularly fond of, and a film he enjoyed making.

Pacino would then go on to make a couple of misfires in *Misconduct (2016)* and *Hangman (2017)* before going back into television.

Chapter 25

Paterno
(TV, 2018)

Written by: Debora Cahn and John C. Richards
Directed by: Barry Levinson
Cast: Al Pacino, Riley Keough, Kathy Baker, Greg Grunberg, Annie Parisse, Ben Cook, Jim Johnson, Peter Jacobson, Larry Mitchell, Darren Goldstein, Kristen Bush, Sean Cullen

Like many of Pacino's projects, *Paterno* had a lengthy process to get to the screen. On September 8, 2012, it was reported that ICM Partners, where John Burnham, Jeff Berg and Adam Schweitzer represented Pacino, would take a package for a film about Joe Paterno with Pacino playing Paterno. A few months later, Brian De Palma was announced as director. HBO picked up the film, then called Happy Valley, but in September 2014, Deadline reported that the film had been halted in pre-production amid budgetary concerns. 'We have not killed the project, so to say so is inaccurate,' the network said in a statement to Deadline. 'We have suspended pre-production for a moment to deal with budget issues, but the project is still intact at HBO with the entire creative team as before.'

By June 2017, the film was once again moving forward, with Barry Levinson now in the director's chair. Riley Keough, Kathy Baker, Greg Grunberg and Annie Parisse joined the cast.

The project tackled one of the most dramatic falls from grace in American sports history. The script written by Debora Cahn and John C. Richards explores the final weeks in the career of Joe Paterno, Penn State's legendary football coach whose legacy was irreparably damaged by the Jerry Sandusky child abuse scandal.

Sandusky, who was Penn State defensive coordinator, sexually abused eight young boys over a period of at least 15 years. Officials at Penn State, the team which represents the Pennsylvania State University in college football, purportedly failed to notify law enforcement after learning about some of these incidents.

'The part that was interesting to me was the idea of, "How do you not know that you know?"' Cahn said to awardsdaily.com. 'How do we wind up in these situations where we say, "Everybody knew." Well, if everybody knew, then how come it continued? This was a particular story where apparently a lot of people knew.'

Cahn came at writing the script with a couple of key questions: How did Paterno hear about these allegations so many times over the years and do apparently nothing? And did he genuinely believe he did everything he could do?

Paterno was an attempt to understand how someone so respected, so revered could become so entwined with such heinous crimes that cast such a dark pall over college football. The film centres on a pivotal two-week period in 2011. On the last Saturday in October 2011, JoePa, as he was affectionately known to everyone on the Penn State University campus in Happy Valley, secured his 409th victory as the coach of the Penn State Nittany Lions, making him the winningest coach in college football history. Six days later, a grand jury indicted Jerry Sandusky on 40 counts of child sex abuse. A week after that Paterno was dismissed from Penn State.

Paterno's downfall was rapid, and the narrow timeframe highlights this as Paterno's reputation unravels as he's faced with questions about what he knew, when he knew it, and what he did—or failed to do—about Sandusky's crimes.

Sara Ganim was a reporter for The Patriot-News in Harrisburg, PA, where she broke the story of a Grand Jury investigation of Sandusky in 2011. That exposé led to her winning the Pulitzer Prize for Local Reporting in 2012, making her, at 24, the third-youngest winner of the prestigious award.

Pacino's portrayal of Paterno is notably restrained, much like his performance in *You Don't Know Jack* was. Criticism of Pacino's acting style usually focuses on his more explosive performances, so it's unfortunate that roles where he showcases more nuance, subtlety and range such as his TV work don't have the same reach his movies do.

Working with longtime makeup artist John Caglione Jr., Pacino physically transformed into the coach, with particular attention paid to crafting the right nose prosthetic. Pacino approached the role through extensive study of archival footage, noting that modern technology allowed him to be 'all but in somebody's living room' while researching Paterno's mannerisms and behaviour.

Beyond studying film Pacino said he tried to be truthful to the script, emphasising that his performance was a 'portrayal' of the character. His goal, he said to the Golden Globes YouTube channel was that hopefully the outside – the make-up and the mannerisms – reaches the inside and he could express what the writers wrote.

He compared the part to Roy Cohn in *Angels in America*, highlighting that in that show he didn't play Roy Cohn but a character called Roy Cohn that Tony Kushner wrote. His work was interpreting Kushner's language and who Roy Cohn was to him. Again, with Paterno he said he wasn't playing that man that people knew but interpreting the character on the page.

The film's most compelling scenes take place within Paterno's home, where the coach is surrounded by family members desperately trying to understand his role in the scandal. Pacino plays these moments with subtle complexity, portraying Paterno as simultaneously defensive, confused, and perhaps harbouring deep-seated guilt he can't fully acknowledge.

'He goes to denial and then guilt and then a kind of contrition,' Pacino said to USA Today. 'He's trying to figure out two things: what he did that has allowed this to happen and how do you cope with it?'

Levinson approached the material, much the way he did with Jack Kevorkian's story, with deliberate ambiguity. Rather than definitively answering questions about Paterno's culpability, the film explores the psychology of a man who had spent decades focusing solely on football, perhaps at the cost of recognising serious crimes happening within his program. The director saw in Paterno's story elements of classical tragedy, describing him as 'The king of Happy Valley' whose fall from grace contained distinctly Greek elements.

The film's narrative is augmented by a parallel storyline following Sara Ganim played by Riley Keough. This subplot provides context and helps illuminate the institutional failures that allowed Sandusky's abuse to continue for so long. Ganim herself served as a consultant on the film, helping ensure its accuracy while emphasising that the story's true importance lay with Sandusky's victims.

Through Pacino's performance, we see a man who had devoted his life to mentoring young athletes and building a successful football program, yet somehow failed to protect vulnerable children from a predator in his midst. The film suggests that Paterno's singular focus on football, which had brought him such success, may have been the very thing that blinded him to Sandusky's crimes.

Rather than offering easy answers, the film presents a complex portrait of moral failure and institutional corruption. It raises uncomfortable questions about responsibility, wilful ignorance, and the dangers of unchecked power within collegiate athletics. While some critics, like Robert Lloyd of the *Los Angeles Times*, found the film's effects 'scattered' and its points sometimes lost in the narrative structure, its central examination of how good people can become complicit in evil remains powerful and relevant.

Critical reception to *Paterno* was generally positive. Critics particularly praised Pacino's nuanced performance, with IndieWire's Ben Travers noting how the actor portrayed Paterno as 'at once wracked with guilt and oblivious to any misdeeds.'

However, the film also attracted controversy, particularly from Paterno's supporters. Three hundred former Penn State players signed a letter protesting the film's portrayal of their coach, arguing that Levinson and his team never consulted anyone who knew Paterno personally.

In *Sports Illustrated* Conor Orr felt the ambiguity was uncomfortable and the sexual abuse scandal merely a subplot. He highlights a line from late in the film, where someone asks Sara Ganim, 'A crime against children happened. Why are we talking about Joe Paterno?'

A film that centred solely on those horrific acts may well have been unpalatable but with its focus on Paterno and his downfall the film serves as both a character study and a broader indictment of institutional power structures that prioritise the protection of reputation over the protection of the vulnerable.

Just two months after he was fired Joe Paterno died of lung cancer at the age of 85.

Chapter 26

The Irishman
(Film, 2019)

Directed by: Martin Scorsese
Written by: Steve Zaillian
Based on the book *I Heard You Paint Houses* by Charles Brandt
Cast: Robert De Niro, Al Pacino, Joe Pesci, Harvey Keitel, Anna Paquin, Ray Romano, Stephen Graham, Bobby Cannavale, Stephanie Kurtzuba, Kathrine Narducci, Welker White, Jesse Plemons

Martin Scorsese and Robert De Niro had been attempting to have *The Irishman* made since 2009. In 2013, the pair gathered alongside Pacino, Joe Pesci, Bobby Cannavale and some other actors, Pacino reckoned they numbered around 70, at the Tribeca Grill in New York to do a reading of Steve Zaillian's script in front of potential backers. The director was looking to secure a $175 million budget.

Scorsese and De Niro hadn't worked together since *Casino (1995)*. In 2007, they were all set to start work on *The Winter of Frankie Machine*, based on the book by Don Winslow, about a retired hitman who thought he was out, but then he was dragged back in. On a conference call with Paramount, where the movie was greenlighted, De Niro mentioned that there was another book he liked. Charles Brandt's 2004 book *I Heard You Paint Houses*. The project switched from a go movie to a development deal.

Brandt's book centred on Frank Sheeran, the character De Niro would play. Brandt had been Sheeran's lawyer. Sheeran claimed to be a mafia hitman, who had been ordered by crime boss Russell Bufalino to kill Teamsters boss Jimmy Hoffa, who went missing in 1975 and was declared legally dead in 1982.

The film was initially set up at Paramount and STX. However, in 2017, Paramount grew concerned about the spiralling budget. That was the point at which Netflix stepped in. Other companies became concerned that ticket sales wouldn't recoup their costs. Netflix didn't have those concerns, and the project coming with big names attached appealed to them.

In September 2017, with Netflix on board and the budget secured, *The Irishman* began production in New York. It would be a 108-day shoot, with more than 160 locations and 28 built sets. There would be 200 characters across four time periods.

At the Italian premiere of *Righteous Kill* in Rome in September 2008, De Niro heard the crowd shout his name as he and Pacino walked along the red carpet. De Niro turned to his co-star, and while he acknowledged the wonderful reaction, he couldn't help but feel disappointed that the movie didn't live up to the fans' fervour. 'It would be nice if they were here for a movie that we really feel proud about,' De Niro said to Pacino. 'Next time, we'll do one we like.'

The de-aging technology used on the film became one of the most notable things about it. *The Irishman* contains 1750 visual effects shots. The technology allowed the actors, then in their 70s, to play characters in their mid-20s to 50s. The actors were concerned that there should not be any interference with their performances, where they intended to ad-lib frequently. They didn't want to wear any headgear, and they didn't want technology to get in the way.

To solve this problem, ILM Visual Effects Supervisor Pablo Helman came up with a three-camera rig, where two additional infrared cameras were set on either side of the primary camera. This would allow a computer model of the actors to be built with information taken from the actors' textures and lighting.

To reassure the filmmaking team that it would work, the visual effects firm Industrial Light & Magic had De Niro reenact the Christmas party scene from *Goodfellas*. The filmmakers were astonished by this initial 10-second test, in which De Niro's character, Jimmy Conway, grows exasperated with his fellow mobsters for lavishing their wives with pink Cadillacs and mink coats with money they stole from a Lufthansa heist. 'It was extraordinary,' Jane Rosenthal, De Niro's longtime producing partner, told *Variety*. 'You put them both side by side, and you could not tell the difference.' The ILM team set out how to turn the bulky test rig into a financially viable and production-friendly model.

Pacino found the process easy and even enjoyed having the little dots applied. 'You'll do anything for the context of the film, whether you put a bonnet on or whatever,' he told *The Independent*. There was someone on the set who would shout out the age the character was supposed to be in the scene. 'Someone would come up to me and say, "You're 39."' Pacino told The Ringer podcast. '[You'd recall] some sort of memory of 39, and your body tries to acclimate to that and think that way. They remind you of it.'

Pacino and De Niro first met in 1968 while walking on New York's 14th Street in the East Village, between Avenues A and B. Pacino was with his then girlfriend Jill Clayburgh, who introduced them. Clayburgh and De Niro had worked together on the film *The Wedding Party (1969)*. Pacino had recalled seeing De Niro in Brian De Palma's *Greetings (1968)*. Clayburgh suggested that the pair should work together. It took them quite some time to share a scene, but their friendship was immediate. As they both rose to sudden fame in the early 1970s, their shared experience and how to deal with it allowed them to form a bond. Pacino found what was going on strange and disconcerting – from being an unknown actor to suddenly someone everyone on the street knew – and he took comfort in speaking with De Niro, who was going through the same thing. They would call each other and compare notes, building a trust that led to their working relationship. 'It was camaraderie that got us together,' Pacino told *The Guardian*.

Pacino explained to *The Guardian* why he and Scorsese had never worked together before, when they seemed like such a good fit. 'Like everything in this business, if you've been in it for a while, you realise that things get started, but then they go in different places and they don't always culminate in a film.'

Nick de Semlyen in *Empire* asked Pacino if he had looked on enviously when Scorsese and De Niro were a force in the 1970s. Pacino said that he had his relationship with Sidney Lumet and with Marty Bregman, so was content that he had his own thing going on. He did say that Francis Ford Coppola once told him he should meet Scorsese. 'This is when I was a youngster. We almost did a film together. We worked on a film, Marty and I, years ago. But like all these things, they take time and then they don't turn out.'

More than once over the years, Pacino and Scorsese had discussed working on films. They had made a start on doing a Modigliani biopic based on Dennis McIntyre's 1979 play in the 1980s but couldn't get finance. Pacino would finally make this project with Johnny Depp directing in 2024, with Pacino, by that time, too old to portray the Italian artist who died at 35, playing art collector Maurice Gangnat.

'He would be someone I'd really want to work with,' Pacino told author Anthony DeCurtis in 2005. 'He's tops. As Bobby once told me, Scorsese can't help making a movie that comes right out of himself. He's a great filmmaker. I marvel at his stuff. Anything he does.'

Pacino had, of course, played real-life figures before, but this time there was no option to go or not go to the source. He had to rely on books, footage and photographs of Hoffa. Pacino's tactic was to inundate himself with it and find its stimulation. Pacino went through all the film he could, listening to Hoffa's voice and assessing his mannerisms. 'You pile it on and see what stays with you,' he told Page Six. In the development of his character Pacino found himself discussing the character with all the departments on set – wardrobe, make-up, hair – as everyone had developed their own takes on Hoffa.

'Hoffa was a real icon in the world and in the United States,' Pacino told goldenglobes.com, 'he was second in popularity only to then-President Kennedy. But somehow, we always had a feeling of him as someone shady, somewhat suspect, even though I found out he was a real visionary when it came to helping the workers.'

While it was the first time Pacino had worked with Scorsese, it was the ninth movie the director had made with De Niro, who played Frank Sheeran, a mobster and Teamsters official who worked for Hoffa.

The film had its world premiere at the New York Film Festival on 27th September. The Associated Press reviewer Lindsey Bahr wrote, 'Pacino doesn't make his entrance into the film for quite some time, but his arrival and gravitas gives the film a jolt exactly when it's needed.'

The film was satisfying for fans of Pacino and De Niro, because The Irishman offered some great scenes for the pair of them to share.

Pacino's Hoffa eats several ice-cream sundaes during the course of the movie. 'He wasn't a drinker, wasn't a smoker,' Pacino told Entertainment

Weekly. 'He liked his ice cream. Ice cream was a pause in his life where he could think and just sit with it – at least, that's the way I thought of it.'

After Pacino saw the movie for the first time he wrote an email to De Niro telling him he was moved by De Niro's performance. De Niro was surprised, but told Pacino that he was moved by his words.

Pacino's performance was widely acclaimed. He was nominated as Best Supporting Actor for an Academy Award, a Golden Globe and a BAFTA. He lost out each time to Brad Pitt for *Once Upon a Time in Hollywood (2019)* a movie in which Pacino co-starred.

Chapter 27

Hunters
(TV, 2020–23)

Created by: David Weil

Cast: Logan Lerman, Al Pacino, Jerrika Hinton, Lena Olin, Saul Rubinek, Carol Kane, Josh Radnor, Greg Austin, Tiffany Boone, Louis Ozawa, Kate Mulvany, Dylan Baker, Jennifer Jason Leigh

Pacino's latest move into television was different from his previous stints. He was now making his first foray into a continuing series.

Hunters was made by Amazon Prime Video and set in New York City in 1977, and followed a band of Nazi hunters who discovered hundreds of high-ranking Nazi officials living among them and planning a Fourth Reich in the U.S. This being TV, the Hunters didn't try to bring the Nazis to a judicial court, but set out to kill them.

Creator David Weil had been brooding on the story for around five years, inspired by stories his grandmother, a Holocaust survivor, had told him. Weil was also inspired by the knowledge of how the U.S. government brought over many high-ranking Nazi officials and put them in positions of power in government. He saw that as an injustice and something that had to be brought to light.

While there is basis in fact in the premise – Operation Paperclip brought more than 1,600 German scientists, engineers and technicians – including many former Nazis – into US Government employment, there were a lot of artistic liberties taken with the plot.

Pacino's agent had read the pilot script and contacted Weil to tell him there was something in it that Pacino would respond to. Pacino met with Weil and the pilot's director Alfonso Gomez-Rejon. Pacino called it one of the craziest and most original stories he'd read. Pacino was drawn to the changes in tone, how the story moved from being horrifying to amusing to tragic. Pacino wanted to read the whole series, so Weil gave him all ten scripts for the first season and they began discussing the character, with Pacino contributing ideas to Meyer Offerman's backstory.

'It was just amazing, witnessing a genius like Al Pacino put this character together, build him from the ground up in these meetings,' Weil told Forbes.

Pacino enjoyed that he had action sequences to get into. He saw it as a challenge that even at the age of 79 he was still up for.

Weil made the decision to give all of the prisoners and survivors in the show tattoos above the number 202,499, which was the highest-recorded number ever given to an Auschwitz prisoner. The show however proved to be controversial.

After the first episode aired the Auschwitz Memorial criticised the fictional version of Nazi atrocities on show. In *The Guardian* Lucy Mangan called Hunters 'dangerously insensitive.' It's true that the show didn't need to invent atrocities for the Nazis in the show to commit when what they really did was horrifying enough. The show presented its own version of history throughout its run. In The Wrap, Phil Owen wrote, 'The key issue with Hunters in season 1 is that it can't decide if it wants to be a fun exploitation story in the vein of Inglourious Basterds or a meditation on righteous revenge a la Munich.' Owen highlights that the Nazis within the world of *Hunters* were planning their own atrocities in the present, making the show less about retrospective justice than preventing the end of the world, which resolved the moral issues the characters may have faced about hunting down and killing elderly Nazis for the crimes of their past.

'Al Pacino has taught me so much about the actor's process, the actor's relationship with the writer and the filmmaker and what matters, and how to create an environment where the actor can play and discover and succeed,' Weil told Backstage in 2021.

Co-star Josh Radnor also remembered advice he had received from Pacino. The *How I Met Your Mother* star took the opportunity to ask Pacino what to do in a scene where as an actor you have no lines, you're only listening to your scene partner.

'He just said, "Never stop thinking. Never stop thinking,"'Radnor told People in 2022. Radnor continued, 'The camera loves thought,' Pacino told Radnor. 'Even if you're thinking about your grocery list, always be thinking.'

'You know, he's a fantastic storyteller,' Radnor told Smashing Interviews Magazine. 'It was just great to both work with him and observe him up close and play with him eventually but also to get a taste of the rich history he's been a part of the last half century of theatre and films.'

Logan Lerman, who played Jonah Heidelbaum the young protagonist of *Hunters* was also thrilled at getting to work alongside someone who had been an acting hero of his since he was old enough to watch movies, taking sick days from school to watch *Serpico* and *Dog Day Afternoon*. 'He has so many incredible stories,' Lerman told the Hollywood Foreign Press Association in 2020. 'We'd find ourselves kind of getting off track of what we were talking about for work that day and just getting into Al's amazing history. It's incredible just to hear it coming from his mouth and all the things that people don't know.'

Hunters ran for two seasons, the first season finale providing an astonishing twist centering around Pacino's character. The second season showed his character in an entirely different light. Although the clues were there – and reviewers went back to check – the critics were largely surprised yet unsatisfied by the shock the show provided, as it was so momentous it threw the show's whole premise off its axis.

Ed Cumming in *The Telegraph* summed the series up well writing of the second season: 'Hunters has its moments. Most of them involve Pacino, seemingly incapable of being unwatchable, even when the dialogue he is given tries its best.'

That Pacino was still doing good work in streaming television harks back to what he thought of Jack Lemmon – that he was never an old actor, he was still fresh on screen.

The release of his autobiography in 2024 saw Pacino go on a promotion campaign doing long interviews for TV channels in America, United Kingdom and Australia, as well as appearing on podcasts and in magazines. In each case his engaging personality shines through and continues to enthral new generations.

He's still revered as an acting legend, even now that the weaker roles have started to outnumber the classics. In his autobiography Pacino jokes that he has more Golden Raspberry nominations than Oscars. There's always been interest in his private life, and that still continues despite Pacino now being in his mid-80s, but the respect for him as one of the enduring A-List stars remains.

Bibliography

Books

Adams, Cindy Heller. *Lee Strasberg: The Imperfect Genius of the Actors Studio* (Garden City, N.Y.: Doubleday, 1980)

Agan, Patrick. *Hoffman vs. Hoffman: The Actor and the Man* (London: R. Hale, 1986)

Alda, Arlene. *Just Kids from the Bronx: Telling it the Way it Was: An Oral History* (New York: Henry Holt, 2015)

Bigsby, Christopher. *Contemporary American Playwrights* (Cambridge: Cambridge University Press, 2000)

Biskind, Peter. *The Godfather Companion* (New York: HarperPerennial, 1990)

Black, Stephen A.; Brietzke, Zander; Bryer, Jackson R.; Hickey Garvey, Sheila. (ed.) *Jason Robards Remembered: Essays and Recollections* (Jefferson, N.C.: McFarland & Co., 2002)

Boyer, Jay. *Sidney Lumet* (New York: Maxwell Macmillan International, 1993)

Brecht, Bertolt. *The Resistible Rise of Arturo Ui* (London: Methuen Publishing Ltd, 2002)

Brenner, Marie. *Going Hollywood: An Insider's Look at Power and Pretense in the Movie Business* (New York: Delacorte Press, 1978)

Brunette, Peter (ed.). *Brian De Palma: Interviews* (Jackson: University Press of Mississippi, 2003)

Butler, Isaac. *The Method: How the Twentieth Century Learned to Act* (New York: Bloomsbury, 2024)

Butler, Isaac; Kois, Dan. *The World Only Spins Forward: The Ascent of Angels in America* (New York: Bloomsbury USA, 2018)

Chapman, Peter. *The Players: Actors in Movies On Television and Videocassette* (New York: Windsor Press, 1994)

Cowie, Peter. *Coppola: A Biography* (New York: Da Capo Press, 1994)

Cunningham, Frank R. *Sidney Lumet: Film and Literary Vision* (Lexington, Ky.: University Press of Kentucky, 2001)

DeCurtis, Anthony. *In Other Words: Artists Talk About Life and Work* (Milwaukee:Hal Leonard, 2005)

Devlin, Albert J.(ed.). *Conversations with Tennessee Williams* (Jackson: University Press of Mississippi, 1986)

Eberts, Jake; Ilott, Terry. *My Indecision is Final: The Rise and Fall of Goldcrest Films* (London: Faber & Faber, 1990)

Evans, Robert. *The Kid Stays in the Picture* (London: Aurum Press, 1994)

Friedkin, William. *The Friedkin Connection: A Memoir* (New York: Harper, 2013)

Fuller, Nick. *Call Me Bud: Jack Lemmon on Film* (Sandy: Authors OnLine, 2006)

Goldman, William. *The Big Picture: Who Killed Hollywood? and Other Essays* (New York: Applause, 2000)

Griffin, Merv; Bender, Dave. *Merv: Making The Good Life Last* (New York: Simon & Schuster, 2003)

Grobel, Lawrence. *Al Pacino The Authorised Biography* (London: Simon & Schuster UK Ltd, 2006)

Haynes, Jim. *Traverse Plays* (Penguin Books: Harmondsworth, 1966)

Heard, Christopher. *Depp* (Toronto: ECW Press, 2001)

Hirsch, Foster. *A Method to Their Madness: The History of the Actors Studio* (New York: W.W. Norton, 1984)

Horovitz, Israel. *Plays: 1* (Methuen Drama: London, 2006)

Hull, S. Loraine. *Strasberg's Method as Taught by Lorrie Hull: A Practical Guide for Actors, Teachers, and Directors* (Woodbridge, Conn.: Ox Bow Pub., 1985)

Johnstone, Nick. *Sean Penn: A Biography* (London: Omnibus, 2000)

Jones, Nesta; Dykes, Steven. *File on Mamet* (London: Methuen Drama, 1991)

Kael, Pauline. *Reeling: Film Writing 1972–1975* (New York: Little, Brown, 1976)

Kael, Pauline. *5001 Nights at the Movies: A Guide from A to Z* (New York: Henry Holt, 1985)

Keaton, Diane. *Then Again* (New York: Fourth Estate, 2011)

Kelly, Richard T. *Sean Penn: His Life and Times* (Edinburgh; New York: Canongate, 2004)

Kolin, Philip C; Kullman, Colby H. *Speaking on Stage: Interviews with Contemporary American Playwrights* (Tuscaloosa: University of Alabama Press, 1996)

Kushner, Tony. *Angels in America: A Gay Fantasia on National Themes* (New York: Theatre Communications Group, 2003)

Lawrence, Jerome. *Actor, The Life and Times of Paul Muni* (New York: G.P. Putnam's Sons, 1974)

Leguizamo, John. *Pimps, Hos, Playa Hatas, and All the Rest of my Hollywood Friends: My Life* (New York: Ecco, 2006)

Lenburg, Jeff. *Dustin Hoffman, Hollywood's Anti-Hero* (New York: St. Martin's Press, 1983)

Lumet, Sidney. *Making Movies* (New York: Alfred A. Knopf, 1995)

Malina, Judith. *Full Moon Stages Personal Notes from 50 Years of The Living Theatre* (Three Rooms Press: New York City, 2015)

Mattanza, Alessandra. *My New York: Celebrities Talk About the City* (White Star, Milan: 2014)

Morgan, Barbara; Perez, Maya (ed.). *On Story: Screenwriters and Filmmakers on Their Iconic Films* (Austin: University of Texas Press, 2016)

Nadel, Ira Bruce. *David Mamet: A Life in the Theatre* (New York: Palgrave Macmillan, 2008)

Osborne, Robert. *Academy Awards 1974 Oscar Annual* (California: ESE California, 1974)

Pacino, Al. *Sonny Boy: A Memoir* (New York: Penguin Press, 2024)

Pellicoro, Paul. *Paul Pellicoro on Tango* (Ft. Lee, NJ: Barricade Books, 2002)

Price, Richard. *3 Screenplays* (Boston/New York: Houghton Mifflin)

Priggé, Steven. *Movie Moguls Speak: Interviews with Top Film Producers* (Jefferson, N.C.: McFarland, 2004)

Probst, Leonard. *Off Camera: Leveling About Themselves* (Stein and Day/Scarborough House: New York, 1978)

Puzo, Mario. *The Making of The Godfather* (New York: Grand Central Publishing, 2013)

Rabe, David. *Plays: 1* (Methuen Drama, London: 2002)

Rapf, Joanna E; (ed.) *Sidney Lumet: Interviews* (University Press of Mississippi, 2006)

Russo, Vito. *The Celluloid Closet: Homosexuality in the Movies* (New York: Harper & Row, 1987)

Sanders, James. *Scenes From the City: Filmmaking in New York, 1966–2006* (New York: Rizzoli International Publications: Distributed by Random House, 2006)

Schoeps, Karl-Heinz. *Bertolt Brecht* (New York: F. Ungar Pub. Co., 1977)

Seal, Mark. *Leave the Gun, Take the Cannoli: The Epic Story of the Making of The Godfather* (New York: Gallery Books, 2021)

Searby, Mark. *Al Pacino: The Movies Behind the Man* (Mark Searby, 2017)

Sheldon, David; McCall, Joan; De Leo, Ed. *When I Knew Al: The Untold Story of Al Pacino* (Augusta: Harbor House, 2005)

Spoto, Donald. *The Kindness of Strangers: The Life of Tennessee Williams* (London: Bodley Head, 1985)

Sutherland, Bryony; Ellis, Lucy. *Annie Lennox: The Biography* (London: Omnibus Press, 2001)

Turan, Kenneth; Papp, Joseph. *Free For All: Joe Papp, The Public and The Greatest Theater Story Ever Told* (New York, Anchor Books, 2010)

Walker, Gerald. *Cruising* (New York: Bantam, 1980)

Williams, Dakin; Mead, Shepherd. *Tennessee Williams An Intimate Biography* (New York: Arbor House, 1983)

Yule, Andrew. *Al Pacino A Life on the Wire* (London: Warner Books, 1992)

Newspapers

Albuquerque Journal	Plain Dealer
Berkshire Eagle	Press and Sun-Bulletin
Boston Globe	Puerto Rico Herald
Carmi Times	Rutland Daily Herald
Central New Jersey Home News	Sacramento Bee
Citizen Register	Southam News
Corpus Christi Caller	Staten Island Advance
Daily Mirror	Sunday News
Daily News	Sydney Morning Herald
Daily Post	Telegraph-Journal
Detroit Free Press	The Berkshire Eagle
East Hampton Star	The Buffalo News
Edmonton Journal	The Central New Jersey Home News
Elizabethton Star	The Daily Progress
Evening Standard	The Danville Register
Fort-Worth Star Telegram	The Herald (Glasgow)
Hartford Courant	The Knoxville Journal
Law Enforcement News (New York, N.Y.)	The Morning Call
Los Angeles Times	The News and Observer
Miami Herald	The News Virginian
New York Daily News	The Sunday Oregonian
New York Times	The Telegraph
Newsday	The Tennessean
Peninsula Times Tribune	Transcript-Telegram
Philadelphia Inquirer	Turlock Journal
Pittsburgh Press	Washington Post

Websites

actorsequity.org	artsfuse.org
arts.gov	avclub.com

awardsdaily.com
awfj.org
backstage.com
bigpicturefilmclub.com
boat-tahoe.com
calculator.net
catalog.afi.com
cbsnews.com
cinephiliabeyond.org
city-journal.org
creativescreenwriting.com
denofgeek.com
diaryofascreenwriter.blogspot.com
digicoll.library.wisc.edu
easthamptonstar.com
edition.cnn.com
empireonline.com
eu.usatoday.com
ew.com
fiftygrande.com
filmmakermagazine.com
forbes.com
fxguide.com
garrettcam.com
georgiatoday.ge
goldenglobes.com
gq.com
hollywoodreporter.com
i-d.co
ibdb.com
imdb.com
independent.co.uk
indiewire.com
insider.com
iobdb.com
latimes.com
leonardrossiter.com
looper.com
mcall.com
movieline.com
movingimagesource.us
news.bbc.co.uk
newspapers.com

newyorker.com
npr.org
nps.gov
nymag.com
nypost.com
nytimes.com
obieawards.com
pagesix.com
people.com
playbill.com
pmc.ncbi.nlm.nih.gov
poynter.org
pricedoutblog.com
richardholman.com
robertcmorton.com
rogerebert.com
rouge.com.au
saada.org
si.com
slate.com
smashinginterviews.com
standard.co.uk
steppenwolf.org
the-numbers.com
theactorsstudio.org
theasc.com
theatrewithin.org
theguardian.com
thehollywoodinterview.blogspot.com
theneweuropean.co.uk
thestudiotour.com
thewrap.com
vancouverisawesome.com
vanityfair.com
variety.com
vulture.com
warholstars.org
web.archive.org
weliveentertainment.com
worldarchitecture.org
youtube.com
zerogravitymanagement.com

Magazines

Details
Empire

Esquire
Gay Sunshine: A Journal of Gay Liberation

GQ
Life
New York Magazine
Playboy

Spin Magazine
The Body Politic
The Godfather Part II Movie Program
The London Review of Books

Podcasts
All About Al
Conan O'Brien Needs a Friend
Maltin on Movies

Movie Geeks United
The Ringer
WTF with Marc Maron

Television
ABC News
Al Pacino: Once Upon a Time in Hollywood (BBC, 2024)
Charlie Rose (PBS)
Film 93 (BBC, 1993)
Mann Made: from LA Takedown to Heat (BBC, 1997)
Omnibus: Quentin Tarantino: Hollywood's Boy Wonder (BBC, 1994)

Films
Looking For Richard (Al Pacino, 1996)
Waldo Salt – A Screenwriter's Journey (Robert Hillmann and Eugene Corr, 1990)

DVDs/Blu-Rays
Carlito's Way Blu-Ray
Cruising 2019 Blu-Ray commentary
Cruising Blu-Ray booklet 2025
Cruising Blu-Ray extras 2025
Revolution Blu-Ray
Scarface Blu-Ray booklet
Scarface Gold Edition
The Dialogue: Learning From the Masters
The Godfather 2001 DVD commentary
The Godfather Part Two 2001 DVD commentary